Reporting Thailand's Southern Conflict

Since 2004, Thailand's southern border provinces have been plagued by violence. There are a wide array of explanations for this violence, from the revival of Malay nationalist movements and the influence from the global trend of radical Islam, to the power play among the regional underground crime syndicates, politicians, and state authorities. The disparate interpretations signal the dynamic and complex discursive contention of this damaging and enduring conflict, and this book looks at how this is played out in the Thai media, and with what possible consequences.

In analysing the southern conflict coverage, this book presents the deficiencies in news coverage as produced by four news organisations of different natures across a seven-year review period, and discusses the professional practices that hinder journalism from serving as a fair arena for healthy and rational democratic debates. Based on in-depth interviews with news workers, it argues that Thai journalism is not always monolithic and static, as shown in the discursive shifts in news content, the variations of journalistic practices, and news workers' disparate stances on the conflict. The book goes on to highlight the less immediately apparent difficulties of political conflict reporting, such as the subtle patterns of intimidation and media manipulation, as well as the challenges of countering socially prevailing hegemonic beliefs in Thai society.

Exploring the political contingencies and socio-cultural influences at play, this book provides an in-depth study of journalism's role in politics in Thailand, and is of interest to students and scholars of Southeast Asian Politics, Media Studies, and Peace and Conflict Studies.

Phansasiri Kularb is a Lecturer in the Faculty of Communication Arts at Chulalongkorn University, Thailand. Her interests include journalism and political conflict, journalism practices, and civic and citizen media. She has participated in research projects on Thai media freedom and media regulation and policy.

Rethinking Southeast Asia
Edited by Duncan McCargo, University of Leeds, UK

Southeast Asia is a dynamic and rapidly changing region which continues to defy predictions and challenge formulaic understandings. This series publishes cutting-edge work on the region, providing a venue for books that are readable, topical, interdisciplinary and critical of conventional views. It aims to communicate the energy, contestations and ambiguities that make Southeast Asia both consistently fascinating and sometimes potentially disturbing.

Some titles in the series address the needs of students and teachers, published in simultaneous in hardback and paperback, including:

Rethinking Vietnam
Duncan McCargo

Rethinking Southeast Asia is also a forum for innovative new research intended for a more specialist readership. Titles are published initially in hardback.

1 **Politics and the Press in Thailand**
Media machinations
Duncan McCargo

2 **Democracy and National Identity in Thailand**
Michael Kelly Connors

3 **The Politics of NGOs in Indonesia**
Developing democracy and managing a movement
Bob S. Hadiwinata

4 **Changing Political Economy of Vietnam**
The case of Ho Chi Minh City
Martin Gainsborough

5 **Military Politics and Democratization in Indonesia***
Jun Honna

6 **Living at the Edge of Thai Society***
The Karen in the highlands of northern Thailand
Claudio O. Delang

7 **Thailand Beyond the Crisis***
Peter Warr

8 **Virtual Thailand***
Media and culture politics in Thailand, Malaysia and Singapore
Glen Lewis

9 **Decentralization and *Adat* Revivalism in Indonesia***
The politics of becoming indigenous
Adam D. Tyson

10 **Truth on Trial in Thailand***
Defamation, treason, and lèse-majesté
David Streckfuss

11 Civil Society in the Philippines
Theoretical, methodological and
policy debates
Gerard Clarke

**12 Politics and Governance in
Indonesia**
The police in the era of *Reformasi*
Muradi

**13 Transnational Islamic Actors
and Indonesia's Foreign Policy**
Transcending the state
Delphine Alles

**14 Reporting Thailand's Southern
Conflict**
Mediating political dissent
Phansasiri Kularb

*available in paperback

Reporting Thailand's Southern Conflict

Mediating political dissent

Phansasiri Kularb

LONDON AND NEW YORK

First published 2016
by Routledge
2 Park Square, Milton Park, Abingdon, Oxon OX14 4RN

and by Routledge
711 Third Avenue, New York, NY 10017

*Routledge is an imprint of the Taylor & Francis Group,
an informa business*

© 2016 Phansasiri Kularb

The right of Phansasiri Kularb to be identified as author of this work
has been asserted by her in accordance with sections 77 and 78 of the
Copyright, Designs and Patents Act 1988.

All rights reserved. No part of this book may be reprinted or reproduced or
utilised in any form or by any electronic, mechanical, or other means, now
known or hereafter invented, including photocopying and recording, or in
any information storage or retrieval system, without permission in writing
from the publishers.

Trademark notice: Product or corporate names may be trademarks or
registered trademarks, and are used only for identification and explanation
without intent to infringe.

British Library Cataloguing in Publication Data
A catalogue record for this book is available from the British Library

Library of Congress Cataloging-in-Publication Data
Names: Phansåasiri Kulåap, author.
Title: Reporting Thailand's southern conflict : mediating political dissent /
    Phansasiri Kularb.
Description: New York : Routledge, 2016. | Series: Rethinking Southeast
    Asia ; 14 | Includes bibliographical references and index.
Identifiers: LCCN 2015036559 | ISBN 9781138847002 (hardback) |
    ISBN 9781315727059 (ebook)
Subjects: LCSH: Thailand, Southern—Politics and government—Press
    coverage. | Political violence—Thailand, Southern—Press coverage. |
    Press and politics—Thailand.
Classification: LCC DS588.S68 P44 2016 | DDC 959.304/4—dc23
LC record available at http://lccn.loc.gov/2015036559

ISBN: 978-1-138-84700-2 (hbk)
ISBN: 978-1-315-72705-9 (ebk)

Typeset in Times New Roman
by Apex CoVantage, LLC

For the people of the far South and those who devote themselves to solving the southern conflict

Contents

List of figures	x
List of tables	xi
Preface	xii
Acknowledgements	xxi

1	Introduction	1
2	News representation of the southern conflict	26
3	Reporting the southern conflict: from the field to the newsroom	55
4	News access and southern conflict reporting	80
5	Disparate roles of journalism in the southern conflict	98
6	Conclusion	116

Appendix A:	*Towards a new paradigm and practices – recommendations for southern conflict reporting*	131
Appendix B:	*Key moments in the southern conflict, Thai politics and media (2001–2014)*	134
Appendix C:	*Profiles of the four media organisations in this study*	153
Appendix D:	*Research methodology*	160
Appendix E:	*List of selected local non-profit media and civil society organisations working on southern conflict issues*	166
Appendix F:	*List of selected publications on the southern conflict by Thai journalists*	168
Index		169

Figures

2.1	An overview of the southern conflict coverage classified by themes	28
2.2	The frequency of the four meta-frames in the southern conflict coverage	31
2.3	The frequency of news frames used to identify the causes of the southern conflict and violence	32
2.4	The frequency of news frames used to describe the uses of force in southern violence	34
2.5	The frequency of news frames used to describe the repercussions of southern conflict and violence	35
2.6	The frequency of news frames used to identify the solutions to the southern conflict	39
3.1	The lines of production of the southern conflict news employed by news organisations	56
3.2	The editorial meeting and daily news production process	59
3.3	The difficulties of southern conflict reporting: in the field and in the newsroom	75
5.1	Factors influencing news production in southern conflict reporting	112
6.1	The Thai news production culture and the roles of journalism in the southern conflict	123
6.2	The diversity and complexity of news ecology in southern conflict reporting	125
B.1	Matichon plc's business structure	153
B.2	*Thai PBS'* organisation structure	155
B.3	*Thai PBS'* news department structure	156

Tables

1.1	Contesting realities: comparison of contending discourses in the southern conflict	11
2.1	Comparison of the four selected news organisations	26
2.2	The frequency of topics in the southern conflict coverage	30
2.3	The comparison of headlines with different *uses of force* frames	35
2.4	The contexts of headlines and introductions concerning the impact of conflict	36
2.5	The comparison between the coverage of impact on state officials and on the locals	37
2.6	The frequency of the references to perpetrators and victims of violence	38
2.7	Comparison of protagonists' views towards peace dialogues as a solution to the southern conflict	40
2.8	Labels of the southern conflict in the headlines and introductions	43
2.9	Labels for the antagonists in the southern conflict in headlines and introductions	44
2.10	The news genres in southern conflict reporting	46
2.11	The actors featured in visual presentation of the news coverage	48
2.12	The contexts of visual presentation in news content	49
4.1	The types of sources quoted in news content	83
4.2	The specialisation of sources presented in news content	85
4.3	The locations and bases of sources in southern conflict reporting	86
B.1	The development of the Isara News Agency's Southern News Desk	158
B.2	Summary of news organisations' similarities and differences	159
D.1	The four meta-frames for the news framing analysis	161
D.2	Components of frames in the *causes of conflict and violence* meta-frame	161
D.3	Components of frames in the *repercussions* meta-frame	162
D.4	Components of frames in the *solutions* meta-frame	162
D.5	List of in-depth interviewees	164

Preface

"A challenging field": so a veteran correspondent succinctly defined reporting the civil conflict in Thailand's southern border provinces. The label seems fitting, given the struggle's complex contexts, multifarious protagonists and dynamic patterns, as well as its interplay with the country's unstable politics and deep-seated beliefs in Thai society. As such, journalists covering this phenomenon – involving a broad range of news specialisms – are often faced with conundrums causing them to rethink the practices and roles that have long been established as routine in Thai journalism.

One news manager pointed out that the best quality of field journalists who reported the southern conflict was not their journalistic skills, but rather, their survival instinct and safety precautions taken in order to remain unscathed in the volatile area. Meanwhile, a southern stringer expressed weariness with dealing with news organisations in the capital city whose staff seemed to assume that "criminal" investigation in the conflict zone should be reported fast and with a typical narrative, in line with similar cases elsewhere. "For some incidents, if we cannot find answers as to who the perpetrator(s) was/were [right away], we will report that the cases were suspected to be a personal dispute or a *sathanakarn tai*,[1] and that the cases remain under investigation. Because if it turns out to be a personal issue and the locals are aware of that, they will say this report is a lie if we say otherwise," said the local freelancer. "But Bangkok [newsrooms] tend to ask us stringers to identify for sure that an incident was a *sathanakarn tai*, so the story will become news and can be 'sold'."

Another reporter questioned whether the profession's golden rule of detachment to maintain neutrality and objectivity would help remedy the problem that involves human suffering. "The first cup of tea we share, it is like we just get to know one another. But with the second cup, you and I get to talk. With the third cup, we become friends,"[2] the field TV reporter said, recalling a quote from a book she had read. "It would be to take advantage of [the locals] if we just get a story and finish. There should be more responsibility when we are in a conflict area, if we really want to help them."

These statements, although seemingly disconnected, lay out various factors that govern, restrict, and facilitate the production of southern conflict coverage, as will be detailed later in this book. At the same time, the testimonies also signal news workers' reflection on their practices and professionalism, as well as their attempt to push existing boundaries in order better to report this enduring and complex violent conflict.

The armed conflict in the southern border region – comprising three provinces: Pattani, Yala, Narathiwat, and four districts of Songkla – has been on-going since January 4, 2004.[3] After more than a decade, more than 6,000 people have been killed and some 11,000 injured, the majority of them civilians, in over 14,000 incidents, including attacks allegedly instigated by insurgents and counter-insurgency actions launched by state authorities (Supaporn et al. 2014). A news report indicates that damage to property resulting from these attacks has been estimated at 154 million baht (approximately 4.7 million US dollars) (Pakorn 2014), while regional economic growth has continually suffered contraction (The National Economic and Social Development Board n.d.). Whilst estimating that there are about 9,161 active insurgents in the area, in 2012 alone the military deployed approximately 150,000 security personnel, including soldiers, paramilitary, and civilian defence volunteers, to safeguard the restive region, rendering the southernmost region a semi-militarised state. However, the extensive presence of the military in the region does little to minimise the conflict (Srisompob 2012). While statistics show a declining rate of violent incidents, the conflict continues to be dynamic in nature. One crucial factor facilitating this conflict's length and evolution over more than a decade is the fact that insurgents have formed loose organisational structures and wide networks that interlink enfranchised members across communities – a "liminal lattice," as Southeast Asian studies academic Duncan McCargo (2008) defines the arrangement. Such strategies enable the insurgents to operate in small groups instantaneously and clandestinely – a "conspiracy of silence" as political scientist Zachary Abuza (2009) puts it, and at the same time make it difficult for authorities quickly to identify the perpetrators. By the same token, the insurgents' anonymity and scattered webs of coordination pave the way for law enforcement and security officers to execute blanket searches, arrests, and prosecutions of the locals – with ramifications for human rights that will be explained shortly. The networks' obscure hierarchy also results in doubts and scepticism towards the authority and influence of those who declare their representation of insurgent groups in official meetings and other public domains.

The calculable toll of the conflict has yet to include the invisible repercussions. While women and young children have accounted for less than ten percent of deaths (Isara News Agency 2014), the loss of husbands and fathers, usually the breadwinner of the family, leaves thousands of widows and orphans struggling to care for themselves and coping with psychological impact on their own (Waeleemah 2014; Hearty Support Group 2015). Attacks on school teachers and premises, along with authorities' directives to suspend and close religious schools suspected of insurgency involvement, or to use schools as makeshift military bases, disrupt both basic educational services and traditional religious teaching (Nasurah and Pakorn 2013; Supaporn et al. 2014).

Since 2004, more than 200 billion baht or over 6 billion US dollars of the state budget have reportedly been allocated for the "Extinguish the Southern Fire xiv *Preface*

[*dub fai tai*]" missions (Krungthep Turakij 2014), with an additional sum of around 5 billion baht (approximately 153 million US dollars) earmarked for "healing" packages for those affected by violence (Pakorn 2014). National security agencies, particularly the Internal Security Operations Command (ISOC) – the military-run governmental unit – received the highest amount of funding in the 2015 fiscal year (Sitthichai and Pakorn 2014). These agencies were tasked with maintaining security in the region, which entails a wide range of operations, including information operation and economic development projects. Meanwhile, of around 9,500 criminal investigations concerning national security, officials were able to identify suspects in only one-fifth of them. Of the 702 cases that reached court, around 60 percent with more than 1,000 suspects were dismissed, mostly due to lack of witnesses and evidence (Isara News Agency 2015). Despite their eventual acquittal, most suspects were detained for months in custody while awaiting trial.

Not only does the southern conflict stand out because of its numerous and enduring repercussions, but also because of its distinctive origin. The region is geographically distant from central administration – approximately 1,000 kilometres or some 630 miles from the capital city. More importantly, the southern border provinces' demographic composition differs vastly from other parts of Thailand. While the majority of its population, the Malay Muslims, share ethnic, cultural, and religious similarities with Thailand's neighbouring Malaysia, they are cast as a minority in the predominantly Buddhist kingdom.[4]

The southern conflict also emerged and has continued as politics in Thailand has arrived at a significant juncture of vigorous ideological contention and unprecedented levels of turbulence. The conflict has outlived six governments, two of which were overthrown by separate military coups.[5] The administrative changes included a series of politicians and state officials, as well as law enforcement and military officers, who were appointed to head related agencies, only to be removed and replaced sometime later by the same or subsequent government. There were sporadic news reports of secretive meetings organised in Thailand's neighbouring countries between the Thai security agencies and insurgent representatives overseas (Liow and Pathan 2010). Nonetheless, the first official and public peace talks only took place in 2013 under the sixth administration, led by Prime Minister Yingluck Shinawatra. Despite scepticism and criticism concerning the political agendas of the Thai government and its Malaysian counterpart, who facilitated the meetings, as well as the representatives of the insurgents' authority over operative militants, the talks were considered a milestone in the southern peace process.[6] However, the process came to a halt when the Yingluck Shinawatra government was toppled later that year in a coup, led by then-Army Commander General Prayut Chan-ocha, following months-long anti-government street protests. The interim coup-installed government made its ultimate goal to "reform" the country in every aspect in order to restore unity and reconcile the deep social divide stemming from national-level politics, prioritising constitutional drafting and eliminating corruption above other tasks (Ministry of Justice n.d.).

The junta administration has attempted to demonstrate "peace"[7] initiatives in the region and has reportedly considered resurrecting peace dialogue.[8] In late

Preface xv

August 2015, a team of Thai negotiators publicly announced their first meeting with representatives from six insurgent groups under a new council called Majlis Syura Patani or Mara Patani in Kuala Lumpur, with Malaysia facilitating the talk. Both sides initially agreed to hold more dialogues to seek peaceful conflict resolution. While the Thai government expected to discuss security concerns such as setting up a safety zone and restoring justice, the movements' umbrella group asserted that the southern conflict should be set as a national agenda to ensure the continuity of policy implementation.[9] Still, scepticism over the influence of this group and the efficacy of peace dialogue remains.[10] The junta prime minister even dismissed recognising the insurgents, because they violated the Thai law, until their ability to reduce the number of violent incidents was proven.[11]

This book is about Thai journalism and the southern conflict, but the introductory section aims first to illustrate the complexity of the southern conflict, and the crucial role of Thailand's multifaceted and dynamic socio-political milieu in this protracted conflict. It also shows the various players involved, from people struggling in their plight, to disparate parties who are tasked with missions to resolve conflicts. As will be elaborated in Chapter 1, the causes and nature of the armed conflict in Thailand's southernmost provinces have been explained variously in a large volume of academic literature, as well as in reports by state agencies, news media, and the civil sector, both domestic and international. These disparate readings of the phenomenon underpin the focus of this study: the southern conflict is a field of vigorous discursive contestation among several players. It is in this contentious discursive field that this study observes *how* Thai journalism and journalists "mediatize" the conflict, and, more importantly, *why* they perform in such ways – from highlighting or silencing competing views and presenting their own readings of the conflict to in some instances becoming active players.

The aim of this book is to explore the Thai news production culture in reporting the southern conflict.[12] The study asks three main questions: 1) *How do journalists make sense of the conflict?* 2) *What roles do they perform, and what roles do they think journalism and journalists should play in this conflict?* and 3) *How do journalists carry out these roles?* In seeking answers to these questions, I analysed news coverage of the conflict from 2004 to 2010, observed various stages of the news production process, and conducted in-depth interviews with journalists who are involved in reporting the southern conflict. To map out an overview of the Thai news production culture, I selected four Thai news organisations of different natures, principles, and media platforms as the primary subjects, due to their continuing coverage of and dedicated spaces for the southern conflict.[13] I also collected views of practitioners from other news organisations who have been consistently reporting the issue and region, as well as advocates whose works focus on communicating about the conflict and peace processes in order to gain perspectives apart from the "professional media"-oriented ones.

Because the study seeks to explain the contending views concerning the conflict, I feel it is important to explain my stance on this issue to readers. Prior to conducting this research, my perspective and experience were associated little with the far South. I am a Buddhist Thai living in Bangkok. My view on the

xvi *Preface*

southern conflict does not completely dismiss the influence of vigorous competitions to maintain the status quo among disparate vested interest groups, such as politicians and officials – both at regional and national levels – underground crime syndicates, and even local opinion leaders on the conflict. Nonetheless, I believe its root cause is the clash between the deeply entrenched and dominant beliefs of Thai nation-state constructs and the Malay Muslim identity, resulting in the deprivation of locals' civil rights. The southern conflict's ground and ramifications are not entirely unique; they share similarity with other conflicts involving underprivileged groups and marginalised ethnicities in Thailand. Thus, the solution should focus upon decentralisation of political structures to empower the locals' civil rights and political participation, ensure justice, and recognise the Malay Muslim identity, which corresponds with the notion of "self-determination" recently advocated by civil society networks in the deep South. Devolution, for a start, is what I argue to be a remedy, not specifically for the southern conflict but for other state-citizen disputes that are prevalent in other parts of Thailand. I also feel that public engagement, deliberative processes, and peace dialogues – structurally and culturally – must take place not only among the population of the far South and with insurgent movements, but also nationwide, to bring about solutions.

My professional and academic background also plays a crucial part in laying out research methodology and analytical approaches. Having worked in news organisations and being a journalism lecturer, I have a rather sympathetic view towards news workers, individually and as an institution, and hope to identify the flaws in news practices in order to reduce these shortcomings via pragmatic means. Therefore, the research was designed so that I could explore the "behind-the-scenes" of news production and employ organisational approaches[14] to tease out and critically examine factors involved in culture of Thai journalism. Being aware of my stances on the southern conflict and Thai journalism, I have attempted to minimise blind spots and personal biases by exploring various literature and materials so that I could form a well-grounded understanding and critical analyses of both issues.

The analytical lens of this book derives mainly from a number of seminal works by scholars studying journalism in global conflicts, and Western academics who specialise in Thai and Southeast Asian studies. Nonetheless, it is also my intention to bring forth a series of academic works by Thai researchers, many of which are masters and doctoral theses. Despite their minimal presence in the international arena, these works offer insightful and valuable analyses, which also provide a solid ground for this study.

Notes

1 This term's literal translation is "southern situation," which has become parlance among officials and news workers in reference to southern insurgency-related incidents.
2 The exact passage is, "The first time you share tea with a Balti, you are a stranger. The second time you take tea, you are an honored guest. The third time you share a cup of tea, you become family . . ." from Greg Mortenson and David Oliver Relin. 2006. *Three*

Cups of Tea: One Man's Mission to Fight Terrorism and Build Nations . . . One School at a Time. New York: The Penguin Group, p. 150.

3 Despite sporadic unrest in the southernmost provinces since late 1980s, the region had been relatively calm; therefore, news reports and academic literature often mark the weapon heist and large-scale attack on the military base in Narathiwat province on January 4, 2004 as the beginning of a new round of insurgency in the southernmost region. For more detail on the history of insurgency in the deep South, see, for example, Thanet Aphornsuvan. 2007. *Rebellion in Southern Thailand: Contending Histories*. Washington, D.C.: East-West Center Washington; John Funston. 2008. *Southern Thailand: The Dynamics of Conflict*. Washington, D.C.: East-West Center; and Duncan McCargo. 2008. *Tearing Apart the Land: Islam and Legitimacy in Southern Thailand*. Ithaca, New York: Cornell University Press.

4 According to the Ministry of Interior's statistics, in 2009, the proportion of the three southern border provinces' population accounted for two percent of the entire Thai population, whereas the number of residents in the capital city of Bangkok accounted for eight percent of the entire population.

5 The new round of violence emerged in 2004, when then-Prime Minister Thaksin Shinawatra neared the end of his first term. Following a landslide election win for his second term in 2005, Thaksin's administration encountered months-long demonstrations accusing his government of corruption and human rights violations, and was later toppled by a military coup led by the army commander at that time, General Sonthi Boonyaratglin, on 19 September 2006. Another military coup took place on 22 May 2014, in which Prime Minister Yingluck Shinawatra, Thaksin's sister, whose party won the election in a similar fashion to her brother's, and, later, faced anti-government street protests, was deposed by another army commander, General Prayut Chan-ocha. The general later appointed himself the premier of the interim junta government. For more detail on key moments in the southern conflict and Thai politics, see Appendix B. For a discussion on the turbulence of Thailand's modern politics, see, for example, Prajak Kongkirati. 2014. The rise and fall of electoral violence in Thailand: Changing rules, structures and power landscapes, 1997–2011. *Contemporary Southeast Asia: A Journal of International and Strategic Affairs*. 36(3), pp. 386–416.

6 For more analyses of the 2013 Kuala Lumpur peace talks, see, for example, McCargo, Duncan. 2014. *Southern Thailand: From Conflict to Negotiations?* [online]. Sydney, NSW: Lowy Institute for International Policy. Available at: www.lowyinstitute.org/publications/southern-thailand-conflict-negotiations [Accessed: 8 June 2015]; and Rungrawee Chalermsripinyorat. 2014. เส้นทางกระบวนการสันติภาพปาตานี [*The Road to Patani Peace Process*]. Pattani: Prince of Songkla University's Institute for Peace Studies and the Southern Thailand Empowerment and Participation Project.

7 The Prayut Chan-ocha administration uses the term สันติสุข [*santisook*] when referring to "peace" in peace process/talk, instead of สันติภาพ [*santiparb*], which has been widely used in public discourse and by the civil society sector. Despite the same English translation, the term *santisook* has been primarily used in military policy concerning the southern conflict. An Isara News Agency article explains that the change of lexis reflects the junta's goal, which "aims to serve people's interests and to answer people's true needs, not the needs of movements who use violence as their device," in hopes to "to create peacefulness in the region and for the people." See Pakorn Peungnetr. 2014. ทำไมต้องเปลี่ยนจาก "พูดคุยสันติภาพ" เป็น "พูดคุยสันติสุข" [Why there needs to be the change from "santiparb talk" to "santisook talk"?] [online]. *Isara News Agency*, 7 August 2014. Available at: www.isranews.org/เรื่องเด่น-สำนักข่าวอิศรา/item/31925-talk_31925.html [Accessed: 1 April 2015].

8 During his official visit to Malaysia in December 2014, Prime Minister Prayut Chan-ocha discussed re-initiating peace talks with insurgent movements and having Malaysia reprise its role as facilitator with Malaysian premier Najib Razak. Following the visit, in January 2015, the Thai prime minister set up the mechanism to push forward the

xviii *Preface*

peace (*santisook*) dialogue process, which comprises three committees. The first two are headed by him, and the last committee, the Area-based Inter-agency Coordination Working Group, is led by the Region 4 ISOC chief. For more on the plan, see, for example, *The Strait Times*. Southern Thailand peace talks on agenda as Thai PM Prayuth visits Malaysia [online]. 1 December 2014. Available at: www.straitstimes.com/news/asia/south-east-asia/story/southernthailand-peace-talks-agenda-thai-pm-prayuth-visits-malaysia#sthash.OCIdaMNe.dpuf [Accessed: 10 May 2015]; *Kom Chad Leuk Online*. เปิดโครงสร้าง 'เจรจาสันติสุข' ดึงทุกฝ่ายเข้าพูดคุยดับไฟใต้ [Reveal the 'peace dialogue' structure; Pulling in every party to talk about extinguishing the Southern Fire] [online]. 12 December 2014. Available at: www.komchadluek.net/detail/20141212/197567.html [Accessed: 10 May 2015]; and Patsara Jikkham and Waedao Harai. 2015. Prayut lays out plan to solve strife in South. *Bangkok Post*, 29 January 2015.

9 Mara Patani comprises six insurgent movements, including the Barisan Revolusi Nasional (BRN), the Gerakan Mujahideen Islam Patani (GMIP), the Barisan Islam Pembebasan Patani (BIPP), and three blocs under the Patani United Liberation Organisation (PULO). Nonetheless, *The Nation* columnist Don Pathan notes that this umbrella group does not receive strong support from most BRN leaders, particularly ones from the movement's military operation. See Don Pathan. 2015. Deep South peace efforts hit another dead end. *The Nation*, 22 May 2015.

10 See, for example, Pakorn Peungnetr. 2015. Watch out, MARA Pattani may be a deception![online]. *Isara News Agency*, 23 June 2015. Available at: http://isranews. org/south-news/english-article/item/39440-beware.html [Accessed: 1 September 2015]; and Don Pathan. 2015. Deep South peace efforts hit another dead end. *The Nation*, 22 May 2015.

11 See, for example, *Matichon Online*. บิ๊กตู่ยังไม่ยอมรับ "มารา ปาตานี" บอกไปทำให้เหตุการณ์รุนแรงในพื้นที่ลดลงก่อน [Big Too (the prime minister's nickname) does not recognise "Mara Patani," saying (they must) first reduce the number of violent incidents in the area] [online]. 28 August 2015. Available at: www.matichon.co.th/news_detail.php?newsid=1440767420 [Accessed: 1 September 2015].

12 The use of "conflict" in this book in reference to the situation in Thailand's southern border provinces is intentional. The phenomenon has been has been characterised variously; most academic publications and reports by international media and watchdog agencies call it "insurgency," clearly indicating the influence of insurgent/separatist movements in the conflict. Meanwhile, vernacular media often labels the situation "unrest" or "violence" or, commonly, with the metaphor "Southern Fire". Notwithstanding the meanings of these terms, I opt for "conflict" here to denote the underlying concept used to explain this phenomenon in this study.

13 See their profile in Appendix C. For more details on the study's research methodology, see Appendix D or Chapter 5 of my PhD thesis: Phansasiri Kularb. 2013. *Mediating Political Dissent: A Study of Thai News Organisations and Southern Conflict Reporting*. Cardiff University, UK.

14 Jackie Harrison explains this group of approaches as "the study of the social organization of newswork" (2006, p. 31), following Michael Schudson (1989, 1996, 2000) and Simon Cottle (2003)'s arguments, which explores the practices of news production. As Harrison points out, the organisational perspective recognises the influence of dominant power structures on the production of news and its meanings in the same vein as the political economist and culturalist approaches. However, the emphasis of the organisational approach is on the types of practices and protocols that news organisations apply to journalists, and the interplay between the agencies, journalists, and external forces in news production. For more detail, see Jackie Harrison. 2006. *News*. Oxon: Routledge.

Preface xix

References

Abuza, Zachary. 2009. *Conspiracy of Silence: The Insurgency in Southern Thailand.* Washington, DC: United States Institute of Peace Press.

Harrison, Jackie. 2006. *News.* Oxon: Routledge.

Hearty Support Group. 2015. โตขึ้นหนูอยากจะเป็น...?:รายงานสถานการณ์เด็กในพื้นที่ความขัดแย้งชายแดนใต้ ประจำปี 2557 [When I grow up, I want to be . . . ?: Report on children's situation in the southern border conflict area 2014] [online]. *Deep South Watch*, 20 January 2015. Available at: www.deepsouthwatch.org/sites/default/files/child_report_dj_2014_updated2.pdf [Accessed: 1 April 2015].

Isara News Agency. 2014. เสียงเงียบจากชายแดนใต้ . . . เมื่อผู้หญิงถูกทำร้ายจากความรุนแรง [Silence from the southern border . . . When women were hurt from violence] [online]. 27 February 2014. Available at: www.isranews.org/south-news/stat-history/item/27580-voice_27580.html [Accessed: 1 September 2015].

Isara News Agency. 2015. 11ปีไฟใต้ . . . ตายครึ่งหมื่น ปืนถูกปล้น 2 พันกระบอก งบทะลุ 2.3 แสนล้าน [11 years of Southern Fire . . . half ten thousands killed. 2,000 guns robbed. Budget surpasses 230 billion] [online]. 3 January 2015. Available at: www.isranews.org/south-news/scoop/item/35565-eleven_35565.html [Accessed: 1 April 2015].

Krungthep Turakij. 2014. 10 ปีไฟใต้ งบทะลุ 2 แสนล้าน [10 Years of Southern Fire, budget surpasses 200 billion] [online]. 5 January 2014. Available at: www.bangkokbiznews.com/news/detail/553854 [Accessed: 1 April 2015].

Liow, Joseph C. and Don Pathan. 2010. *Confronting Ghosts: Thailand's Shapeless Southern Insurgency.* Sydney, NSW: Lowy Institute for International Policy.

McCargo, Duncan. 2008. *Tearing Apart the Land: Islam and Legitimacy in Southern Thailand.* Ithaca, New York: Cornell University Press.

Ministry of Justice, The. n.d. คำแถลงนโยบายของคณะรัฐมนตรี พลเอกประยุทธ์ จันทร์โอชา นายกรัฐมนตรีแถลงต่อสภานิติบัญญัติแห่งชาติ วันศุกร์ที่ ๑๒ กันยายน ๒๕๕๗ [Policy statement of the Cabinet. General Prayut Chan-Ocha, the Prime Minister, delivers to the National Legislative Assembly on Friday 12 September 2014] [online]. Available at: www.moj.go.th/intro/policystatment.pdf [Accessed: 10 May 2015].

Nasurah Jeh-ha and Pakorn Peungnetr. 2013. ถอดหัวใจครูน้อยชายแดนใต้ ปิดโรงเรียนไม่ใช่วิธีแก้ปัญหา [Teachers in southern border reveal closing schools is not a solution] [online]. *Isara News Agency*, 15 December 2013. Available at: www.isranews.org/isranews-article/item/18254-ถอดหัวใจ-ครูน้อยชายแดนใต้-ปิดโรงเรียนไม่ใช่วิธีแก้ปัญหา.html [Accessed: 1 April 2015].

Office of the National Economic and Social Development Board, The. n.d. แผนการพัฒนาพื้นที่พิเศษ 5 จังหวัดชายแดนภาคใต้ ปี 2552-2555 [Development plans for the Special Region of 5 Southern Border Provinces 2009–2012] [online]. Available at: http://eris.nesdb.go.th/pdf/351000–001.pdf [Accessed: 1 April 2015].

Pakorn Peungnetr. 2014. 10 ปีไฟใต้งบเยียวยา5พันล้าน ชดเชยทรัพย์สิน-ธุรกิจ900ล้าน [10 Year of Southern Fire. Healing budget 5 billion. Compensation for properties and business 900 million] [online]. *Isara News Agency,* 11 April 2014. Available at: www.isranews.org/south-news/stat-history/item/28562-pension.html [Accessed: 1 April 2015].

Sitthichai Nakonwilai and Pakorn Peungnetr. 2014. เอกซเรย์งบปี 58 เทคับไฟใต้ 2.5 หมื่นล้าน "กลาโหม-กอ.รมน." เฮได้เพิ่มถ้วนหน้า [X-ray 2015 budget. 25 billion poured into extinguishing Southern Fire. "Defence-ISOC" all given raises] [Online]. *Isara News Agency*, 14 August 2014. Available at: www.isranews.org/isranews-article/item/32087-budget_32087.html [Accessed: 1 April 2015].

xx *Preface*

Srisompob Jitpiromsri. 2012. 9 MONTHS INTO THE 9TH YEAR: Amidst the enigmatic violence, the Pa(t)tani Peace Process still keeps on moving [online]. *Deep South Watch*, 23 December 2012. Available at: www.deepsouthwatch.org/en/node/3803 [Accessed: 9 February 2013].

Supaporn Panasnachee et al. 2014. สรุปสถิติเหตุการณ์ความไม่สงบในพื้นที่จังหวัดชายแดนภาคใต้ประจำปี 2557: ปีที่มีจำนวนเหตุการณ์น้อยที่สุดในรอบ 11 ปี [Statistical summary of unrests in southern border provinces 2014: the year with the least number of incidents in 11 years] [online]. *Deep South Watch*, 27 December 2014. Available at: www.deepsouthwatch.org/node/6596 [Accessed: 1 April 2015].

Waeleemah Pusu. 2014. เหตุรุนแรงชายแดนใต้!หญิงม่าย-เด็กกำพร้าพุ่ง [Violent incidents in southern border cause the number of widows and orphans to rise] [online]. *Krungthep Turakij*, 26 November 2014. Available at: www.bangkokbiznews.com/news/detail/619842#sthash. ljkZOSS5.dpuf [Accessed: 1 April 2015].

Acknowledgements

This study would have remained a mere doctoral thesis, not a published research monograph, had it not been for my PhD supervisor, Professor Simon Cottle at Cardiff University's School of Journalism, Media and Cultural Studies, who encouraged me to submit the proposal to the publisher in the first place. Therefore, it is only fitting that I first express him my sincere gratitude for laying the foundation of this book. While Professor Cottle's insightful academic works and perspectives have tremendously helped steering this study into a clear direction, his understanding and calm composure have been absolutely accommodating in the long, challenging, and at times disheartening, undertaking of thesis writing.

My appreciation also goes to the management of Chulalongkorn University and of the Faculty of Communication Arts, for without them I would not have had a golden opportunity to pursue my PhD study and bring this research into fruition. Many thanks as well to the wonderful staff and peers at Cardiff University's JOMEC who have helped facilitating and polishing this study in one way or another.

At the heart of this study is the information gleaned from the many hours I spent with journalists and media practitioners; therefore, my deepest gratitude goes to those who have facilitated my observations and interviews, namely Isara News Agency's Pakorn Peungnetr as well as Nasurah Jeh-ha and Abdullah Wangni, to both of whom I am forever indebted, Sopit Wangwiwattana and Yenjit Sathiramongkolsuk at Thai PBS, Piyachote Intaraniwas and his team at ASTV Manager's Southern News Centre, and Srisuda Jantarasima at Matichon. I am also very much thankful to the interviewees for their valuable time and insights: Ahmad Ramansiriwong, Don Pathan, Korkhet Jantalertluck, Muhammad Ayup Pathan, Muhammadpares Lohasan, Nattha Komolvadhin, Nuannoi Thammasatien, Patchara Yingdamnoon, Prasong Lertrattanawisut, Ramadan Panjor, Roseeda Pusu, Sawas Wansalae, Seksan Kittitaweesin, Sermsuk Kasitipradit, Somkiat Jantaraseema, Sonthaya Kaewkam, Supara Janchidfah, Surapan Boonthanom, Thitinob Komolnimi, Tichila Puttarasapan, Tuwaedaniya Meringging, Waeleemoh Pusu, Wanchai Tantiwittayapitak, Yah Alee, and many others whose names do not appear here. Talking to them and witnessing part of their works have been a privilege, which also gives me a glimmer of hope for Thai journalism during these gloomy times.

xxii *Acknowledgements*

Many thanks to the attentive people at Routledge and associates who have helped transforming a simple document into a sophisticated (to my eye, at least) publication. Most importantly, I am truly grateful to the series editor, Professor Duncan McCargo – an integral person who has made this book possible. Not only have his extensive and laborious researches about Thai press, politics and the southern conflict essentially laid a solid ground for my study, making it a much less overwhelming endeavour, but his keen interest and critical input have also helped sharpened the manuscript profoundly. I am honoured to have worked with him, and believe that under his guidance, the book can contribute to the studies and works of Thailand's southern conflict.

The final paragraph is saved for my close and loved ones, without whom I would not have been able to maintain my wit and sanity – little as they may be. Whilst there are not too many to be named, I fear leaving anyone out, given my occasional clumsiness, will create yet another conflict. Accordingly, many massive, heartfelt thanks to my kind friends, mentors, and colleagues, for all your continuing help that comes in various forms. My amazing parents deserve my greatest gratitude. Their caring and unwavering support is the backbone of my being, and their lives the testament of integrity – a dignified path for me to follow. As such, any merits this book may have belong to all the people involved in its making and those whose stories are told here, while I alone humbly take full accountability for any shortcomings that may remain.

1   Introduction

The resurgence of violence in Thailand's southern border provinces, including Pattani, Yala, Narathiwat, and four districts in neighbouring Songkla, presents distinct political and socio-cultural contexts. Nonetheless, this decade-long phenomenon shares one similarity with political conflicts in other parts of the world: hostility and vigorous discursive contention among protagonists with unequal resources. It is in this contentious and complex setting that news practitioners operate, along with other protagonists in the conflict. Thus, similar to the analyses of other players' actions and movements, the performance of Thai journalists and journalism has also been constantly evaluated.

Notwithstanding existing findings on Thai journalism's shortcomings in response to the phenomenon, this book attempts to argue and demonstrate that journalists do not always act as passive players who simply report, or "mediate," the southern conflict. There appear to be pivotal moments when the news media "mediatize"[1] the on-going violence, which sometimes results in productive consequences or adverse repercussions. At the same time, as the violence progresses, journalists demonstrate professional reflexivity[2] – a development that sometimes signals their aims to carry out constructive roles with respect to political conflict and violence.

This introductory chapter is divided into four parts. The first discusses the disparate interpretations of the conflict to provide the political and socio-cultural setting, as well as the underlying outlooks, wherein Thai journalists operate. The second and third parts look at key theoretical approaches used in this study, namely, the sociology of journalism and the relations between news media and conflict. The last part lays out the outline of this book, which presents findings and discussion concerning news media content and journalists' performance in the southern conflict.

A contested sphere: contending discourses of the southern conflict

To understand the re-emergence of violence in Thailand's southern border provinces, it is crucial to be sensitised to discussions on the long history of political struggles and movements in the region that involved Malay nationalism and its

2 *Introduction*

distinctive Islamic nuance (Thanet 2007; Wattana 2007; Funston 2008; McCargo 2008, 2012). The region is home to the predominantly Muslim and Malay-ethnic population (Malay Muslim),[3] which has been cast as the minority in the Buddhist-dominated kingdom. The region itself has been recognised as one of the country's significant battlefields of political struggle, from the royal dispute over sovereignty during the fifteenth to eighteenth centuries,[4] to the Malay separatist- and Communist-driven armed conflicts in the mid-twentieth century. This means that the re-emerged violence does come from a cultural vacuum; it reflects the conflicting views that have long been entrenched in the Malay Muslim and remaining Thai communities.

The histories of the Patani[5] empire were eclipsed when the central Thai administration enforced a number of national assimilation (or "Thai-ification") policies (Kajadpai 1983; Che Man 2005, pp. 88–89; Connors 2007, p. 145) to ensure the standardised practices and customs of what it claimed to be "Thai-ness" when the territory became subsumed under the Thai kingdom. The implementation of "cultural regulation" as part of the civilised nation-building scheme was ever more rigorous in the era of nationalist and military-groomed Prime Minister Plaek Phibunsongkram, from 1938 to 1944. The government intervention into many Islamic Malay traditions marked a pivotal point in the relations between the central administration and the southerners. In particular, the state's interference in the practice of *adat melayu* (Malay customary law) and the registration of *pondok* (community-based Islamic religious school) (Thanet 2007, p. 33, 57; McCargo 2008, pp. 39–41) resulted in the conflict that descended from the elite locals to the middle class and grassroots communities in both Thai and Patani society (Thanet 2007, p. 33, 57).

Lacking an official and formal forum to voice their dissatisfaction, while being under-represented in centralised politics and administration systems,[6] the locals attempted to challenge the central power via unconventional means. Nevertheless, the accounts of political struggles in the deep South from Thai and local perspectives were inconsistent. The Thai officials' version implied that the arrest of and the treason charge against prominent religious leader Haji Sulong Abdulkader[7] and the "Dusun Nyor Rebellion"[8] were the triggering points for separatist movements in modern politics. On the contrary, locals, and later academics, argued that the Duson Nyor incident in 1948 was the villagers' attempt to guard themselves against the Chinese Communist Party of Malaya and was unrelated to separatism movement (Chaiwat 2007).

During the 1960s and 1970s, separatist movements sprang into action, and violent incidents were prevalent. A number of armed insurgent groups were formed, including the three most prominent: the National Front for the Liberation of Patani (*Barisan Nasional Pembebasan Patani* – BNPP), the National Revolutionary Front (*Barisan Revolusi Nasional* – BRN), and the Patani United Liberation Organisation (PULO) (Funston 2008, p. 9). Founders and members came from varied backgrounds and deployed different approaches,[9] but they all pursued the same goal: independence for the Patani state. However, in the 1980s,

Introduction 3

the Prem Tinsulanond government initiated a set of policies, similar to ones used to suppress Communist militant activities in late 1970s, to minimise insurgent movements and enable Malay Muslims, particularly those in the top echelon of the community, to enter politics (McCargo 2008, p. 2). Analysts saw the situation had taken on a positive turn, as violence subsided afterward. For the following two decades, the region remained relatively undisturbed, as former separatists were given amnesties and underwent rehabilitation programmes. Meanwhile, two state agencies, the Southern Border Provinces Administrative Centre (SBPAC), and the Civil-Police-Military joint command unit 43 (CPM 43), were set up in the region to gather intelligence and maintain security, while slowly working towards installing a fair and efficient administrative system and establish public trust in the hopes of bridging the wide and deep rift between the locals and the authority (Funston 2008, pp. 15–18).

The violence abated during the 1980s and 1990s before resurfacing in the twenty-first century during the first term of Prime Minister Thaksin Shinawatra, who took office in February 2001. The patterns of the re-emerged unrest have differed markedly from those of previous uprisings (Funston 2008; Liow and Pathan 2010). From December 2001 to 2003, the region saw sporadic attacks on police posts and school torching (McCargo 2008, p. xxiii). The event that marked the beginning of the new round of political violence was the large-scale weapons heist at a military armoury depot in Narathiwat on January 4, 2004. Thereafter, attacks and killings have become more frequent, and with discernible patterns. Some studies and investigative reports concluded that the administration's incompetence in intelligence-gathering and its failure to foster a good relationship with the southern inhabitants and local religious leaders facilitated the growth of anti-state sentiment and insurgent movements (Kingoua 2006; Deep South Bookazine 2007a; Deep South Bookazine 2008). The Thaksin government's disbandment of the southern-based SBPAC and CPM 43 during his first term was believed to have contributed to the deficiency in southern governance. Nonetheless, Mark Askew argues that during the 1990s, both entities gradually lost their grip in regional intelligence gathering. With this argument, he indicates that the abolishment of both agencies did not strike the final blow to the region's relatively violence-free decades, because the conflict had been brewing in the region long before 2004, even under the two agencies' purview. The violence, however, was accelerated by the Thaksin administration's iron-fist policies, since the insurgency resurfaced during this time (Askew 2007, pp. 38–53).

Disparate stakeholders, including academics, have different readings of the current phenomenon and its causes, and, consequently, offer diverse solutions to the problem. Here, three discourses[10] concerning the southern conflict – *crime and conspiracy, minority's grievance,* and *Malay nationalism and Islamism* – are highlighted due to their prevalence in media reports, academic literature, and public debates. These discourses will be later used to analyse news content and journalists' understandings of the conflict.

4   *Introduction*

Crime and conspiracy

The notion of various influential cliques competing with one another to maintain their interests in the southern border region is not entirely new, given the long history of power struggles and periodic violence prior to 2004. Thus, when the mass weapon heist occurred in Narathiwat in January 2004, then-Prime Minister Thaksin Shinawatra called the incident an act of "banditry and lawlessness" (McCargo 2008, p. 6). Authorities also came up with a convoluted version of conspiracies, where local vested interest groups – organised crime syndicates involved in illegal drug, cross-border trades, and human trafficking, as well as state officials and influential local politicians – teamed up to stir up unrest in the region to gain and protect their interests. The belief that the web of local high-profile public figures were behind the insurgency led to surveillance of these people and treason charges against veteran politicians and local elites in the early years of resurgent violence (see Appendix B). Such a perspective resulted in the enforcement of a hard-line approach that relied heavily on crime control, security measures, and the state's long-time reluctance to hold open dialogues with insurgent groups. The following interview excerpt of a regional army commander best reflects this discourse.

> Lieutenant General Udomchai Thammasarorat, commander of the Region 4 Army, said the current unrest situation is caused, up to 80%, by **"additional threats,"** which are underground vested interest groups, drugs lords, illegal dealers of fuel and other products. [The incidents caused by] actual separatist movement was only 20%.
>
> The illegal interest groups hired armed forces from the **"jihadist"** (which means to enter warfare and willing to sacrifice for religious belief) separatist groups to instigate various types of violence, especially bombing attacks, to cause concerns among officers or lure them into pouring forces into any particular spot, which will then pave way for other routes or areas to be used in trafficking illicit drugs and illegal products.
>
> "We have obtained evidence of money transfer from illegal traders to accounts of members of separatist networks. When I have received this information, I ordered to arrest them all. Therefore, there are frequent bombings to retaliate [the army's action] recently," the Region 4 Army chief indicated.
>
> [. . .]
>
> Lt.Gen. Udomchai pointed out that [separatist] perpetrators, accounted for 20% [of the overall perpetrators], were not innate criminals, but were instilled with wrong historical and religious beliefs, prompting them to take up weapon and fight the state. Therefore, he proposed **"amnesty"** to be granted to this group of people. They should then be brought into rehabilitation training to change their attitude. At the same time, every group of people who have been affected by the unrest is to be treated, and the military should oversee the entire process.[11]

Authorities also claim that poverty, caused by unemployment and drug addiction, particularly among the youth, also contributed to violence. As a result, apart from

Introduction 5

offering perpetrators amnesty and rehabilitation as the incentive to end violence, the Thaksin administration and its successors have proposed economic development schemes in the region as a way to eradicate poverty and restore peace.[12]

Although the unfavourable ramifications of the government's iron-fist approaches, as described in the previous section, cast doubts on the problem diagnosis, a study by Marc Askew (2007) asserts that the explanation of the conspiring networks of illegal business operators and influential figures may still be valid, given that the perpetrators of violence, and their modus operandi, have been kept clandestine and obscure. The schemes to generate unrest, Askew argues, might have been devised in the southern border region by groups who share similar interests, from underground crime syndicates to local politicians and state officials. Therefore, there is a possibility that "the competing, fissured, and predatory agencies of the Thai state have been central agents in reproducing this disorder" (2007, p. 67) in the southernmost region, in order to maintain their status quo and to reap benefits from the disorderly border. At the same time, the notion of the southernmost region as the prime scene of unrest and instability has enabled insurgents to exploit the locals' distrust towards the state workers by implicating officials as the attackers in many incidents. As a result, another vested interest group that has kept the southernmost provinces vulnerable is separatist groups and leaders themselves, who, like the aforementioned antagonists, remained secretive and unapproachable.

The *crime and conspiracy* discourse highlights violent actions and asserts that networks of political cliques and illegal trade in the region are a front of this conflict. It still, however, makes little reference to historical and cultural nuances and the record of mistreatment and suppression. Although injustice against the Malay Muslims and separatist movement are mentioned, they are undermined by the more salient aspects of the conflict, namely violence, as threats to national security and public order.

Minority's grievance

The second discourse sees the conflict as the locals' revolts against the central ruling structure, which has denied their political and cultural identity. This discourse states that the Malay Muslims have long been mistreated and marginalised in the predominant Thai-Buddhist convention due to their different customs and beliefs, particularly when the "Thai-ification" policies were implemented. Calling this conflict a "millenarian revolt," historian Nidhi Aeusrivongse (2004) bases his interpretation on the April 28, 2004 uprisings (see Appendix B) and argues that the synchronised attacks were carried out as a form of resistance against the Thai state. He downplays the influence of criminal organisations and the separatist movements' goal of autonomy, explaining that the perpetrators of violence were "small people" who took a stand against authorities for what they believed in.

A master's thesis by King-oua Laohong (2006)[13] provides evidence that the violence was fuelled by the growing resentment against the state, particularly among the Malay Muslim communities – a result of the authorities' abuse of

6 Introduction

power during the recent decade. King-oua finds that current residents of the southern border provinces, especially young Muslims who are often targeted as new recruits for the insurgent groups, do not dwell much on the past grievances or the revered Haji Sulong's seven-point autonomy proposal from the 1950s. Instead, the study suggests that dissent has been cultivated among Malay Muslim youths by insurgents using recent unjust incidents, such as the Kru-Ze Mosque attack in Pattani, the clampdown on protestors in Tak Bai District in Narathiwat, and numerous unprecedented searches and arrests, to instigate their anger (King-oau 2006, p. 228).

The following excerpts from a seminal report by the National Reconciliation Commission (NRC)[14] exemplify key features of the *minority's grievance* discourse, from the problem diagnosis to the proposed solutions.

> *To solve the problem of violence in the southern border provinces, Thai society must understand that although the conflict in the area may have structural causes not unlike those in other parts of rural Thailand–poverty, brutal competition with external economic forces over natural resources, low-quality education, injustice at the hands of state officials and shortcomings in the judicial process–its color is different due to factors which include differences in religions, ethnicity, languages, and understandings of history, all of which could easily be used to justify violence. Therefore, to overcome the problem of violence in the southern border provinces, political measures should be of paramount importance, with the aim of reordering relationship between the state and the people, and between majority and minority populations, both within the area and throughout the country, to solve the problems at the structural level and address the justifications for violence at the cultural level.*
>
> . . .
>
> *The National Reconciliation Commission is of the view that whoever uses violence to harm or kill the innocents, or to destroy the property of people and the state, are committing criminal acts and must be made accountable for such acts. However, from a certain angle, the violence that took place in the area was a reaction to the state's excessively harsh tactics and measures, which resulted from miscalculated strategies and circumstantial assessments . . .*[15]

The message is in line with the following passages, extracted from an article by the leader of the United Front for Patani Independence (*Barisan Bersatu Kemerdekaan – BERSATU*),[16] Dr. Wan Kadir Che Man. The statements indicate the causes of the conflict and support the paths to peace recommended by the NRC.

> One answer of this violence is, this is a retaliation against numerous acts of injustice in which [Malay Muslims in the deep South] were victimised, be it the mass arrests of suspects, the mysterious disappearance of Malay Muslims in the region, and the state officials' privilege to carry out unjustified search

Introduction 7

in people's houses and Islamic religious schools. The number of these unjust acts has increased ever since the enactment of martial law in the area. . . .

As for the long-term policies, the Thai government needs to accept the fact that Malay Muslims are not Thai, and they are indigenous groups in the region. Therefore, the policies to be implemented must consider these issues. . . . And please understand, give trust, and be open for [public] participation in as many activities as possible, and always keep in mind to avoid any coercive policies.[17]

The *minority's grievance* discourse places the state's disregard of the region's distinct culture and ethnicity at the heart of the conflict; hence, the marginalisation of the Malay Muslims. Therefore, it is crucial for the authorities and the Thai public to recognise and honour the differences. Changes must be made at all levels, through public participation processes, from individuals' attitudes and practices to structural conditions such as local governance and administration of religion-related affairs. Additionally, some proponents suggest that public discussions and debates are crucial, as they would pave the way for long-term solutions.

Regardless of its seemingly well-rounded problem diagnosis and proposed remedy, this discourse still faces criticism for highlighting cultural distinctiveness but downplaying the influence of Malay nationalism and Islam, including the roles of *pondok* and religious teachers, in this conflict. Conceding that violence may have been the locals' acts of resistance against the state's suppression, a former insurgent leader, among other critics, argues that such a perspective has romanticised Malay Muslim ways of living as idyllic (Deep South Bookazine 2007b, pp. 84–86). Such interpretations may not produce solutions that truly tackle the problem at its roots.

Malay nationalism and Islamism

Contrary to the state's initial explanation that violence is part of the network of underground criminals and corrupted officials, the third discourse centres around the long history of entrenched Malay nationalism, as discussed in the second section, and the global trend of Islamism in the new millennium. Countering the explanation which pinpoints the region's inferior socio-economic development as the cause of the recurred insurgency, historian Thanet Aphornsuvan summarises: "The conflict is not socioeconomic but mainly 'ethnic, religious, and nationalist'" (Thanet 2007, p. 59).

It should also be noted that by pairing Malay nationalism together with Islamism in one discourse, this study does not imply that both concepts are identical. Nonetheless, these two notions were put together because they both approach the conflict from ideological angles rather than purely structural and socio-cultural ones. The *Malay nationalism and Islamism* discourse moves further from *minority's grievance* by not only acknowledging the cultural distinctiveness in the far South, but also critically analysing how these differences are embedded in the region's social and political structures, and how they challenge Thailand's predominant beliefs

8 *Introduction*

and systems in the process. As such, the conflict cannot be solved merely by accepting cultural diversity, but by legitimising the Malay Muslim identity via political means.

Despite similar diagnoses of the conflict's roots, this explanation carries an array of different analyses. Duncan McCargo (2007, 2008, 2012), for instance, analyses how this ideological clash results in vigorous political contention between the Thai state, insurgents, and the locals. He suggests that the power struggle in national-level politics plays an integral part in this conflict, arguing that the Thaksin Shinawatra administration's hard-line policing and security approaches at the beginning of the violence were used to stabilise the ruling coalition's authority and discredit the opposition parties, which have long enjoyed popularity in the region. More importantly, the government's move was meant to challenge the royal legitimacy, or what he calls the "Network Monarchy," in the far South. However, the government's plan backfired. Instead of decreasing the locals' loyalty to the royal family and their associates, the schemes gave rise to more resentment and distrust against the political ruling establishment.[18]

Some analyses are based on studies of insurgency and terrorism,[19] or trace back to the strategies of southern Communist movement and Islamic separatist networks in the 1960s and 1970s,[20] in order to comprehend insurgents' tactical strategies in the current wave of violence. These studies implicate key underground organisations that battle for independence of the Patani state, particularly the BNPP, BRN, PULO, and BERSATU, as well as the influence of religion and transnational terrorism in the southern armed conflict. This set of literature has laid ground for other academics to further explore the foundations and operative strategies of separatist movements. Nevertheless, they make little reference to the socio-cultural aspects, despite attempting to explain the significant role that local religious institutions play in this insurgency. Critics also point out the limitations in the national security/insurgency-oriented approach, as some of these studies were heavily based on the authority's accounts and official dossiers, which may have swayed the findings to favour the state's view (Connors 2007; Funston 2008): hence, leaning towards the *crime and conspiracy* rather than the *Malay nationalism and Islamism* discourse.

Subsequent works that discuss separatism and Malay nationalism bridge the two notions with the unique societal customs and deep-seated anti-Siam sentiment in the three southern border provinces, hence, bringing in debates on Islamic elements, the changing patterns of violence from the 1960s–1970s unrest, and the obscure goals of insurgents.[21] Some studies and reports go further with the investigation of information warfare strategies deployed by insurgents to justify the violence and to delegitimise the state's presence and policies concerning the region.[22] The following excerpt from an interview with a PULO leader illustrates that the insurgent group's anti-Thai state stance and Malay nationalism are the driving force behind their actions.

The Patani society and the Thailand society are two different societies. Patanis are Muslim; Thai people believe in Buddhism. We speak the Malay language;

Introduction 9

Thai people speak the Thai language. . . . Our ancestors established the Patani Islamic Kingdom and lived freely in their own land. In addition, the Patani culture is not at all similar to the Thai culture. In spite of all these differences, the Thailand government occupied our land and wants to alienate us from our own culture. Our ancestors showed great resistance against the attacks of the Buddhist Thailand Kingdom in order to protect our own religion and culture. In the same way, we will continue our resistance in order to protect our religion and culture.[23]

Meanwhile, the influence of Islamism and radical Islam has been brought up in the discussion of southern violence, in particular after the April 28, 2004 orchestrated uprising. Reports said police found copies of *Berjihad di Patani*, a statement declaring war against the Thai state in the fight for Patani's liberation, in the hands of slain suspects. Wattana Sugunnasil's study on the use of Islamic rhetoric in separatist movements indicates that in this monograph, the authors employ an interpretation of the Qu'ran to legitimise the use of force against the Thai state, which has deprived the Malay Muslims of their rightful territory and their religious belief and customs. By proclaiming a *jihad* against the Thai government, the *Berjihad di Patani*, among other interpretations, encourages the locals to sacrifice themselves for martyrdom and to join in armed battles to liberate Patani from the state's suppression. At the same time, the booklet provides a convincing rationale for the attacks on state officials, or even *infidel* Muslims who take sides with the Thai state (Wattana 2007, emphasis in original).

Scholars note that the radical Islamic rhetoric in the fight for Patani's independence was not born in a social and cultural vacuum, but stemmed from the confusion and division of religious sects that have been rooted among the Muslims in the region (Wannata 2007, pp. 132–133; McCargo 2008, pp. 19–54; McCargo 2012, pp. 47–66).[24] The Islamic reform initiated in the 1970s has significantly intensified Muslim religiosity and has deepened the division from the dominant Buddhist communities (Funston 2008); by the same token, Buddhist establishments and communities in the region and nationwide perceive this conflict as a threat to the Thai nation-state, widening the gap further.[25] The developments have also empowered some *ustadz* (religious teachers), enabling them to be among the driving forces of insurgent movements. Together with the long history of Malay nationalism, which is itself entrenched with the notion of Islam, separatist organisations have succeeded by conflating both concepts in the secular nationalist struggle for autonomy (Deep South Bookazine 2007a; Wattana 2007). Similar to debates concerning religious movements elsewhere in the world, the interpretations of religious scriptures have become highly contested, prompting religious authorities to counter by imparting a white paper in the hopes of correcting the misinterpreted version of Islamic beliefs promoted by the insurgents.

Insofar as the explanation regarding religious extremist movements has become prevalent, there has been a discursive shift – following the arrest of a Jemaah Islamiyah member suspected in the 2002 Bali bombing in Thailand in 2003 – from the local Islamist-separatist concept to the potential connection with transnational

10   *Introduction*

jihadist networks. Such a hypothesis has been supported by analysts from Western intelligence agencies and has been in line with the US-led global war on terror campaigns (Funston 2008; McCargo 2008, p. 7; Abuza 2009). However, scholars in Thai studies argue that there is no solid evidence to verify the link between the southern organisations and transnational extremist movements, except for the similar religious undertone. Moreover, the fact that the violence has been contained within the deep South emphasises the insurgents' aim for regional autonomy. As McCargo asserts, "The primary emphasis of the militants is on historical and political grievances, not religious ones" (McCargo 2008, p. 188).

Table 1.1 summarises the key features of the three discourses. A clear demarcation is challenging, especially when similar rhetoric is used to identify the causes and propose solutions. These seemingly overlapping territories also signal the fluidity in the discursive contention, which often hinders decision-makers, academia, news workers, and the general public in sufficiently recognising the complexities at work in the southern conflict (Supalak 2009). The separation of discourses proposed here is rather simplified and perhaps does not thoroughly delineate all the complexity and disparity among the competing discourses. Nevertheless, the categorisation helps tease out the key differences among the contending discourses, and forms a pragmatic foundation for further analyses.

Compared with other discourses, *crime and conspiracy* is evidently distinctive, as it highlights the violent nature of the conflict and describes the phenomenon as criminality and national security threats. Claiming that the primary perpetrators of violence are vested interest groups and a small group of underground insurgents, the *crime and conspiracy* discourse proposes that the conflict can be resolved by maintaining tight security and public order. While agreeing with the latter two discourses that truth and justice are keys to appeasing those affected by violence and mistreatment – be it local Malay Muslims, civil servants, or other societal groups, this discourse views the established presence of law enforcement and security officers in the region as vital to the peace-keeping process. Despite making suggestions about a special administrative body for the region, this discourse discusses little political decentralisation, and sees a centralised administrative system where the Bangkok-based political and military authorities ultimately make the decisions.

The complexity of the discursive contention is more discernible in the remaining two discourses. As discussed previously, the *minority's grievance* and *Malay nationalism and Islamism* discourses point to similar causal explanations: that the resurgent conflict was propelled by a long history of political suppression and cultural marginalisation. Although the *minority's grievance* discourse promotes public sensitivity towards cultural differences and empowerment of the locals' participation, it still operates under the dominant Thai nation-state paradigm – a "unitary state" formed by three pillars: "nation, religion, king" (McCargo 2012, pp. 122–126).[26] As such, key members of the National Reconciliation Commission who exemplified this discourse were ambivalent towards the idea of autonomy and self-determination proposed in the *Malay nationalism and Islamism* discourse (McCargo 2012, pp. 82–84, p. 131). Meanwhile, questioning the existing political

Table 1.1 Contesting realities: comparison of contending discourses in the southern conflict

Discourses	Crime and conspiracy	Minority's grievance	Malay nationalism and Islamism	
Description of problem	Criminality and security threats	Marginalisation and injustice	Insurgency	
Primary causes and perpetrators	1. Vested interest groups maintain status quo, facilitated by poverty and poor life quality in the region 2. Separatist movements seeks separation from the Thai state	Locals rebel against discriminatory and unjust practices and structural inequality caused by centralised administration	Locals and insurgent movements challenge political centralisation and dominant beliefs	
Problem solutions	*State as command centre; top-down* 1. Crime control and security enforcement; information and psychological operations 2. Projects to boost local economy as well as standardised and religious education 3. "Healing" compensation for victims of violence 4. "Moral correction" rehabilitation programmes and amnesty for defected insurgents 5. Secretive peace talks with insurgent leaders overseas	*State as facilitator; multi-lateral* 1. Recognition of local identity (Malay nationalism and Islam) 2. Public participation and deliberative democratic processes such as community empowerment projects 3. Reconciliation with the locals such as open dialogue, rectification of unjust treatment/abuses, revelation of "truth," and free flow of information 4. Peace talks with insurgent groups and dissidents	*State as facilitator; Civil sector as active player; multi-lateral* 'Political approach' Similar to solutions proposed in *minority's grievance*: recognition, public participation, reconciliation, peace dialogues	'Radical approach' 1. Intimidation and information warfare 2. Intervention by and recognition from international forum
Ideal political structures	*Restructuring* 1. A special administrative body 2. Replace martial law with state of emergency decree	*Reform* Region-specific administrative system	*Revolution* Autonomous local administration	Independence
Political Goals	Centralisation	Devolution	(semi) Autonomy	

12 *Introduction*

and socio-cultural conventions that subjugate the locals' rights, the *Malay nationalism and Islamism* discourse calls for an autonomous administrative structure in which residents of the deep South from all ethnicities and social groups can join in the debates and have more, or even ultimate, decision power concerning their livelihood – even if those debates and decisions may challenge the Thai nation-state constructs.[27]

These discourses are most prevalent in academic researches, reports, publications, and media coverage. It should also be noted that the literature and excerpts of statements used to explain each discourse do not necessarily reflect the authors' or speakers' endorsement of that discourse. At the same time, it is premature to label any political or social groups promoters or supporters of a particular discourse, as the complexity of each political and social group makes it difficult clearly to identify their members' collective outlook, and it is not this study's objective to find such correlations.[28] Additionally, there may be other interpretations which differ from the three presented here, but have not been brought to light due to the lack of evidential support. However, the fact that the above interpretations have become widely presented and explored illustrates an integral characteristic of the southern conflict: certain discourses are promoted to be recognised, and perhaps to supersede others, in order to legitimise the protagonists' agenda.

The making of news and news workers: understanding news production culture

This section now turns to a discussion of how journalists operate and how journalism plays roles in political conflict. Here, the sociology of journalism is used as the primary analytical lens to study Thai news organisations and the southern conflict. The sociology of journalism argues, broadly, that news media are shaped by social, political, economic, and technological determinants, as opposed to being solely determined by journalistic features or one particular force outside the news organisations.[29] As Michael Schudson puts it, "the decisions inherent in the manufacture of news have more to do with the marketplace, the nature of organizations, and the assumptions of news professionals than with individual bias" (Schudson 2003, p. 47). Along this line, Stephen Reese proposes the *hierarchy-of-influences* model (2001): the five cascading levels of factors that shape news operation, performing both independently and along with one another. He points out that while individual journalists' attitudes, training, and background are the first mould that shapes journalists' actions and outputs, routines – the "ongoing, structured, deeply naturalized rules, norms, procedures that are embedded in media work" (Ibid., p. 180) – become the second mould that builds occupational conformity. Routines then fall in line with the news organisation's larger and formal structure, such as editorial policies and company rules, and the power plays inside the organisation, such as line of command and self-censorship. The model then suggests the investigation into extra-media influences, which include the government, advertisers, and other media organisations. Reese concludes that, ultimately, the ideological level subsumes the previous four factors, so that they work to sustain particular

Introduction 13

ideological goals, and leads the news media as a social force to maintain its status quo and be part of a social control system. Meanwhile, the news media also react to and interact with the political settings surrounding them,[30] as well as the economic system in which they operate.[31] Therefore, news workers invent and amend their norms, professional and moral judgment, practices, and outputs in accordance with the political culture they work in. At the same time, market demands also determine the use of presentation formats of journalism, as seen in the hybrid *infotainment* or *popular journalism* (Bourdieu 1996; McNair 1998).

Regardless, the sociology of journalism does not see journalism as a passive domain. Contrary to the *dominance paradigm* (McNair 1998, p. 25), which sees elite groups as the sole promoters of dominant discourses and the media as faithfully legitimising and maintaining such dominance, Brian McNair argues that there is no guarantee that any ideology will stay in the superior position. As a result, "the media functions not always or necessarily as a tool of ideological domination, but often as an arena for a real competition of ideas and interpretation of events" (Ibid., p. 29), while recognising the unequal distribution of power among members of stratified social groups. The analysis is in line with Gadi Wolfsfeld's *political contest* model, which sees journalism's role as that of a forum for competing discourses in political conflict, and recognises that there are opportunities for protagonists to challenge the control of dominating discourses (Wolfsfeld 1997, 2004). Some studies also indicate that the development of technology and the globalised flow of information redefine journalism as well as enabling new forms, genres, and practices of journalism to emerge, effectively broadening the news ecology (Cottle 2006; McNair 2006; Waisbord 2013). Such an impact, as demonstrated in McNair's *cultural chaos paradigm* (2006), minimises the power of dominant discourses by allowing minority and alternative voices to be heard more than before, although their presence may not entirely outdo the existing dominant discourses.

The sociology of journalism moves beyond a media-centric view by proposing an analytical framework that considers the political and cultural milieux as equally influential in shaping news media's performance; nevertheless, it does not downplay the influence of journalistic characteristics embedded in the news production culture. This framework enables the examination of three "major factors" that shape the news coverage of politics, suggested by Rodney Benson: "a) commercial or economic, b) political, and c) interorganizational field of journalism" (2004, p. 280). Given that political conflicts are defined by contending discourses, some of which come from contradictory viewpoints, the sociology of journalism helps shed light on relevant protagonists on the news stage.

A symbiotic and dynamic relationship: the roles of news media in conflict

The interplay between journalism and other protagonists in political conflict has been theorised as dynamic and changeable (Hallin 1989; Wolfsfeld 1997). Moreover, the relationship is often dialectical – meaning it is an interdependent,

14   *Introduction*

negotiated, and reciprocal relationship. It can also be governed by political and economic imperatives (Herman and Chomsky 1988) and influenced by the surrounding geopolitical settings (Sonwalkar 2004). Various stakeholders' perspectives towards political conflict/violence contribute to news media's understanding of the conflict, and thus, the representation of conflict in news content. At the same time, these views also determine protagonists' expectations of how news media should portray political conflict (Schlesinger, Murdock, and Elliott 1983; Nossek 2007).

To locate the positions of news media in political conflict/violence, Hillel Nossek (2007) proposes three approaches to explain the symbiotic relation between political violence (in his study, terrorism) and journalism. The first, the *classical approach*, sees journalism serving terrorism in three ways: 1) providing publicity, 2) giving legitimate causes for their actions, and 3) becoming an arena where terrorists from different camps can learn their tactics and strategies from one another, contributing to the so-called contagion effect (Brosius and Weimann 1991 cited in Cottle 2006, p. 146; Dobkin 1992 cited in Nossek 2007, p. 274). The spectacle of terrorist acts prompts news media to present the stories to a mass audience (Carruthers 2000; Nacos 2002); hence, serving as the "oxygen provider" for terrorism (Nossek 2007, p. 275). Also, knowing how dramatic scenes can grab the media's attention, perpetrators also opt for extreme violence as their messenger. By providing platforms to publicise terrorists' use of weapons and tactics, the media helps glorify, legitimise, and rationalise terrorist groups' activities (Carruthers 2000; Nacos 2010).

While the *classical approach* sees news media effectively taking sides with the anti-establishment perpetrators, the second approach, proposed by Nossek, the *critical approach,* offers a contrasting analysis. Based on Edward Herman and Noam Chomsky's *propaganda model* (Herman and Chomsky 1988), this approach argues that in reporting terrorism, the news media in fact serve the state's aims by amplifying panic among the public, which subsequently legitimatises the state's uses of force to control any forms of public order disruption, and strengthens the government's position. This perspective points to economic interests as the main cause for the news media's favour for sensational presentation and the occlusion of the conflict's contexts (Herman and Chomsky 1988; Tumber 2007). The impact of this dramatised coverage, the *critical approach* suggests, is in the interest of the state rather than that of terrorist groups. The lack of substantial information prevents the public from forming a clear understanding of the complexity of the conflict's political nature, let alone sympathising with the terrorists' goals. Furthermore, siding with the state, intentionally or unknowingly, the media tend to ignore "terrorism from above" – violence instigated by the state, which "seeks to sow terror in the public mind so that people will obey and overlook government actions that violate their rights and weaken their ability to criticise government" (Nossek 2007, p. 276). A clear example of this case was Chomsky's work in 2002 (cited in Nossek 2007, p. 277) on the US military operation in Afghanistan, where the American media failed to challenge the administration's decision to invade

Introduction 15

another country, or Justin Lewis' studies (2007, 2008) on the media's support of US and UK military budget allocation.

From this perspective, therefore, the media can be seen as the state's accomplice in publicising homogenous and hegemonic views towards political violence among the public, usually the views of the dominant elites. People are likely to place trust in authorities to eradicate criminal disruption and restore public order when they feel threatened by terrorists (Schlesinger et al. 1983, pp. 24–27). The continuing portrayal of aggressions can give rise to fear and terror among the public (Altheide 2002, 2006), and the "us versus them" perspective (Sonwalkar 2004, 2005) towards those identified with the insurgents. While carrying apathy or resentment towards "the Others," be it insurgents or the people with whom they identified, the public may justify the use of forces against the "deviant" to protect their own safety, if governmental protection measures are deemed insufficient.

Prominent elements of political conflict, as viewed by both approaches, are the state's measures to limit information access, such as censorship, the military's press handler system, and national security law. Still, the two perspectives have different readings on such restrictions. The *classical approach* sees these restrictions as the state's attempt to weaken news media's information-gathering ability, preventing them from further spreading the terrorists' messages. On the contrary, the *critical approach* views the state's deployment of *structural constraints* (Schlesinger et al. 1983) as a way to ensure the elite hegemonic view as the sole representation of the conflict.

Regardless of their arguments, both approaches contain blind spots in their analyses of journalism's roles in political conflict. The *classical approach's* "contagion" effect, which draws causal links between media and terrorism, remains debatable due to insufficient empirical evidence (Picard 1991; Nacos 2010), and the portrayal of news media as promoters of blood frenzy does not do justice to other journalistic efforts, such as peace journalism, which promote conflict resolution. In the same vein, although critics from the *critical approach* have placed a strong accusation against news media as the state's guard dog, they have yet to form a clear answer when it comes to the desired role of journalism in reporting conflict. Overall, both approaches see news media as passive, yet influential, protagonists whose job is to spread propaganda, be it for government or anti-state movements. At the same time, this shared presumption does not recognise constructive professional values, such as being a "public watchdog" and maintaining objectivity.

In the third perspective, the *functional or professional approach*, news media are still criticised for underperforming in resolving political conflicts. But contrary to the previous two approaches, this perspective does not label news media as a servant of the state or co-conspirator with terrorists purely because of market imperatives or dominant political perspectives. Instead, this approach attempts to explain that the political, socio-cultural, and media environments which encompass news organisations are major variables that shape journalists' perspectives towards political violence, and must therefore be granted heightened theoretical

16 *Introduction*

recognition. This is similar to Gadi Wolfsfeld's *political contest* model (1997), which positions the media as the central stage on which political conflict key players compete to rally the public's support, and not simply the prime campaigner for either the state or its antagonists. Similarly, Daniel Hallin's *sphere of legitimate controversy* (1989) argues that news media play a responsive role to elites' consensus and disagreements. As a result, they are unlikely to break away from the agreed discourse that dominates the debate so as to avoid being cast as dissident. However, when there is a disagreement among political leaders, news media become proactive in promoting a different stance from the elite and other news media.

While accepting that the news media favour the dramatised and sensational elements of political violence to gain financial interests, this approach admits that there are other professional conventions that explain why not all violent events are selected to be in the news. The "newsworthiness" of political violence and how it is portrayed also depend on journalistic conventions like frames and narrative styles (Picard and Adams 1991; Fawcett 2002) or geopolitical interests (Sonwalkar 2004). Moreover, journalists' choice of news sources are not solely determined by their economic interests, political beliefs, or structural restrictions, but professional requirements such as deadline and the source-indexing system (Bennett 1990 cited in Wolfsfeld 2004, p. 21) and human experiences of being in hostile situations and bonding with their military companions (Morrison and Tumber 1988 cited in Tumber 2004, pp. 192–193; Cottle 2006, p. 190) can also shape journalists' outlook of the conflict. Similarly, keeping confidentiality of news sources and off-record information for the purpose of ensuring the safety of informants rather than abiding by authorities' rules is another factor that compels news media to leave certain stories in the dark when covering wars and conflicts (Tumber 2005). The desirable role of journalism, in this perspective, involves the exercise of media self-regulation and the social responsibility principle.

The three approaches reflect different positions on journalism's roles in political conflict and enable us to be sensitised to the varied rationales of news organisations and other stake-holders' decisions, policies, or actions towards the conflict. While this study uses the *functional/professional approach* to explore and analyse the roles of Thai journalism in reporting the southern conflict, it is crucial to be aware of other approaches, as they suggest the logic behind different protagonists' views on the roles of Thai news media in this phenomenon.

The outline of this book

This book sets out to explore the roles of Thai journalism in the southern conflict by examining news content, news production culture, and factors influencing news-making processes. Chapter 2 looks at the news output of four selected organisations to answer how the conflict was reported and how journalists make sense of the phenomenon. The chapter will lay out the predominant themes, news frames, and labels used to characterise the conflict and its participating factions. Along with the analysis of the types and specialisations of most frequently used

Introduction 17

news sources and the presentation formats, this chapter illustrates how the news coverage of the southern conflict tends to support the state authority's perspectives and marginalise other interpretations of the problem.

Chapter 3 will present an overview of news production practices and discuss difficulties in reporting the southern conflict, which helps explain deficiencies in news output, such as the prevalence of state official sources and their perspectives in news content. The discussion in this chapter will take into account the tension of professional conventions at work as well as the dynamic political and media environments at play.

Chapter 4 will then elaborate on the interdependent relationship between journalists and their sources, and how diversity of sources is used as a proof of professional objectivity. The analysis in this chapter will observe the interplay between journalists and their sources, and how this interaction affects the representation of different discourses in news media. Chapter 5 will discuss three prominent journalistic perspectives on the southern conflict, and how journalists translate those stances into journalism's anticipated roles in the conflict. Discussion and debate concerning key journalistic ideologies and practices will be brought in, such as the notion of objectivity, criteria for story selection and presentation styles, and recommendations to improve the quality of conflict reporting, such as peace journalism[32] and other variation in journalistic presentations.[33] Chapter 6 will then recapitulate the findings and discuss the interplay between Thai journalism and the fierce and dynamic discursive contestation of – and disparate protagonists in – the conflict, which contributes to the production of southern conflict coverage.

Overall, the book argues that while the prominent themes and voices in the news coverage generally echo the state authority's outlooks, the shifting paradigm of news professionalism, as well as the dynamism, diversity, and complexity of Thai news ecology could enable the marginalised interpretations of the southern conflict to emerge in news coverage, producing "contra-flows" of information against the hegemonic discourses. These opportunities could be manifest through mechanisms such as the variations of news presentation formats, journalistic and organisational principles, and professional reflexivity.

Notes

1 The recently conceptualised notion of "mediatization" encourages media researchers to explore how media organisations and technology actively influence power transformations in society through "media logic," while also being shaped by such transformations because they are a societal member (Livingstone 2009; Lundby 2009). As opposed to "mediation," which refers to the communication processes wherein news media merely convey information from one party to another, mediatization sees news media as being "capable of enacting and performing conflicts as well as reporting and representing them" (Cottle 2006, p. 9). As a result, the news media's role is more than a neutral purveyor of information; they often have a "*performative* involvement and *constitutive* role within them" (Ibid., original emphasis). Despite being debatable, the concept nevertheless offers an outlook into the media's association with and its overtone in many aspects of daily life, as well as the varied effects of the complexity within the media ecology. For the overarching discussions on mediatization, see

18 *Introduction*

Lundby, K. ed. 2009. *Mediatization: Concept, Changes, Consequences.* New York: Peter Lang; Sonia Livingstone. 2009. On the mediation of everything: ICA presidential address 2008. *Journal of Communication,* 59(1), pp. 1–18; and Cottle, S. 2006. *Mediatized Conflict.* Maidenhead: Open University Press, for conflict mediatization.

2 Following Laura Ahva's explanation, professional reflexivity in this study refers to "journalists' capacity for self-awareness; their ability to recognize influences and changes in their environment, alter the course of their actions, and renegotiate their professional self-images as a result" (Ahva 2013, p. 791). For more discussions on this concept generally, see, for example, Ahva, L. 2013. Public journalism and professional reflexivity. *Journalism,* 14(6), pp. 790–806; and Cottle, S. 2005. In defence of 'thick' journalism; or how television journalism can be good for us. In: Allan, S. ed. *Journalism: Critical Issues.* Berkshire: Open University Press, pp. 109–124. For more discussions on professional reflexivity and war coverage, see, for example, Nohrstedt, S. A. 2005. Media Reflexivity in the War on Terror. Three Swedish Dailies and the Iraq War. In: Ottosen, R. and Nohrstedt, S.A. eds. *Global War – Local Views: Media Images of the Iraq War,* Gotherburg: Nordicom, pp. 327–348; and Hanitzsch, T. 2004. Journalists as Peacekeeping Force? Peace Journalism and Mass Communication Theory. *Journalism Studies* 5(4), pp. 483–495 on professional reflexivity and peace journalism

3 The use of "Malay Muslims" to refer to the natives of Pattani, Yala, and Narathiwat who are Muslim and speak the local language of Patani Malay has raised debates among academics and conservative officials (McCargo 2007: ix). The Thai authority uses the term "Thai Muslims" in official documents, in line with references to Thai citizens of other ethnic backgrounds and religious beliefs, as in Chinese Thai or Thai Buddhist. However, political scientist and peace studies scholar Chaiwat Satha-Anand has opted for the term "Malay Muslims" to distinguish the Muslims in the southern border provinces from other Islamic believers in other parts of the country, and also as recognition of the region's long history, which relates to the notions of Islam and Malay descent. Despite the National Reconciliation Commission's (2006) suggestion of "Thai Muslims of Malay descent," many scholars follow Chaiwat's application. In this study, I also use "Malay Muslims" to maintain the originality of the cited literatures, and in accordance with Chaiwat's argument.

4 See, for example, Syukri 1985; and Thanet 2007. Ibrahim Syukri's *Sejarah Kerajaan Melayu Patani (SKMP)* [History of the Malay Kingdom of Patani] was originally published in the late 1940s in Malaysia's Kelantan state, and was banned in Thailand due to its contradictions of the Thai state's accounts. Later, the monograph became a sought-after underground book for new generations of Patani intellectuals. Here, I refer to Thanet's analysis of the English translation by Connor Bailey and John N. Miksic, published in 1985 by Ohio University Center for International Studies.

5 Many academics in the study of southern Thai conflict suggest that the use of "Patani" as a reference to the ancient territory connotes political implication. Although the Thai pronunciation of the ancient empire and the modern southern border province is alike, "Pattani" was used in reference to the province in line with the official spelling, while "Patani" refers to the empire that existed from the fifteenth to seventeenth centuries and covered the three southernmost provinces, some part of Songkla (itself a former ancient state, Singora), and some northern Malaysian states. "Patani" also follows the Malay spelling of the region. While McCargo (2007, p. viii) notes that the usage of "Patani" may reflect the authors' political stance, in this book I follow the original term used in the cited literature.

6 No Malay Muslim politicians were able to garner a seat in the general MP elections from 1938 to 1948 (Thanet 2007, p. 34).

7 Haji Sulong Abdulkader was regarded as a prominent religious leader. A graduate of Mecca, he pioneered Islamic education reform in southern Thailand in the

Introduction 19

1940s. Gaining respect from the locals, Haji Sulong later expanded his campaigns to establishing networks of religious leaders and scholars, and worked to negotiate the government's interference with local customs, as he saw that such actions would cause Muslims to stray from the proper way of life. His 1947 seven-point proposal (McCargo 2008, pp. 60–61) demanded certain degrees of autonomy and the endorsement of Islamic elements in the region's political, judicial, and cultural structures. However, the proposal was turned down by the then government and Haji Sulong was later arrested and charged with treason. He was reported to have disappeared and was presumed dead in 1954. His family has also been regarded as a political legacy in Pattani Province, particularly his son, Den Tohmeena, who is a veteran politician. See McCargo 2008, pp. 63–75, for more detail on Den Tohmeena's role in politics.

8 The data concerning the Dusun Nyor incident remains debatable and inconsistent, starting with the date when the event took place (the 25th, 26th, or the 28th of April 1948). Malay Muslim residents of Dusun Nyor village in Narathiwat Province gathered and brought with them their choice of primitive arms, then performed superstitious rituals, including the sacred oil-bathing ceremony, which villagers believed would make them invincible against weapons in their fight against the widespread Communist guerrillas. However, police suspected the villagers were forming an armed revolt against the state, provoked by the arrest of Haji Sulong. The authorities dispatched a number of law enforcement and security officers to the scene, and opened fire on the villagers. Thirty police were killed in the incident, but the deaths of villagers, believed to be far more, were uncounted. Some official Thai accounts referred to Haji Sulong as the mastermind of the incident, but the record also showed that the religious leader was in jail at that time. See more details of and debates on the Dusun Nyor incident in Chaiwat Satha-Anand. 2007. The Silence of the Bullet Monument: Violence and "Truth" Management, Dusun-nyor 1948, and Kru-Ze 2004. In: McCargo, D. ed. *Rethinking Thailand's Southern Violence*. Singapore: NUS Press, pp. 11–34.

9 As Funston classifies, "the BNPP represented a coalition of the aristocracy and conservative Islamic class; the BRN had a more radical Islamic "republican orientation, with its base in the *pondok*; and PULO focused more on secular nationalism than Islam (although from time to time also emphasized Islam)" (2008, pp. 9–10).

10 The term "discourse" used here refers to the wider, socially prevailing beliefs or ideologies that cohere as recognisable perspectives. This explanation follows Kevin William's definition, which derives from the works of Michel Foucault: "a systematically organized set of statements that gives expression to the meanings and values of an institution. [. . .] A discourse provides a set of possible statements about a given area, and organizes and gives structure to the manner in which a particular topic, object, process is to be talked about" (2003, p. 160).

11 An excerpt from *Isara News Agency*. 2011. สำรวจนโยบายดับไฟใต้ – เพื่อไทยจ่อตั้งกอส. 2 – ทหารฯ อภัยโทษ [A survey of policies to distinguish southern fire. Puea Thai to establish NRC 2 – Military suggests amnesty] [Online]. 15 August 2011. Available at: www.isranews. org/south-news/scoop/38–2009–11–15–11–15–01/3160-สำรวจนโยบายดับไฟใต้-เพื่อไทยจ่อตั้ง-กอส-2-ทหารฯ-อภัยโทษ.hmtl [Accessed: 6 January 2013] – Translation from Thai by the author, [original emphases].

12 This is contrary to Srisompob Jitpiromsri and Panyasak Sobhonvasu (2007)'s findings, which argue that, while financial deficiency might have been a valid factor in the past, the economy in the southernmost region has improved significantly in the new millennium. The study concludes that poverty alone might not prompt the locals to stage uprisings, and the government's financial boosts have done little to ease the regional tension.

13 The thesis was later published as a pocket book in 2008, titled ถอดรหัสไฟใต้ [*Decoding the Southern Fire*] by Krungthep Turakij Publisher.

20 *Introduction*

14 The National Reconciliation Commission (NRC) was an independent body set up by the Thaksin Shinawatra cabinet on March 28, 2005. It was tasked with conducting fact-finding missions and peace-initiative projects. The team was headed by a high-profile statesman, and its members included cabinet members, academics, human rights campaigners, and social activists. For more detail, see Appendix B.

15 An excerpt from The National Reconciliation Commission. 2006. *Report of the National Reconciliation Commission: Overcoming Violence Through the Power of Reconciliation* [online]. Translated from Thai by Asian Human Rights Commission. Bangkok, pp. 3, 11. Available at: http://thailand.ahrchk.net/docs/nrc_report_en.pdf [Accessed: 11 January 2013] [original emphases].

16 BERSATU was established in late 1980s as a loose umbrella organisation of four prominent separatist groups: PULO, BRN, BIPP (*Barisan Islam Pembebasan Patani* or the Islamic Liberation Front of Patani – formerly known as BNPP), and the Patani Mujahidin Movement (GIMP). The objective of BERSATU was to coordinate among the member groups in terms of shared political goals, as well as their strategies in warfare, international recognition, and talks with the Thai government.

17 An excerpt from Che Man, Wan Kadir. 2005. Conflict and Conflict Resolution: Malay Muslim Liberation Movement in Thailand. Translated from English by Parinya Nuanpian and Nipon Soh-heng. ฟ้าเดียวกัน *[Fah Diew Kan]*. April–June 2005, pp. 97–98

18 For more discussions on the Thaksin administration's deficiency in southern conflict resolution and the attempts to destabilise the Network Monarchy's political authority and legitimacy, see McCargo, D. 2007. Thaksin and the Resurgence of Violence in the Thai South. In: McCargo, D. ed. *Rethinking Thailand's Southern Violence*. Singapore: NUS Press, pp. 35–68; and Ukrist Pathmanand. 2007. Thaksin's Achilles' Heel: The Failure of Hawkish Approaches in the Thai South. In: McCargo, D. ed. *Rethinking Thailand's Southern Violence*. Singapore: NUS Press, pp. 69–88.

19 See, for example, Gunaratna, R. et al. 2005. *Conflict and Terrorism in Southern Thailand*. Singapore: Marshall Cavendish Academic; and Abuza, Z. 2009. *Conspiracy of Silence: The Insurgency in Southern Thailand*. Washington, D.C.: United States Institute of Peace Press.

20 See, for example, Kitti Rattanachaya. 2004. จุดไฟใต้ ตั้งรัฐปัตตานี *[Southern Fire Ignition, Establishment of Patani State]*. Bangkok: So. Pijit Karn Pim; Surachart Bamroongsook. 2006. การก่อความไม่สงบในภาคใต้ของไทย [Insurgency in Southern Thailand] [online]. จุลสารความมั่นคงศึกษา *[Security Studies Monograph]*. 10(1). Available at: http://stability.trf.or.th/default.aspx [Accessed: 11 Janaury 2013]; and Kitti Rattanachaya. 2006. ถอดรหัสไฟใต้ *[Decoding the Southern Fire]*. Bangkok: Duang Kaew Publishing.

21 See, for example, Funston 2008; McCargo 2008; Liow and Pathan 2010; Rungrawee et al. 2013.

22 See, for example, King-oua 2006; Deep South Bookazine 2007a, pp. 28–77; Srisompob and Panyasak 2007; Deep South Bookazine 2008, pp. 32–66.

23 An excerpt from Özköse, A. 2009. Patani capital: Istanbul. The new leader of the Patanis, Nur Abdurrahman, spoke first with the World Bulletin [Online]. *World Bulletin*, 4 December 2009, paragraph 22. Available at: www.worldbulletin.net/?aType=haber Archive&ArticleID=50818 [Accessed: 11 January 2013].

24 Another noteworthy reading is Baroon (pseudonym)'s ญิฮาดสีเทา *[Grey Jihad]*. The compilation of essays written by this news magazine columnist highlights the influence of Islam in the current round of violence from a local and former insurgent's perspective. Interestingly, while his outlook on the southern conflict exemplifies the *minority's grievance* discourse, despite certain *crime and conspiracy* discourse' rhetoric, his analysis of the role of Islam in local communities – which is not sufficiently mentioned in the previous two discourses – resembles that of *Malay nationalism and Islamism*. See Baroon. 2005. ญิฮาดสีเทา *[Grey Jihad]*. Bangkok: Sarika.

25 See more discussion on the roles of Thai Buddhism in the southern conflict in McCargo 2012, pp. 16–46.

Introduction 21

26 For more discussion on the clash between the notion of Thainess and Malay Muslim identity, and its impact on the Malay Muslim's citizenship, see McCargo. 2012. "Contested Citizenship," pp. 111–128.

27 For more discussion on the proposals of autonomy in the southern border region, see McCargo. 2012. "Autonomous Futures," pp. 129–152.

28 For instance, to simply conclude that every Malay Muslim sympathises with the insurgents and endorses the *Malay nationalism and Islamism* discourse would be an overstatement, and to infer that every state official supports the *crime and conspiracy* discourse may not be entirely accurate. The previously mentioned *Grey Jihad* (2005) was an example of a former insurgent refuting the influence of Malay nationalism and not identifying himself as a "Malay Muslim," although he highlights the significance of Islam in this conflict. This finding is in line with Sorayut Aiemueayut's analysis (2013, pp. 95–97, 111) on how the Malay Muslims have the "sense of belonging" towards the Thai state. However, the authorities' and military's practices of separating the "us" (Thai citizens) from the "them" (insurgents) often results in the branding of Malay Muslims as "insurgent sympathisers".

29 See, for example, Schlesinger 1990; McNair 1998; Schudson 2003.

30 See, for example, Hallin 1989; Pharr 1996; Wolfsfeld 1997; McCargo 2000; Wolfsfeld 2004; Archetti 2010.

31 See, for example, Hallin and Mancini 2004.

32 See, for example, Hanitzsch 2004, 2005; Lynch and McGoldrick 2005; McCargo 2006; Supapohn 2006; Walakkamol 2007; Witchayawanee 2009; Walakkamol 2013.

33 See, for example, online news reporting (Allan 2002); live discussion and debate television programme (Cottle 2002); regional television and the use of *contextual objectivity* (Iskandar and El-Nawawy 2004); other forms of 'thick' journalism (Cottle 2005); civic community radio (Chalisa 2007).

References

Abuza, Zachary. 2009. *Conspiracy of Silence: The Insurgency in Southern Thailand.* Washington, DC: United States Institute of Peace Press.

Ahva, Laura. 2013. Public journalism and professional reflexivity. *Journalism* 14(6), pp. 790–806.

Allan, Stuart. 2002. Reweaving the Internet: Online News of September 11. In: Zelizer, B. and Allan, S. eds. *Journalism After September 11*. London: Routledge, pp. 119–140.

Altheide, David. 2002. *Creating Fear: News and the Construction of Crisis*. New York: Aldine de Gruyter.

Altheide, David. 2006. *Terrorism and the Politics of Fear*. Oxford: AltaMira Press.

Archetti, Christina. 2010. Comparing international coverage of 9/11: Towards an interdisciplinary explanation of the construction of news. *Journalism* 11(5), pp. 567–588.

Askew, Mark. 2007. *Conspiracy, Politics, and a Disorderly Border: The Struggle to Comprehend Insurgency in Thailand's Deep South*. Washington, DC: East-West Center Washington.

Baroon. 2005. ญิฮาดสีเทา *[Grey Jihad]*. Bangkok: Sarika.

Benson, Rodney. 2004. Bringing the sociology of media back in. *Political Communication* 21(3), pp. 275–292.

Bourdieu, Pierre. 1996. *On Television and Journalism*. London: Pluto Press.

Carruthers, Susan. 2000. *The Media at War*. Hampshire: Palgrave Macmillan.

Chaiwat Satha-Anand. 2007. The Silence of the Bullet Monument: Violence and "Truth" Management, Dusun-nyor 1948, and Kru-Ze 2004. In: McCargo, D. ed. *Rethinking Thailand's Southern Violence*. Singapore: NUS Press, pp. 11–34.

22   Introduction

Chalisa Magpanthong. 2007. *Participatory Community Media: Three Cases Studies of Thai Community Radio Stations*. PhD Dissertation, Ohio University.

Che Man, Wan Kadir. 2005. Conflict and Conflict Resolution: Malay Muslim Liberation Movement in Thailand. Translated from English by Parinya Nuanpian and Nipon Sohheng. ฟ้าเดียวกัน *[Fah Diew Kan]*. April–June 2005, pp. 86–100.

Connors, Michael K. 2007. War on Error and the Southern Fire: How Terrorism Analysts Get It Wrong. In: McCargo, D. ed. *Rethinking Thailand's Southern Violence*. Singapore: NUS Press, pp. 145–173.

Cottle, Simon. 2002. Television Agora and Agoraphobia Post-September 11. In: Zelizer, B. and Allan, S. eds. *Journalism After September 11*. London: Routledge, pp. 178–198.

Cottle, Simon. 2005. In Defence of 'Thick' Journalism; or How Television Journalism Can Be Good for Us. In: Allan, S. ed. *Journalism: Critical Issues*. Berkshire: Open University Press, pp. 109–124.

Cottle, Simon. 2006. *Mediatized Conflict*. Maidenhead: Open University Press.

Deep South Bookazine. 2007a. Cover Story. สงครามความคิด: การต่อสู้ยืดเยื้อ [Cover Story. War of Ideas: The Prolonged Fight]. In: Muhammad Ayup Pathan and Apiwat Supreechawuttipong. eds. *Deep South Bookazine*. December 2007(2). Bangkok: Pap Pim Publishing, pp. 28–77.

Deep South Bookazine. 2007b. สัมภาษณ์อิสกันดาร์ ธำรงทรัพย์ [Interview with Iskandar Thamrongsap]. In: Muhammad Ayup Pathan and Apiwat Supreecha-wuttipong. eds. *Deep South Bookazine*. December 2007(2). Bangkok: Parbpim, pp. 82–100.

Deep South Bookazine. 2008. Cover Story. สงครามความรู้สึก: ปมลึกไฟใต้ [Cover Story. War of Feelings: A Deep Knot of the Southern Fire]. In: Pakorn Puengnetr and Muhammad Ayup Pathan. eds. *Deep South Bookazine*. April 2008(3). Bangkok: Pap Pim Publishing, pp. 32–63.

Fawcett, Liz. 2002. Why peace journalism isn't news. *Journalism Studies,* 3(2), pp. 213–223.

Funston, John. 2008. *Southern Thailand: The Dynamics of Conflict*. Washington, DC: East-West Center.

Hallin, Daniel. 1989. *The "Uncensored War": The Media and Vietnam*. London: University of California Press.

Hallin, Daniel and Mancini, Paolo. 2004. *Comparing Media Systems: Three Models of Media and Politics*. Cambridge and New York: Cambridge University Press.

Hanitzsch, Thomas. 2004. Journalists as peacekeeping force? Peace journalism and mass communication theory. *Journalism Studies* 5(4), pp. 483–495.

Herman, Edward and Chomsky, Noam. 1988. *Manufacturing Consent: The Political Economy of the Mass Media*. New York: Vintage.

Isara News Agency. 2011. สำรวจนโยบายดับไฟใต้ – เพื่อไทยจ่อตั้งกอส. 2 – ทหารชูอภัยโทษ [A survey of policies to distinguish southern fire. Puea Thai to establish NRC 2 – Military suggests amnesty] [online]. 15 August 2011. Available at: www.isranews.org/south-news/scoop/38–2009–11–15–11–15–01/3160-สำรวจนโยบายดับไฟใต้-เพื่อไทยจ่อตั้ง-กอส-2-ทหารฯ-อภัยโทษ.hmtl [Accessed: 6 January 2013].

Iskandar, Adel and El-Nawawy, Mohammed. 2004. Al-Jazeera and War Coverage in Iraq: The Media's Quest for Contextual Objectivity. In: Allan, S. and Zelizer, B. eds. *Reporting War: Journalism in Wartime*. Oxon: Routledge, pp. 315–332.

Kajadpai Burutpat. 1983. ชนกลุ่มน้อยในไทยกับความมั่นคงของชาติ *[Minorities in Thailand and the National Security]*. Bangkok: Wangburapa.

King-oua Laohong. 2006. *การปฏิบัติการข่าวสาร ข่าวลือ และแบบแผนพฤติกรรมฝูงชนวุ่นวาย: กรณีศึกษาเปรียบเทียบ เหตุการณ์โจรนินจา และเหตุการณ์จับนาวิกโยธินในภาคใต้ของประเทศไทย [Information Operation, Rumor*

Introduction 23

and Pattern of Mob Behavior: A Comparative Case Study of Ninja Bandit and Marine Hostages in the Southern Region of Thailand]. MA Thesis, Chulalongkorn University.

Lewis, Justin. 2007. The Power of Myths: The War on Terror and Military Might. In: Nossek, H., Sreberny, A., and Sonwalkar, P. eds. *Media and Political Violence.* Cresskill, NJ: Hampton Press, pp. 341–354.

Lewis, Justin. 2008. The role of the media in boosting military spending. *Media, War & Conflict* 1(1), pp. 108–117.

Livingstone, Sonia. 2009. On the mediation of everything: ICA presidential address 2008. *Journal of Communication* 59(1), pp. 1–18.

Lundby, Knut. ed. 2009. *Mediatization: Concept, Changes, Consequences.* New York: Peter Lang.

Lynch, Jake and McGoldrick, Annabel. 2005. *Peace Journalism.* Stroud, Gloucestershire: Hawthorn Press.

McCargo, Duncan. 2000. *Politics and the Press in Thailand: Media Machinations.* London: Routledge.

McCargo, Duncan. 2006. Communicating Thailand's southern conflict. *The Journal of International Communication* 12(2), pp. 19–34.

McCargo, Duncan. 2007. Thaksin and the Resurgence of Violence in the Thai South. In: McCargo, D. ed. *Rethinking Thailand's Southern Violence.* Singapore: NUS Press, pp. 35–68.

McCargo, Duncan. 2008. *Tearing Apart the Land: Islam and Legitimacy in Southern Thailand.* Ithaca, New York: Cornell University Press.

McCargo, Duncan. 2012. *Mapping National Anxieties: Thailand's Southern Conflict.* Copenhagen: NIAS Press.

McNair, Brian. 1998. *The Sociology of Journalism.* London: Arnold.

McNair, Brian. 2006. *Cultural Chaos: Journalism, News and Power in a Globalised World.* London: Routledge.

Nacos, Brigitte L. 2002. *Mass-Mediated Terrorism: The Central Role of the Media in Terrorism and Counterterrorism.* Lanham, MD: Rowman & Littlefield.

Nacos, Brigitte L. 2010. Revisiting the contagion hypothesis: Terrorism, news coverage, and copycat attacks. *Perspectives on Terrorism, North America* 3(3), pp. 1–13.

National Reconciliation Commission, The. 2006. *Report of the National Reconciliation Commission: Overcoming Violence Through the Power of Reconciliation* [online]. Translated from Thai by Asian Human Rights Commission. Bangkok. Available at: http://thailand.ahrchk.net/docs/nrc _report_en.pdf [Accessed: 11 January 2013].

Nidhi Aeusrivongse. 2004. มองสถานการณ์ใต้ผ่านแว่นกบฏชาวนา [Looking at the southern situation through the millenarian revolt lense]. ศิลปวัฒนธรรม [*Silapa Wattanatham*]. 8 June 2004, pp. 110–125.

Nossek, Hillel. 2007. Terrorism and the Media: Does the Weapon Matter to the Coverage. In: Nossek, H., Sreberny, A., and Sonwalkar, P.. eds. *Media and Political Violence.* Cresskill, NJ: Hampton Press, pp. 269–303.

Pharr, Susan. 1996. Media as Trickster in Japan. In: Pharr, S. and Krauss, E. eds. *Media and Politics in Japan.* Honolulu: University of Hawaii Press, pp. 19–41.

Picard, Robert G. 1991. News Coverage as the Contagion of Terrorism: Dangerous Charges Backed by Dubious Science. In: Alali, A.O. and Eke, K.K. eds. *Media Coverage of Terrorism: Methods of Diffusion.* Newbury Park, CA: Sage, pp. 49–62.

Picard, Robert G. and Adams, Paul D. 1991. Characterizations of Acts and Perpetrators of Political Violence in Three Elite U.S. Daily Newspapers. In: Alali, A.O. and Eke, K.K. eds. *Media Coverage of Terrorism: Methods of Diffusion.* Newbury Park, CA: Sage, pp. 11–22.

24 Introduction

Reese, Stephen D. 2001. Understanding the global journalist: A hierarchy-of-influences approach. *Journalism Studies* 2(2), pp. 173–187.

Schlesinger, Philip. 1990. Rethinking the Sociology of Journalism: Source Strategies and the Limits of Media-Centrism. In: Ferguson, M. ed. *Public Communication – The New Imperatives: Future Directions for Media Research*. London: Sage, pp. 61–83.

Schlesinger, Philip, Murdock, Graham, and Elliott, Philip. 1983. *Televising 'Terrorism': Political Violence in Popular Culture*. London: Comedia Publishing Group.

Schudson, Michael. 2003. *The Sociology of News*. New York: W.W. Norton.

Sonwalkar, Prasun. 2004. Out of Sight, Out of Mind?: The Non-Reporting of Small Wars and Insurgencies. In: Allan, S. and Zelizer, B. eds. *Reporting War: Journalism in Wartime*. Oxon: Routledge, pp. 206–233.

Sonwalkar, Prasun. 2005. Banal Journalism: The Centrality of the 'Us-Them' Binary in News Discourse. In: Allan, S. ed. *Journalism: Critical Issues*. Berkshire: Open University Press, pp. 261–273.

Sorayut Aiemueayut. 2013. "อยู่กับความรุนแรง" ความรุนแรงในพื้นที่ทางโลกย์ของมลายูมุสลิมในสามจังหวัดภาคใต้ ["Living with Violence" Violence in the Malay Muslim's secular spaces in the three southern provinces]. *ฟ้าเดียวกัน [Fah Diew Kan]*. January–June 2013, pp. 87–112.

Srisompob Jitpiromsri and Panyasak Sobhonvasu. 2007. Unpacking Thailand's Southern Conflict: The Poverty of Structural Explanations. In: McCargo, D. ed. *Rethinking Thailand's Southern Violence*. Singapore: NUS Press, pp. 89–111.

Supalak Ganjanakhundee. 2009. ชุมโจรในจินตนาการ:ว่าด้วยภูมิรู้ของทหารไทยเกี่ยวกับผู้ก่อความไม่สงบในภาคใต้ [Imagined Bandit's Den: Thai soldier's knowledge about instigators in the South]. *ฟ้าเดียวกัน [Fah Diew Kan]*. January–March 2009, pp. 56–71.

Supapohn Kanwerayotin. 2006. *Peace Journalism in Thailand: A Case Study of Issara News Centre of the Thai Journalists Association*. MA Thesis, Chulalongkorn University.

Syukri, Ibrahim. 1985. *Sejarah Kerajaan Melayu Patani [History of the Malay Kingdom of Patani]*. Translated by C. Bailey and J.N. Miksic. Athens, Ohio: Ohio University Center for International Studies.

Thanet Aphornsuvan. 2007. *Rebellion in Southern Thailand: Contending Histories*. Washington, D.C.: East-West Center Washington.

Tumber, Howard. 2004. Prisoners of News Values? Journalists, Professionalism, and Identification in Times of War. In: Allan, S. and Zelizer, B. eds. *Reporting War: Journalism in Wartime*. Oxon: Routledge, pp. 190–205.

Tumber, Howard. 2005. Journalism and the War in Iraq. In: Allan, S. ed. *Journalism: Critical Issues*. Berkshire: Open University Press, pp. 370–380.

Tumber, Howard. 2007. The Media and International Conflict: A Theoretical Overview. In: Nossek, H., Sreberny, A., and Sonwalkar, P. eds. *Media and Political Violence*. Cresskill, NJ: Hampton Press, pp. 23–39.

Ukrist Pathmanand. 2007. Thaksin's Achilles' Heel: The Failure of Hawkish Approaches in the Thai South. In: McCargo, D. ed. *Rethinking Thailand's Southern Violence*. Singapore: NUS Press, pp. 69–88.

Waisbord, Silvio. 2013. *Reinventing Professionalism: Journalism and News in Global Perspective*. Cambridge & Malden, MA: Polity.

Walakkamol Changkamol. 2007. สื่อสันติภาพ: จริยธรรม การจัดการ และข้อเสนอแนะเพื่อการพัฒนา *[Peace Journalism: Ethics, Management and Suggestions for Development]*. Pattani: Prince of Songkhla University, Pattani Campus.

Walakkamol Changkamol. 2013. Peace Journalism: How Thai journalism applied it: A case study of violent conflict in the Southern border provinces. *Paper Presented at the 1st Annual PSU Phuket Conference 2012 Multidisciplinary Studies on Sustainable*

Development on 10–12 January 2013 at Prince of Songkla University, Phuket Campus. Available at: www.conference.phuket.psu.ac.th/conference2012/proceedings/pdf/o_FIS07%20Walakkamol.pdf [Accessed: 20 July 2015].

Wattana Sugunnasil. 2007. Islam, Radicalism, and Violence in Southern Thailand: Berjihad di Patani and the 28 April 2004 Attack. In: McCargo, D. ed. *Rethinking Thailand's Southern Violence*. Singapore: NUS Press, pp. 112–136.

Witchayawanee Choonui. 2009. *บทบาทของโต๊ะข่าวภาคใต้ สถาบันอิศรากับการเป็นสื่อเพื่อสันติภาพ กรณีเหตุการณ์ความไม่สงบในสามจังหวัดชายแดนภาคใต้ [The Role of the Southern News Desk, Issara Institute as Peace Journalism: In the Case of Insurgency in the Three Southernmost Provinces]*. MA Thesis, Chulalongkorn University.

Wolfsfeld, Gadi. 1997. *Media and Political Conflict: News From the Middle East*. Cambridge: Cambridge University Press.

Wolfsfeld, Gadi. 2004. *Media and the Path to Peace*. Cambridge: Cambridge University Press.

2 News representation of the southern conflict

This chapter seeks to examine how the southern conflict is represented by the Thai news organisations by examining the news content from 2004, when the armed conflict re-emerged, to 2010, produced by four selected media outlets (see their profile in Appendix C): the *Matichon* daily newspaper, the Thai Public Broadcasting Service television channel (hereafter *Thai PBS*), the Manager Online news website (hereafter *Manager*), and the Isara News Agency's Southern News Desk news website (hereafter *Isara*). The analysis reveals the dominant themes and preferred sources in the coverage, which also indicate the news media's inclination towards and marginalisation of the political discourse used to explain the conflict.

The news organisations selected in this study differ in their main presentation platforms, sizes, management structures, and journalistic and operational principles. The *Matichon* daily newspaper and the *Manager* website are commercial media. The remaining two, in spite of being non-profit, vary in terms of their journalistic principles. *Thai PBS* television station upholds the public service broadcasting ethos, while the *Isara* website's goal is to be an alternative source of news from the far South. The main differences among these organisations can be described in Table 2.1.

Table 2.1 Comparison of the four selected news organisations

	Matichon	*Thai PBS*	*Manager*	*Isara*
Type of organisation	Public company	National public service broadcaster	Privately owned company	Professional organisation
Ownership	Matichon Group (a listed media corporation)	Public Broadcasting Organisation of Thailand (an independent state agency)	Manager Group (a medium-size media company)	Isara Institute (a professional organisation)
Primary source of revenue	Advertising	Allocation of two billion baht (approx. 61 million US dollars) from excise tax for annual budget	Advertising	Various domestic and international civil society organisations and corporations

	Matichon	Thai PBS	Manager	Isara
Other media operations under the same ownership	• 2 newspapers: (1 tabloid-style daily, 1 business weekly) • 1 weekly and 3 monthly magazines: (1 news and current affairs, 1 history and culture, 2 small business-oriented) • 1 publishing house	1 digital radio station	• 1 daily newspaper • 1 financial weekly magazine • 1 news and current affairs monthly magazine • 1 satellite TV channel	The Southern News Desk is a section of the Isara News Agency's website, which also hosts: • 1 Community News Centre webpage • 1 Public Policy News Centre webpage • 1 Investigative News Centre webpage
Newsroom operation	• HQ in Bangkok • no news centre in South • stringers based in southern provinces – under regional news desk	• HQ in Bangkok • the Southern news centre based in Hat Yai, Songkla • stringers based in southern provinces – under regional news desk	• HQ in Bangkok • 2 southern news centres; one based in Hat Yai, Songkla and one in Phuket • stringers based in southern provinces – under southern news centre	• no official HQ/ editor based in Bangkok • no office in southern provinces, reporters mostly based in Pattani • stringers and contributors based in southern provinces
News content orientation	Politics	Public policy	General news and politics	The southern conflict and the southern border provinces
Main presentation platform	Newspaper	Television	Website	Website
General presentation of southern conflict stories	Front page, regional news section, feature section	• 7 regular newscasts • 5 hourly bulletins[1]	Homepage, Southern News website (covering stories from the entire South, but not specifically about southern conflict)	The entire website content is dedicated to the subject
Regular section for southern conflict reports	None	• One 5-minute weekly package on Sunday prime-time newscast • One 30-minute magazine programme on Monday afternoon slot	None	The entire website content is dedicated to the subject

[1]This study only analyses stories presented on the channel's regular newscasts, not on other forms of programmes.

28 *News representation*

The chapter is presented in four parts. The first part discusses the news themes, frames, and labels of the southern conflict and its protagonists. The second explores the presentation formats used in the southern conflict reporting and the trends of coverage during the seven-year review period. The final part then concludes with key arguments derived from the findings. The analysis of source attribution in the coverage will be featured in Chapter 4, which discusses the journalist-source relationships.

The volatile deep South: news themes and frames in the southern conflict coverage

This part presents the analysis of headlines and anchor introductions in the case of broadcast news to identify the dominant news themes, frames, and labels of the conflict and its protagonists. It first examines the recurring themes and news frames, and second the labels that news organisations use to describe the conflict and its protagonists.

Themes in the southern conflict coverage

The headline and introduction topics are categorised into three thematic groups: 1) *governance and politics*,[1] 2) *security and public order*,[2] and 3) *socio-economy and culture*.[3] As Figure 2.1 illustrates, the most highlighted theme is *security and public order*, such as stories about attacks, authorities' investigations, suspect arrests, security reinforcement, and the connection between the narcotics trade and southern violence. Meanwhile, the *socio-economy and culture* theme scores slightly higher than *governance and politics*. Based on this finding, the frequent

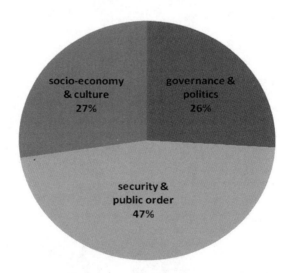

Figure 2.1 An overview of the southern conflict coverage classified by themes

News representation   29

coverage of security and public order-related issues could signal journalists' support for the *crime and conspiracy* discourse. However, journalists argue that these reports are the most frequent because of the constant aggression in the far South. Not to report them would be considered concealing facts from the public.

This finding presents an interesting discussion point. When looking at the frequency of topics, as shown in Table 2.2, stories concerning violent incidents are most reported. However, episodes with direct reference to terrorist or separatist movements are rarely highlighted. The findings suggest that, despite seeing violent incidents in the southern border provinces as part of their routine coverage, journalists often refrain from identifying perpetrators or connecting these occurrences to insurgent movements unless authorities state so. With minimal context and background about the assailants, the depiction of violence in the news coverage gives more support to the *crime and conspiracy* discourse than the *Malay nationalism and Islamism* discourse. The following headlines and anchor introduction demonstrate how an incident was typically reported.

> Southern bandits attack border rangers – railway personnel, killing 3.
> (*Matichon* 19 July 2004)[4]

> 4 Buddhist Thais, the last group in Bajo, brutally killed. Victims' children ask for transfer, revealing "death is definite" if continue to stay.
> (*Matichon* 20 September 2010)[5]

> Southern bandit(s) snipes villagers in Nara[thiwat], killing 1.
> (*Manager* 15 December 2009)[6]

> Last night, perpetrators opened fire on villagers and a village chief in both Pattani and Yala Provinces. Four people died and another two were injured. This made officials specially increase surveillance in the areas.
> (*Thai PBS* 28 August 2010)[7]

In addition, human rights and religious education, which are key elements of the *minority's grievance* and the *Malay nationalism and Islamism* discourses, are among the least reported topics, compared to other topics relevant to these discourses, such as the impact on livelihood, history and culture, and religion. This finding suggests that, while allowing the interpretations of *minority's grievance* and *Malay nationalism and Islamism* discourses to emerge, journalists chose to bring forward the aspects that the general public could sympathise with or relate to over subjects that people may find too abstract or less familiar, such as human rights or specialised education systems. Interestingly, as will be later elaborated, the human rights topic has a better chance of making headlines when the sources of information are influential international figures.

It should be noted that when comparing the outputs among the four organisations, despite their different news orientations, the *security and public order* theme still dominates. Unsurprisingly, with its emphasis on political news, the *Matichon*

Table 2.2 The frequency of topics in the southern conflict coverage

a. Governance and politics

Topics	Frequency (percentage)
Southern policy	18
International affairs	3
Political contention and election campaign	2
Local and national administration	2
Human rights	1
Total	*26*

b. Security and public order

Topics	Frequency (percentage)
Violent incidents	20
Law enforcement and judicial process	13
Local and national security	9
Drugs	3
Separatism	1
Terrorism	1
Total	*47*

c. Socio-economy and culture

Topics	Frequency (percentage)
Impact on livelihood	10
Education	5
Economy	4
History and culture	4
Religions	2
Medical and healthcare services	1
Religious education	1
Total	*27*
Others[1]	1
100	

Total (*n* = 793)

[1]"Others" refers to the stories that were not directly pertinent to the conflict, but in which the southern conflict was mentioned. These stories included the life of a respected senior citizen in the region, problems with garbage collection mismanagement in a southern village, the life of a grandmother and her blind grandchild, and a helicopter accident that killed a team of forensic scientists working in the area.

daily scores higher than others in the *governance and politics* theme. Meanwhile, the online *Manager* and *Isara*'s frequent *socio-economy and culture* reports may benefit from the proximity of their southern-based staff in the region and their dedicated space for news from the South.

The news frames in the southern conflict coverage

While the frequency of topics presented above gives an overview of the themes of the coverage, the news framing analysis, which examines the contexts of headlines and introductions, illustrates which aspect of the conflict is highlighted (see detail of the news frame matrix in Appendix D). As shown in Figure 2.2 below, the *solutions* meta-frame is reported most, closely followed by the *uses of force* meta-frame. While the high frequency of the *uses of force* meta-frame buttresses the previous analysis, where violent incidents are the most reported topic, it also elicits an interesting point. This discovery shows that, although news organisations primarily report about violence and bloodshed, they also give considerable attention to the solutions to this enduring conflict. Nonetheless, as will be discussed later, the solutions presented in the news content are varied and support different discourses. As a result, while signalling the news media's move to help end the conflict, the disparate subcategories in the *solutions* meta-frame also reflect journalists' and news organisations' dissimilar political perspectives.

It is also interesting to see that the reports on the *causes of conflict and violence* are relatively minimal compared with other meta-frames. The small number of

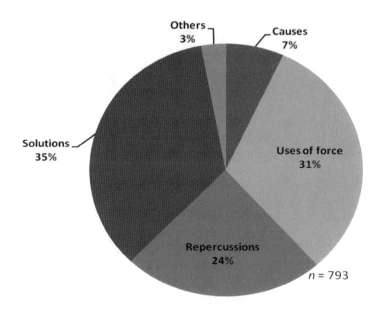

Figure 2.2 The frequency of the four meta-frames in the southern conflict coverage

32 News representation

reports about the causes of conflict suggests that the news media tend to focus on the problem at hand and how it should be resolved, rather than questioning what caused the conflict. It can be argued that, in order to bring the conflict to an end, the news media prioritise acknowledging the problem and introducing solutions before investigating the causes. Nevertheless, the insufficient investigation into its causes could also lead to misjudgement and ineffective remedies for this complex and dynamic conflict.

The examination of the disparate frames, which are the components of each meta-frame, further reveals the complexity of the discursive contention of the southern conflict, particularly in the *causes* and *solutions* meta-frames. In the *causes* meta-frame, five frames are used to explain the rationales behind the southern conflict and violence, as shown in Figure 2.3. Three frames – *retaliation against authority*, *transnational radical Islam*, and *identity politics* – give the nuance of resistance against the state (see the detail of frame components in Appendix D). Regardless of this, these frames underline different reasons for the struggle. The *transnational radical Islam* frame emphasises a link between the southern conflict and the transnational terrorist movements heralding religious fanaticism, while the *identity politics* frame highlights Malay Muslims' grievance of being deprived of their local identity and rights. However, the *retaliation against authority* frame, which is used most, omits reasons as to why local armed groups retaliate. Moreover, the fact that the active insurgent groups seldom speak to the media, openly voice their demands, or publicly claim responsibility for

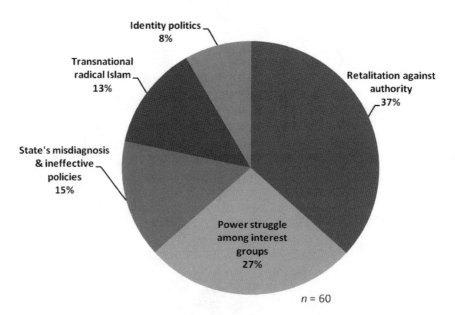

Figure 2.3 The frequency of news frames used to identify the causes of the southern conflict and violence

the attacks enables authorities to become the "primary definers" of the southern conflict. This point will be discussed again in subsequent chapters, regarding the state authorities' media strategies and relationship with journalists. Therefore, the *retaliation against authority* frame renders these insurgents scattered, faceless, irrational, and vindictive, rather than a collective group of people who fight for a cause.

The two remaining frames approach the southern conflict differently by downplaying the ideological influences suggested in the previous three frames. The *power struggle among interest groups* frame points to influential factions who cause unrest in the far South to maintain their status and benefits in the region, such as their political power, financial gains through illegal businesses, and social influence. Similar to the *retaliation against authority* frame, this frame sees the conflict as organised criminal activity that needs to be eradicated rather than pacified. Meanwhile, the *state's misdiagnosis and ineffective policies* frame scrutinises the government's mishandling of the conflict: inefficient military-led strategies and intelligence, irregular budget spending, state officials' incompetency and mistreatment of the locals, and the power struggle in national politics. Regardless of this, the frame is based on two grounds: first, the counter-insurgency viewpoint sees the conflict as a military combat; and second, the political contention perspective regards politicians' proposals as mere rhetorical campaigns rather than productive endeavours. Despite eliciting a critical stance against state authorities, the frame does not delve into why the conflict was initiated in the first place.

Because the most frequently used frames are the *retaliation against authority* and *power struggle among interest groups*, the conflict is, therefore, often depicted as crimes committed by clandestine armed groups and local underground syndicates, in line with the military's "additional threats" theory, which was discussed in Chapter 1. The *state's misdiagnosis and ineffective policies* frame questions the government's actions, but the basis of these criticisms remain on the same ground as the previous two frames: this conflict is a combat situation. As such, the majority of coverage inadvertently supports the *crime and conspiracy* discourse, despite the attribution to separatist groups and locals' dissent and suffering. Explanations of relevant concepts such as the Malay Muslim identity and Islamism are minimal. As a result, the cultural and ideologically based discourses, namely, the *minority's grievance* and *Malay nationalism and Islamism,* are undermined.

The second meta-frame, *uses of force*, comprises the elements that underpin the aforementioned argument about the generalisation of the agents of visible violence. Five frames are discovered: 1) *use of force by unknown actors*, 2) *use of force by authorities*, 3) *arrest and suspect surrender*, 4) *search*, and 5) *security reinforcement*.[8] As illustrated in Figure 2.4, the *uses of force by unknown actors* frame takes up more than half of the entire coverage, while the four latter frames, which refer to the actions in which state officials are in command, still fall behind. Additionally, these actions are reported in ways that affirm the state's legitimacy to suppress violence, whereas the strikes launched by unknown perpetrators are generally described as having a considerable degree of cruelty.

34 *News representation*

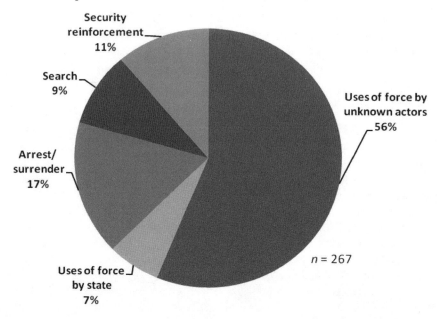

Figure 2.4 The frequency of news frames used to describe the uses of force in southern violence

Moreover, the actions by unknown perpetrators are often depicted in detail, such as "bomb-attacked then shot in the head," and coloured with adjectives and exclamation marks. On the other hand, the outcome of the state officials' actions is usually described as triumphant ("annihilated," "smashed"). Table 2.3 illustrates the examples of headlines using such lexical choices. While it can be argued that the brutality of violence and the loss of life could invoke public sympathy and pressure the authorities to attend to the situation quickly, this kind of portrayal only sheds light on one aspect of the problem. It also allows the authorities' actions to go unquestioned. Together with the eulogy-style storytelling in the cases where officials were killed and the use of criminological labels for the antagonists, which will be discussed later, these frames tend to support the *crime and conspiracy* discourse rather than the *minority's grievance* and *Malay nationalism and Islamism* discourses.

The third meta-frame, *repercussions*, comprises three main frames: 1) *governance*, 2) *impact on stakeholders*, and 3) *public reactions*. As shown in Figure 2.5, the *impact on stakeholders* frame is used most to explicate how people involved are affected by the conflict and violence. The *governance* frame, which looks at the administration's and political elites' reactions to the problems, as well as the trial and investigations, is also considerably featured. The *public reactions* frame registers how people who are not directly affected by the conflict respond to the problems, such as by making donations or raising funds for the victims. This frame reflects the sentiment of the general public, as well as influential public figures, particularly the royal family, and how they make sense of the southern conflict.

Table 2.3 The comparison of headlines with different *uses of force* frames

Uses of force by unknown actors	Uses of force by authorities
Extremely cruel. 7 special forces killed. Bomb-attacked then shot in the head. 7 M16s seized and stolen. (*Matichon* 17 July 2007)[1] Southern bandit makes a harsh insult!! 'Wan Nor's' relative sniped. (*Manager* 24 May 2005)[2] Car-bombing in Yaha! A major sacrifices his life with subordinates. (*Isara* 17 July 2009)[3]	Mujahedeen Aiyerweng-attackers cornered at border, arrested – pressed in interrogation for more info. (*Matichon* 17 March 2005)[4] Southern bandit rakes fire, injuring 3 border patrol officers. 2 bandits annihilated. (*Manager* 25 January 2009)[5] Bomb-producing site smashed. 2 suspects captured. (*Isara* 21 April 2008)[6]

[1] สุดโหดบึ้มแล้วยิงจ่อขมับ7รบพิเศษดับยึดเอ็ม16เจ็ดกระบอกหนี. *Matichon*. 17 July 2007
[2] โจรใต้หยามหนัก!! ลอบยิง ญาติ"วันนอร์". *Manager*. 24 May 2005
[3] คาร์บอมบ์ยะหา! พันตรีพลีชีพพร้อมลูกน้อง. *Isara*. 17 July 2009
[4] จับมุจาฮีดีนทีมถล่มอัยเยอร์เวงจนมุมชายแดน-เค้นสอบขยายผล. *Matichon*. 17 March 2005
[5] โจรใต้กราดยิง ตชด.เจ็บ 3 นาย เด็ดหัวโจรตาย2. *Manager*. 25 January 2009
[6] ทลายแหล่งผลิตระเบิดพร้อมรวบ 2 ผู้ต้องสงสัย. *Isara*. 21 April 2008

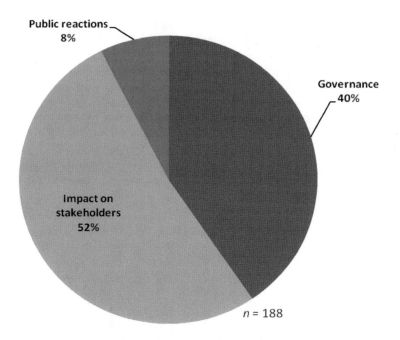

Figure 2.5 The frequency of news frames used to describe the repercussions of southern conflict and violence

36 *News representation*

Table 2.4 The contexts of headlines and introductions concerning the impact of conflict

Types of contexts		Frequency (percentage)
Heroic acts		24
Impact on state officials		20
Impact on residents' livelihood		19
Impact on victims and families		15
Impact on local education		11
Success stories		7
Impact on suspects and families		4
	Total ($n = 111$)	100

The analysis of stories about the impact of the conflict and violence on the livelihood of community members and people involved produces interesting findings. Among 111 reports relevant to this issue, the majority of coverage centres on state officials, such as teachers, police officers, and soldiers, as shown in Table 2.4. The stories often tell how these officials perform their duty amidst the hostility and difficulties, and are often honoured for their bravery, devotion, and sacrifice. On the contrary, there are far fewer reports about how local victims, suspects who were later exonerated, and their families deal with the plights. The finding corresponds with a remark made by a news editor who pointed out that as the conflict continues, stories about people's sufferings from conflict and violence become repetitive and considered "old news". For instance, if a family member was killed in a random shooting incident, it would be unlikely for this case to make news. However, the loss of four members from the same family in separate violent incidents could be deemed more newsworthy. Because of such a notion, the coverage concerning the locals' sufferings appears less frequently because these cases are regarded as "too common".[9]

Notwithstanding the primary protagonists in the news, it can be argued that this type of coverage still underlines the humanitarian aspect of the conflict. The audience can better relate to people's grief when individual subjects are singled out from the seas of the sufferers. Nonetheless, a closer look at the description of how people are affected by and cope with the conflict and violence renders quite an interesting contrast. As demonstrated in Table 2.5, while state officials are depicted as courageous and dedicated, the affected locals are often cast as strong-willed people who strive to carry on with their lives, but are powerless. In addition, by featuring state officials individually or in a small group, the coverage seemingly separates the state agents from their institutional attachment and portrays them as mere human beings in stressful situations. Still, in the end, the reports usually link the officials with the professional values and obligations of their institutions, and praise these officials for upholding such merits despite being in life-threatening situations.

Table 2.5 The comparison between the coverage of impact on state officials and on the locals

Impact on state officials	Impact on the locals
a. Heroic acts	*a. Heroic acts*
Privy councillor praises Teacher Juling, like the candlelight leading education. (*Matichon* 5 June 2006)[1]	Open heart [feelings revealed – researcher] . . . Southern kids smile to combat the southern situation. (*Matichon* 1 February 2007)[3]
Nearly a thousand of Nakhon people welcome home the body of "Major Pansak," hero of the southern border. (*Manager* 9 August 2009)[2]	Khueng Naruemol, the strong lady of Baan Pan (*Isara* 6 May 2008)[4]
b. Impact on state officials (teachers)	*b. Impact on residents' livelihood*
Story title: Southern teachers concerned about the unrest	Thai Buddhists in Yala begin moving out of the area as violence continues. (Manager 25 November 2006)[6]
Anchor introduction:	Some thousands of Buddhist Thais at Sabayoi [District] gather, demanding the military rangers not to be removed from the area following a *pondok* attack at Baan Kuan Lan. (*Isara* 26 March 2007)[7]
The [attack] on the teacher guard team at the Bangnang Guwae School of Bannang Sata District in Yala Province this morning prompted the school to be closed immediately. Meanwhile, teachers in the nearby areas were fearful about the incident while trying to come to terms with it. They also hope the shooting skill they have been trained would help protect their life. (*Thai PBS* 18 May 2009)[5]	
	c. Impact on victims/ suspects and their families
	2 Years after Kru-Ze-Tak Bai. Southern border still weeps. (*Matichon* 28 April 2006)[8]
	Husband disappears . . . in the southern fire. (*Manager* 8 January 2009)[9]
d. Success stories	*d. Success stories*
Cultivator of the seeds of friendship. The life of "military doctor" in the Red Zone. (*Isara* 29 October 2005)[10]	Buddhist and Muslim communities must learn to love and unite. The lesson to fight the southern fire crisis of Kirikhet people. (*Isara* 18 December 2006)[12]
Bad never wins Good, and the today's life of "Noppadol Pueaksophon" the steel-willed vice commander. (*Isara* 16 August 2007)[11]	**Story title:** City monitor network
	Anchor introduction:
	The problem of the explosive detector GT 200's deficiency and the losses from several bombing incidents in Songkla's Hat Yai commercial district previously lead to the birth of the people's city watch network, which can set a boundary of insurgent movement in a limited area. . . . (*Thai* PBS 21 February 2010)[13]

[1] องคมนตรีฯยกครูจูหลิงดั่งเทียนส่องการศึกษา. *Matichon*. 5 June 2006

[2] ชาวนครฯ ร่วมพันรับศพ "พ.ต.พันธ์ศักดิ์" วีรบุรุษชายแดนใต้. *Manager*. 9 August 2009

[3] เปิดใจ..เด็กใต้ยิ้มสู้..สถานการณ์ไฟใต้. *Matichon*. 1 February 2007

[4] เขื่อง นฤมล หญิงแกร่งแห่งบ้านแป้น. *Isara*. 6 May 2008

[5] ครูใต้วิตกเหตุการณ์ไม่สงบ. *Thai PBS*. 18 May 2009. 19:00 news bulletin

[6] ชาวไทยพุทธ จ.ยะลา เริ่มอพยพออกนอกพื้นที่ หลังเหตุรุนแรงยังเกิดขึ้นต่อเนื่อง. *Manager*. 25 November 2006

[7] ไทยพุทธที่สะบ้าย้อย ชุมนุมร่วมพันไม่ต้องการให้ถอนทพ.ออกจากพื้นที่ หลังกรณีถล่มปอเนาะที่บ.ควนหลัน. *Isara*. 26 March 2007

[8] 2ปีกรือเซะ ตากใบชายแดนใต้ยังสะอื้น. *Matichon*. 28 April 2006

[9] สามีหายไป. . .กลางไฟใต้. *Manager*. 8 January 2009

[10] ผู้หว่านเพาะเมล็ดพันธุ์แห่งมิตรภาพ ชีวิต"หมอทหาร" ในพื้นที่สีแดง. *Isara*. 29 October 2005

[11] ความชั่วไม่มีทางเอาชนะความดี และวันนี้ของ "นพดล เผือกโสมณ" รองผู้การกระดูกเหล็ก. *Isara*. 16 August 2007

[12] ชุมชนพุทธ-มุสลิมต้องรู้รักสามัคคี บทเรียนฝ่าวิกฤติไฟใต้ของคนคีรีเขต. *Isara* 18 December 2006

[13] เครือข่ายเฝ้าระวังเมือง. *Thai PBS*. 21 February 2010. 19:00 news bulletin

38 *News representation*

This observation will be brought up again in the subsequent chapters, when some reporters who are based in the far South and those who have been following the situation for many years revealed that they sometimes faced a dilemma when assigned to do a profile piece on state officials killed in the region. As these journalists explained, there were several episodes in which the officials were killed in a personal dispute. However, the incidents were filed as a result of the unrest, so that police investigators would approach the cases differently from typical criminal acts, and the victims could then earn compensation payment. Certain officers who were called heroes by their peers for their long and decorated careers did not receive the same degree of admiration from the locals. Regardless, the Bangkok headquarters sees civil servant casualties as newsworthy and deserving of a tribute for their sacrifice.

Therefore, collectively, the constant glorifying coverage reinforces the portrayal of state officials as rescuers and protectors, and subtly supports the institutions they associate with, particularly the military, police, and standardised education. By commending state officials' bravery and devotion, the news media endorse these institutions and support the *crime and conspiracy* discourse, which maintains the Thai nation-state constructs while overlooking the challenges against these establishments raised by other discourses.

The examination of the references to perpetrators and victims of violence in news headlines and introductions reveals that state official casualties are more mentioned than civilian ones, as demonstrated in Table 2.6. Interestingly, references to Buddhist victims are also slightly more frequent than to Malay Muslim victims. These reports contradict the statistics of violent incidents from 2004 to 2009, compiled by a Pattani-based Prince of Songkla University political scientist, which place the number of civilian and Muslim casualties at the top (Srisompob 2010).

The last meta-frame, *solutions*, comprises seven key frames drawn from the disparate policies, initiatives, and proposals brought up in a bid to solve the

Table 2.6 The frequency of references to perpetrators and victims of violence

References to people involving in and affected by violence		*Frequency (percentage)*
Perpetrators	Unnamed perpetrators	28
	Identified perpetrators	3
Victims	State officials	27
	Suspects/ insurgents	17
	Civilians	15
	Unidentified victims	3
	Buddhists	2
	Muslims	2
Damages	Damage to property	4
	Total ($n = 401$)	100

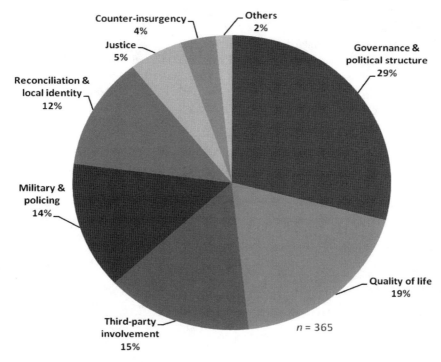

Figure 2.6 The frequency of news frames used to identify the solutions to the southern conflict

conflict. As seen in Figure 2.6, the most featured solutions fall into the *governance and political structure* frame, which suggests the changes from administrative agencies. The proposed solutions range from the rectification and improvement of ineffective political mechanisms such as governmental policies and budget spending on southern conflict affairs, Thailand's relationships with Islamic countries and stance on the conflict in the global forum, to political parties' strategies and the debates on administrative reform in the region, such as the special administrative models. The prominence of this frame affirms that news media represent the conflict as a political problem that requires solutions from the state. However, most solutions and criticisms are still based on the current political structure – essentially, representative democratic politics. The only solution that could challenge Thailand's political convention is the debates and discussions about special administrative models and autonomy. Nevertheless, the subject was brought up after the conflict entered its fourth year in 2007, and the coverage of this issue, particularly on autonomy, is more disapproving than supportive.

Similar to the proposal on autonomy and region-specific administrative models, the *reconciliation and recognition of local identity* and *counter-insurgency* frames, which include solutions that acknowledge cultural diversity and different political beliefs, and which propose dialogue with insurgents and local people as a way to

40 News representation

pacify the conflict, are among the least-used frames. The use of these frames, additionally, does not guarantee positive views towards the proposed solutions. For instance, the stories about dialogue, especially with insurgent movements, demonstrate the government's ambivalent stance towards this action, whereas insurgents and third parties seem more supportive of the idea, as shown in Table 2.7. Meanwhile, the *justice* frame, which suggests the scrutiny and overhaul of the justice system, human rights protection, and healing for the affected parties, is also eclipsed.

On the contrary, the *quality of life* frame, which focuses on the improvement of southerners' well-being, particularly in standardised education, community development, and healthcare services, fares better. This discovery shows that the majority of solutions are aimed at dealing with the social problems at hand and expect discernible results, such as better living, certified education degrees, or employment, rather than dealing with abstract notions such as marginalisation of local identity and human rights abuse.

Table 2.7 Comparison of protagonists' views towards peace dialogues as a solution to the southern conflict

Thai government	Insurgents/ third-party
PM indicates the southern troublemaker[1] leaders asking for dialogue is a good sign, but he has not received the report. (*Manager* 11 October 2006)[2]	Mahathir's son[6] reveals secret discussions with 50 southern troublemaker leaders [indicating] no expectation for secession. (*Matichon* 11 October 2006)[7]
Defence Minister states Government is ready for dialogue with southern troublemaker groups; shuts the door[3] on special administrative zone or autonomy proposals. (*Isara* 2 July 2007)[4]	PULO leader suggests Government to organise dialogue to distinguish southern fire. (*Matichon* 21 April 2008)[8]
Anchor intro: Government affirms that there was no secret dialogue with terrorist movements in the southern border provinces, after the dissemination of one month ceasefire declaration in Narathiwat Province. (*Thai PBS* 14 July 2010)[5]	

[1] Literal translation of the term ป่วนใต้ [Puan Tai], frequently used in news media headlines in reference to insurgents and perpetrators in general. See more discussions in the subsequent section on labels for antagonists

[2] นายกฯ ระบุแกนนำป่วนใต้ขอเจรจาเป็นสัญญาณที่ดี แต่ยังไม่ได้รับรายงาน. *Manager.* 11 October 2006.

[3] Literal translation of the term ปิดประตู [Pid Pratu], which means "to refuse"

[4] รมต.กลาโหม ชี้รัฐฯพร้อมเจรจากลุ่มป่วนใต้ ปิดประตูเขตปกครองพิเศษ หรือข้อเสนอปกครองตนเอง (Autonomy). *Isara.* 2 July 2007

[5] (no story title). *Thai PBS.* 14 July 2010. 12:00 news bulletin

[6] Referring to Mukhriz Mahathir, a son of Dr. Mahathir Mohamad, who was the prime minister of Malaysia from 1981 to 2003

[7] ลูกมหาธีร์ผยถกกลับ50แกนนำป่วนใต้ไม่หวังแยกดินแดน. *Matichon.* 11 October 2006

[8] แกนนำพูโลแนะรบ.เปิดโต๊ะเจรจาดับไฟใต้. *Matichon.* 21 April 2008

News representation 41

Interestingly, the *third-party involvement* frame introduces protagonists who may not be directly accountable for or affected by the conflict but still exert subtle influence over conflict solutions. This frame registers a number of contributions from the international community, particularly the Southeast Asian nations, such as the role of Malaysia as facilitator in the peace talks between Thailand and insurgent leaders, as well as the lessons on peace negotiation and autonomous administrative models in Indonesia and the Philippines. Another type of input comes in the forms of assessment on the Thai government's performance in maintaining universal civil rights, the results of which often fail to impress international scrutiny. The coverage of the international community's concerns and recommendations for southern conflict solutions shows that, despite the government's assertion that the southern conflict is an internal affair, the problem still garners considerable attention from overseas because of certain shared elements, from cultural and religious similarity and the regional security to the protection of basic civil and human rights.

Other protagonists are the general public and the royal institution. People in other parts of the country sometimes express concern about the on-going violence and contribute aid to the locals through donations and fund-raising. Also frequently displaying their stance on the conflict are the royal family and associated agencies. The recurring media coverage of the monarchy and associates, such as the attendance of royal members at slain civil servants' funerals, the Queen's unequivocal condemnation of violence, and the deputy chief of the royal aide-de-camp's adamant view on the necessity of weapon training for villagers, signals the influence of the royal institution on political elites and the conflict solution processes, despite not being a constitutional political player (see more detail of the royal patronage projects for southern conflict relief in Appendix B). The following headlines exemplify this observation.

HM Queen tells PM to solve southern problem with understanding.
(*Matichon* 4 February 2004)[10]

Deputy royal aide-de-camp reveals strategy in training village defence volunteers, "Don't bring spies in for weapon training."
(*Isara* 29 October 2005)[11]

HM Queen concerned about southern problem, establishing "Teacher Centre" for teachers to stay safely together.
(*Isara* 12 August 2008)[12]

Mark [Prime Minister Abhisit Vejjajiva] to follow the royal guidance in extinguishing southern fire.
(*Matichon* 2 January 2009)[13]

The "Old City" organises *tod pha pa* [Buddhist offering ritual] for HM Queen to help teachers in southern border.
(*Matichon* 10 November 2006)[14]

42 *News representation*

Muslims in Yala join in du'a praying to bless [HM Queen] on "National Mother's day".

(*Manager* 12 August 2008)[15]

The last two headlines reflect the influence of the monarch, as well as religious institutions, on the Thai community. While these headlines demonstrate that the general public is concerned about those suffering in the far South, its acts also show loyalty towards the royal family. Thus, this type of coverage illustrates how the beliefs considered to be an integral part of Thai society are played out in the conflict.

In summary, this section demonstrates the preferred themes and news frames in the southern conflict coverage. The wide array of disparate frame components discovered in this study indicates that the complexity and fluidity of the discursive contention are played out in the coverage. However, these components are not equally featured. The salience of certain news frames shows that the southern conflict is represented with a simplified and narrow set of explanations rather than a variety of interpretations based on different perspectives and approaches, evenly presented and contested.

The analysis suggests that the most used news frames are more inclined towards the *crime and conspiracy* discourse than others. As discussed above, the predominant news theme – *security and public order* – alludes to violence as the most discernible reality of the conflict. The news framing analysis, which indicates how the conflict is explained, shows similar results. It can be argued that the violent aspect of the phenomenon is most evident and its ramifications, particularly for ordinary people, can invoke public sympathy. Nonetheless, the salience of the hostile situations undermines other interpretations of this multifaceted conflict, and justifies the use of some solutions without much scrutiny or protestation.

Interestingly, the overall findings do not indicate major discrepancies among outputs of public service and alternative media outlets, namely *Thai PBS* and *Isara*, and mainstream commercial organisations like *Matichon* and *Manager*. Nonetheless, there are a few distinctive dissimilarities which prompt further discussions. The first is that the *power struggle among interest groups* frame is used to identify the causes of conflict more in the reports produced by *Thai PBS* and *Isara* than in ones produced by the commercial media. As will be discussed further in the following chapter, the expertise of journalists who are primarily responsible for southern conflict reporting in these organisations could contribute to the frequent presence of the *power struggle among interest groups* frame. Mostly specialising in security affairs, these reporters tend to follow the military's intelligence and investigations to explore the modus operandi of militia groups and underground crime syndicates.

Another striking difference is the non-mainstream commercial media's emphasis on the *impact on stakeholders* frame, whereas the commercial organisations' focus is on authorities' reactions in the *governance* frame. The last discernible difference between the commercial and not-for-profit organisations is in the *solutions* meta-frame. The commercial media underline the political and administrative

News representation 43

approaches to maintain public order, as apparent in the *governance, quality of life,* and *military* frames. Meanwhile, the public service broadcaster and alternative media outlet emphasise more the conflict's cultural distinctiveness, as shown in the *reconciliation, justice,* and *counter-insurgency* frames. This signals the attempts of public service and alternative media organisations to present the underreported explanations about the conflict.

The news media's labels for the southern conflict and its protagonists

As discussed in the previous sub-section, the hostility and public order aspects are the principal depiction of the southern conflict. This subsection looks into another practice where journalists' inclination towards certain discourses can be detected, which is how the problem and its antagonists are characterised.

The label analysis examines 150 stories in which headlines and anchor introductions directly mention the phenomenon. As illustrated in Table 2.8, a wide array of terms is used to describe the conflict. Interestingly, the most frequently used term is the metaphorical "Southern Fire," in line with a study that finds the constant use of "Southern Fire" in newspaper coverage, depicting the deep South as a perilous zone (Krisadawan Hongladarom and Soraj Hongladarom 2006). The analysis also reveals that more than half of the labels are based on the "Southern Fire" metaphor, for example, "Southern Fire problem," "Southern Fire situation," "poison of the Southern Fire". Additionally, generic terms that identify the conflict

Table 2.8 Labels of the southern conflict in headlines and introductions

Labels of the southern conflict	Frequency (percentage)
Metaphors	*(54)*
Southern Fire, Fire	51
Others relevant terms: Poison of Southern Fire, southern danger, southern seeds	3
Characteristics	*(33)*
Southern problem	13
Southern mishaps, chaos, violent incidents	9
Southern unrest, unrest problem	9
Southern situation, southern border situation	3
Geographical location	*(11)*
South, Southern provinces, Southern border	11
Terrorism-oriented term	*(2)*
"Red Village"[1]	1
Terrorism	1
Total (*n* = 150)	100

[1] The term "Red Village" or "Red Zone" refers to the areas where militia movements are highly active and attacks are prevalent

44 *News representation*

as "problem," such as "southern problem," "unrest," "southern situation" are commonly used, although not as prevalent as the metaphoric labels. Lastly, in many cases, the use of geographical terms such as "South" and "southern border" also refers to the conflict. Despite the wide range of names, the labelling of the conflict resonates with the dominance of the *security and public order* theme – that is, the conflict's restive, violence-prone, and problematic features are highlighted, often with the connotation of ferocity and brutality.

Among the 793 stories sampled, the references to perpetrators of violent incidents and suspects appear 204 times, 24 stories with identifications and 180 with unnamed perpetrators. The study of the latter group reveals that antagonists in the conflict are given various labels; nevertheless, the most-used terms allude to criminality rather than insurgency. As Table 2.9 shows, the terms involving criminal acts, such as "bandit," "instigator," "turbulence maker" are widely used,

Table 2.9 Labels for the antagonists in the southern conflict in headlines and introductions

Labels for antagonists	*Frequency (percentage)*
Criminals	*(64)*
Southern bandit	29
Criminal/ bandit	21
Trouble maker	7
Instigator	6
Ruthless/ brutal southern bandit, Pattani bandit	1
Legal terms	*(14)*
Suspect	7
Accused/ offender	7
Insurgents	*(12)*
(Southern turbulence-making) leader	4
(Southern turbulence-making) ally/member/sympathiser	4
Terrorist/ terrorist group	4
Action-based terms	*(6)*
Shooter/ sniper	3
Bomber	1
Arsonist	1
Motorcyclist attacker	1
Judgment on characters	*(4)*
Ruthless South/ Unlawful South	2
Commander/ringleader/chief/"uncommon thief"	2
Social groups	*(2)*
Trouble teens	2
Total (*n* =180)	102[1]

[1] The numbers are rounded up/down. Therefore, the total is not 100%.

News representation 45

particularly the term "southern bandit". Other oft-cited labels, such as legal terminology and action-based terms, also signal the illegality of their actions. The explicit identification of terrorists and separatists appears less frequently, in line with a small number of stories with terrorism and separatism topics.

Similar to the observation of the themes and news frames, journalists for vernacular media tend not to label perpetrators or suspects with military terms that connote the sense of civil warfare or insurgency, such as "insurgent," "militia," or "guerrilla movement," but choose to describe them according to their actions, such as "shooters," "snipers," and "bombers". The generic criminological characterisation helps prevent journalists from making a premature assumption about the assailants (Picard and Adams 1991); however, the use of these neutral terms inadvertently underpins the *crime and conspiracy* discourse, which portrays the perpetrators as faceless, with obscure backgrounds, and the incidents as frequent but random. Such labelling, despite its non-judgmental tone, also prevents the general public from learning more about the perpetrators and their motives, and essentially undermines other discourses, which give explanations beyond what are deemed unlawful acts.

In summary, looking back at the prominent themes, news frames, and labels, it is apparent that the news media's depiction of the southern conflict tends to highlight violence and its discernible consequences and solutions rather than providing explanations for the causes or invisible impact. Describing the far South as a restive region where outlaws roam freely and launch daily strikes, journalists often turn to state authority and the military for prescriptions to alleviate the conflict. As a result, the coverage's main focuses are on political and military elites' actions and responses, rather than those of other players.

"Thin" and straight-forward: the news genres and visual presentation in southern conflict reporting

While the previous sections discussed the analyses of texts and lexicon choices in news reports, this section moves on to examine journalistic genres and visual presentation to explicate the ways that stories about the southern conflict are told. The last subsection also presents observations on the coverage's trends during the seven-year review period to analyse the changes in southern conflict reporting as the conflict progressed.

Summarising what happened and what people said: the common mode of southern conflict reporting

The examination of the presentation formats identifies four categories of news genres, based on their characteristics, in the southern conflict reporting: 1) *summary and immediacy*, 2) *depth*, 3) *up close and personal*, and 4) *verbatim*. These genres require different writing styles and emphases. *Summary and immediacy* includes general news stories, breaking news and live reports, which mainly recapitulate events and interviews. *Depth* refers to stories with literary writing styles that elaborate on emotional elements and provide analytical perspectives, such as

46 *News representation*

feature articles, short TV documentaries, analyses, and investigative reports. *Up close and personal* refers to stories that focus solely on the accounts or opinions of a person or people involved, mostly through interview or profile pieces. As opposed to *depth*, which centres on an issue or event, this genre highlights the interviewed subject's outlooks and feelings. The last category, *verbatim*, refers to the word-for-word publication of raw data such as reports and studies, government dossiers, regulations, statistics, and speech transcripts. Generally, *verbatim* goes through little or no editing.

It should be noted here that the sample came in "relatively closed" forms,[16] which allow little room for discussion and counter-argument. Nevertheless, these genres still show journalistic variations and enable further investigation into how these variations may highlight or downplay certain angles of the conflict.

The findings in Table 2.10 show that the most frequently used genre in southern conflict reporting is *summary and immediacy*, with news format topping the chart. Stories in other genres appear far less. This implies that the coverage tends to tell what happened and what people said rather than explaining the contexts of these incidents and statements. With the minimal use of exploratory and in-depth presentation modes, the reports on the southern conflict seem to stay on the surface and provide few explanations for this complex phenomenon.

Table 2.10 The news genres in southern conflict reporting

News genres	Frequency (percentage)
Summary and immediacy	*(74)*
News	68
News brief[1]	5
Others: live reports, breaking news	1
Depth	*(18)*
Feature articles/ short TV documentary	12
Analysis articles/ investigative reports	6
Up close and personal	*(5)*
Interviews, live interviews	4
Profiles of key players	1
Verbatim	*(5)*
Reports	2
Detail of projects/ announcements	1
Transcripts of speeches	1
Summary/ chronology of events/ statistics	1
Total ($n = 793$)	101[2]

[1] "News brief" is used here in reference to reports containing a few sentences or a short paragraph, generally used in newspapers and on websites. Despite the brevity, "news brief" does not reflect a sense of urgency, as opposed to "breaking news," which is presented in similar patterns.
[2] The numbers are rounded up/down. Therefore, the total is not 100%.

Despite their different platforms (print, broadcast, online), the prevalence of news genres found in four organisations' outputs is similar. Nonetheless, the coverage of two online news agencies presents an interesting contrast, reflecting the organisations' different approaches in utilising the medium. The majority of *Manager* reports are in the *summary and immediacy* genre, whereas *Isara* scores highest in the *depth* genre. It can be inferred from this discovery that the *Manager* website optimises the new media's benefits of fast and straightforward delivery more than other features. The company also takes advantage of its multimedia and interactive functions by posting video and audio clips produced by its sister media outlets to accompany some stories. On the contrary, *Isara* focuses more on the benefits of virtually unlimited space and a flexible structure, and is able to offer a wider variety of news genres compared to other outlets, despite its much smaller operation costs. Moreover, the use of hyperlinking in *Isara*'s reports also supplements the coverage with additional background and perspectives on the issue, making the reports more comprehensive and contextualised.

Another noteworthy point is the high frequency of the *depth* genre in *Isara*'s and *Thai PBS*' reports, which implies that broadcast media could also facilitate explanatory reporting such as in the forms of documentary-style and analytical packages. Apart from maximising the advantages of their respective platforms, these organisations' news concentration can also enable journalists to create various presentation formats and genres.

Seen but not heard: the visual presentation of southerners and insurgents in news content

This analysis finds that the visual presentation enhances the textual description and helps shed light on certain features of the conflict that are left unexplained in the texts. Some findings even contradict the analysis on source attribution. The visual presentation in the print, broadcast, and online news coverage varies only slightly, featuring similar actors and contexts, as shown in Table 2.11.[17] While police and military officers are still among the most featured actors, the presence of the locals, victims of conflict and violence, as well as insurgents and suspects, is highly prominent, especially in print and online news content. The findings are contrary to the source attribution analysis, where these sources are rarely quoted, particularly in the case of insurgents and suspects. Instead of interviewing these sources, journalists present them by featuring the locals' way of life, their participation in events, or their facial expressions, in photographs and video footage. While the textual analysis points out that the reports often describe insurgents as unknown, clandestine, and faceless, the visual presentation helps match the face to the description. However, it should be noted that the portrayal of insurgents and suspects remains incomplete. The mug shots of suspects, pictures of them in custody, or shots of their actions from CCTV footage, do not offer additional contexts or explanation, as they lack details about their backgrounds or motives. Rather, such depiction emphasises the authority's allegation that these people committed crimes and should be publicly admonished.

48 *News representation*

Table 2.11 The actors featured in visual presentation of the news coverage

a. print and online news content

	Actors	Frequency (percentage – each)
1	Locals	20
2	Military	19
3	Police	14
4	Insurgents and suspects	9
5	Victims of conflict and violence	8
6	Government	7
7	State officials	6
8	Others[2]	4
9	Parliamentarians Civil Sector Academics	3
10	Members of inde-pendent agencies*	2
11	Private sector Royal family members and associates*	1
	Total (*n* = 802)	100

b. broadcast news content

	Actors	Frequency (percentage – each)
1	Police	26
2	Locals	24
3	Military	15
4	State officials	11
5	Government	7
6	Others[1] Victims of conflict and violence	4
7	Civil sector	3
8	Insurgents and suspects	2
9	Academics	2
10	Parliamentarians	1
11	Private sector	1
	Total (*n* = 1,206)	100

*These groups of actors were not featured in the broadcast news sample

[1] Miscellaneous protagonists, such as religious leaders, reporters and camera crews, non-locals/ visitors, or unidentified persons.
[2] Miscellaneous protagonists, such as representatives from overseas organisations, members of the press, non-locals, or unidentified persons.

Meanwhile, the analysis of the visual presentation's contexts reverts to agreeing with the analysis of the preferred theme, news frames, and sources. The majority of visual presentation revolves around organised events and the immediate aftermaths of violence, such as inspection at the scene of incidents, security reinforcement, casualties, and arrests, as demonstrated in Table 2.12. Other elements of the conflict, such as the southern residents' ways of life, human suffering, and history and culture, are also featured, but not to the same degree as the violence-related incidents. This discovery raises two interesting points. The first is that the brutality aspect of the conflict is once again highlighted. The second point is related to journalistic practices. The fact that organised events are photographed most shows that news workers tend to make use of the occasions arranged by sources rather than finding the subjects on their own. It seems journalists are likely to wait for news to come to them, instead of being proactive to seek out a story.

Tables 2.12 The contexts of visual presentation in news content

a. print and online news content

Contexts		Frequency (percentage – each)
1	Organised events	29
2	Scenes of violent incidents	15
3	Ways of life[1]	13
4	Security measures[2] Casualties[3]	9
5	Arrests/searches/ suspect's surrender	7
6	Human suffering[4] History and culture[5]	5
7	Visits[6]	4
8	Others Protests	2
	Total (*n* = 692)	100

b. broadcast news content

Actors		Frequency (percentage – each)
1	Scenes of violent incidents	26
2	Ways of life	18
3	Organised events	16
4	Security measures	13
5	Others (such as sources giving interview)	7
6	History and culture Casualties Arrests/searches/ suspect's surrender	5
7	Human suffering	3
8	Visits	2
9	Protests	1
	Total (*n* = 1,565)	100

[1] General activities of the locals such as people shopping at local market, people praying at mosque, students in the classroom.
[2] Military activities such as army patrol, soldiers guarding schools and temples, weapon training and military equipment.
[3] Corpses, injured people, funerals.
[4] People affected by conflict/ violence expressing and/or demonstrating grief and difficulties, situations that elicit grief and difficulties in life.
[5] Local heritage such as ancient mosques, people performing traditional dance
[6] Photo opportunities of public figures/state officials visiting villages, locals, or injured people

The fluctuating and oscillating coverage: the dynamism and variability of southern conflict reporting

This sub-section examines the trends of the coverage to identify the changes in the way that the southern conflict has been reported during the seven years. To do so, the study looks at the length of story and the number of sources to determine if the conflict has received the same degree of media attention as the situation continues. The analysis also takes note of the consistency and recurrence of news frames to find out if there are any discursive shifts in news representation.

Contrary to the previous discussions, the analysis in these areas shows discrepancies between the four selected media organisations, which reflect the diversity in Thai journalism. The evaluation of story length indicates a downward direction in the coverage of commercial media, namely the daily *Matichon* and *Manager*,

50 *News representation*

but a consistent trend in that of the non-profit organisations, *Thai PBS* and *Isara*. The coverage becomes shorter from 2008 onwards, even in the case of *Isara*, possibly because the crisis in national politics started brewing. Similarly, there is a declining tendency in the number of source attributions in *Matichon*'s and *Manager*'s news content, and an unchanging situation in *Thai PBS*'s, whereas the coverage from *Isara* sees a rising trajectory.

The inverse relationship between the story length and the number of sources in commercial media, and the progression of the conflict, also signals the waning interest of journalists in the issue. To them, the matter is no longer as ground-breaking as when it began. Meanwhile, the consistent coverage in not-for-profit news media could be a result of the organisations' dedicated spaces for the issue. *Thai PBS* allocates specific time slots for the southern conflict-related content, while *Isara* was purposively established to report the conflict and about the far South. Such policies ensure that there will always be a fair amount of space for such reports. These findings reflect the degree of attention given to this issue by different media organisations' editorial teams. They also imply that, although the issue was reported regularly throughout the seven years, the frequency of coverage does not necessarily result in detailed and multi-perspectival explanations.

The statistics of news frames' frequency are too inconclusive to form a clear correlation between the presence of news frames and political situations. Nonetheless, there are cases where the link becomes discernible. Moreover, the fluctuating trend of certain key frames still shows the subtle fluidity of the contending discourses, and reflects the shifts in the news representation of the southern conflict. This finding is in line with studies, which suggest that the interpretations of the southern conflict are not only disparate, but may also be contested and amended as the situation continues.

In the *cause* meta-frame, for instance, the *power struggle among interest groups* frame rarely appears at the beginning of the conflict, but becomes more evident in 2007 and after, following the military's introduction of the "additional threats" theory. On the other hand, the presence of the *identity politics* frame becomes less noticeable in the latter years of the conflict than when it began. At the same time, the *uses of force by unknown actors* frame is on the rise. These observations suggest that elements of the *crime and conspiracy* discourse remain predominant in southern conflict reporting during the seven years, whereas those of other discourses tend to fade into the background.

The fluctuation of some frames could also be a consequence of journalistic practices. For instance, the frequency of the *impact on stakeholders* frame, part of the *repercussions* meta-frame, starts to drop significantly as the conflict entered its fifth year. This corresponds with the earlier observation that, as the situation continued, journalists no longer give the same degree of attention to such stories, considering them "old news". This attitude may change when new angles are introduced or if the stories can be linked to current phenomena.

The connection between news representation and Thai politics could be detected, particularly in the *solutions* meta-frame. For example, the frequency of the *governance and political structure* frame goes up as the debate and discussion on the regional administrative policy for the far South are prevalent in national politics in 2009. Most notably, the special administrative model for the southern border provinces (a component of the *governance and political structure* frame) is not brought up until 2007 – the fourth year of the conflict – and even then, the proposal is presented with negative responses. A few years later, when the topic received more attention from a new government and civil society sector, constructive debates concerning the special administrative model and autonomy then emerge. Similarly, Samatcha Nilaphatama and Rungrawee Chalermsripin-yorat (2014) observe some discursive shifts in the media's coverage of the 2013 formal peace talks between Thai authorities and putative BRN leaders – the process that had been kept closed and secretive in preceding governments. Despite the discrepancies between discourses manifest in the mainstream media's reports and those of alternative outlets and the media of the dissenters, they observe, the coverage still presented fresh debate concerning various options to remedy the conflict, apart from existing and inept ones. By contrast, the frequency of the *reconciliation and recognition of local identity* frame, which sees its peak in 2006, in line with the appointment of the National Reconciliation Commission, declines as the conflict continues. This is partly because the agency concluded its work in the subsequent year; hence, the disappearance of a key proponent of the frame from the media's radar. These discoveries correspond with Daniel Hallin's *spheres of consensus, legitimate controversy and deviance* model (1989, pp. 116–118), which indicates the influence of political elites' sentiment in public discussions on certain issues. At the beginning of the resurgence of violence, key political players were ambivalent towards – if not rejecting – the notion of autonomy for the deep South, and peace talks with "separatists" were kept confidential (see Chapter 1 and Appendix B for more detail). As such, the subjects were in the *sphere of deviance*, and the reports on such issues were minimal. Nonetheless, in late 2009, the debate on self-determination and peace processes was pushed forward in public forums, and the political elite showed disagreeing views. By then, the subject moved into the *sphere of legitimate controversy*, and news media became more independent to explore the previously "taboo" topics, for example, an *Isara* series which interviewed different stakeholders on their diverse views about autonomy for the southern border provinces.

This chapter also demonstrates that the presentation styles of southern conflict coverage have a tendency to favour the *crime and conspiracy* discourse over others. The study of news genres demonstrates that the southern conflict reports are mostly straightforward and presented without much context. The visual presentation could help shed light on the marginalised players, such as affected stakeholders and suspected insurgents. However, the representation remains one-dimensional and fragmented. At the same time, the frequent depiction of violence-related incidents is in accordance with the most highlighted theme, news frames, and sources. The analysis also shows the limitation of journalistic presentation and practices to generate multi-perspectival depictions of this complex and dynamic conflict.

52 *News representation*

Nonetheless, the study of news reports during seven years indicates that the coverage is not always static. The examination of the story length and number of sources reveals a decline, particularly in the reports produced by national-level commercial media. As the conflict entered its fourth year, the attention of national-level news organisations on this issue started to wane, with shorter reports and fewer informants. On the contrary, the average story length and number of sources in the public service and alternative media's reports remained steady. This shows that the news organisations with dedicated spaces for this issue played a significant role in southern conflict reporting, because they could ensure the constant and ample presence of the matter. In a similar vein, as will be discussed in the subsequent chapters, southern-based alternative media and their partnerships with civil society organisations in the far South could keep the subject circulated in regional public forums, and sometimes successfully push the matter forward to the national media.

The subtle changes in the coverage could be denoted from the fluidity of news frames throughout the seven-year review period. Despite the fluctuation of news frames' frequency, the analysis indicates that the *crime and conspiracy* discourse remains in a dominating position, while other discourses are recurring but mostly kept in the background. The rise and fall of news frames in certain periods of the conflict could have been contributed to by the prevalent discussions in national politics, the emergence of new protagonists, or the interests of the news media on the issue. This discovery also provides a basis for further investigation into the relationships between news media, protagonists, and political settings in the following chapters.

Conclusion

This chapter presents the examination into various elements of news content to explain how the southern conflict is represented. Overall, the study suggests that the preferred theme and news frames together render a depiction of the southern conflict that buttresses the *crime and conspiracy* discourse over others. The analysis of the coverage's trends also shows an inverse relationship between the conflict's continuation and the news media's interest in the subject. Although there is some fluidity and dynamism in the coverage throughout seven years, the most recurring themes and news frames remain steady, keeping the predominant discourse in place and revealing minimal discursive shifts. Meanwhile, journalistic variations such as news genres, platforms, news orientations, and organisation principles, contribute little to balancing the discursive contestation. These findings question why news media portray the conflict similarly despite their differing natures, and how alternative explanations can emerge despite these conditions. These queries will be discussed in the following chapters.

In all, the similar patterns of news coverage produced by the commercial and not-for-profit media organisations are more prominent than their differences. The similarities could be a consequence of the general journalistic nature shared by these agencies, from how editors and reporters make news judgements to their relationship and access to news sources. This argument will be discussed more in detail in the subsequent chapters.

Notes

1 The *governance and politics* theme comprises five topics: 1) policy, which refers to the government's decisions and actions concerning the southern conflict, such as policies, measures, and regulations, 2) local and national administration, which refers to actions, measures, and policies carried out by administrative officials, such as provincial governors, district chief-officers, or village chiefs, 3) political contention and election campaigning, 4) human rights, and 5) international affairs, which refers to the relationship with other countries and international agencies and forums, as well as their involvement in the southern conflict.

2 The *security and public order* theme covers six topics: 1) regional and national security, 2) violent incidents, 3) terrorism, which counts the direct attribution to terrorism, insurgency, and unrest, 4) separatism, which refers to the direct attribution to secessionist movements, 5) law enforcement and the justice system, which refers to decisions and actions carried out by law enforcement officers (such as police, forensic teams, investigators), and those in the justice system, and 6) drugs, which refers to illicit drug trade and trafficking.

3 The *socio-economy and culture* theme comprises seven topics: 1) religions, 2) religion education, 3) history and culture, 4) education, which refers to the standardised education system, 5) economy, 6) medical and healthcare service, and 7) the impact of conflict on the livelihood of southern community and the general public.

4 โจรใต้ถล่มตชด.-คนรถไฟดับ3. *Matichon.* 19 July 2004.

5 ฆ่าโหด4ไทยพุทธชุดสุดท้ายบาเจาะ ลูกเหยื่อขอย้ายเผยอยู่ต่อ"ตายแน่". *Matichon.* 20 September 2010.

6 โจรใต้ลอบยิงถล่มชาวบ้านในนราฯ ดับ 1. *Manager.* 15 December 2009.

7 เหตุยิงหลายพื้นที่ในปัตตานี [Shootings in several areas in Pattani]. *Thai PBS.* 28 August 2010. 12:00 news bulletin.

8 The four latter frames refer to the actions taken by state authorities; nevertheless, they carry different emphases. The *use of force by authorities* frame focuses on the officials' attacks on suspects, which often lead to the deaths of suspects, or officers, or both. The *arrest and suspect surrender* frame emphasises the capture of suspects, and when the suspects surrender or report themselves to state officials. The *search* frame highlights the authorities' examination of an area believed to harbour the suspects, such as the suspect's house and village. The *security reinforcement* frame focuses on the intensification of policing and security measures.

9 *Isara* editor. Interview. 25 January 2012.

10 พระราชินีทรงรับสั่งนายกฯแก้ปัญหาใต้ด้วยความเข้าใจ. *Matichon.* 4 February 2004.

11 รองราชสมุหองครักษ์เปิดยุทธวิธีฝึกอบรบ."อย่านำใส้ศึกมาฝึกอาวุธ". *Isara.* 29 October 2005.

12 พระราชินีทรงห่วงปัญหาใต้ ทรงตั้ง"ศูนย์ครู"ให้อยู่รวมกันอย่างปลอดภัย. *Isara.* 12 August 2008.

13 มาร์คใช้แนวทางพระราชทานดับไฟใต้. *Matichon.* 2 January 2009.

14 กรุงเก่า ทอดผ้าป่าทูลถวายพระราชินีช่วยครูชายแดนใต้. *Matichon.* 10 November 2006. The "Old City" is referred to Ayuttaya Province in central Thailand.

15 ชาวมุสลิมยะลาร่วมสวดดุอาร์ถวายพระพร "วันแม่แห่งชาติ". *Manager.* 12 August 2008.

16 In the study by Schlesinger et al. (1983, pp. 34–36), a "relatively open" form refers to television programmes which enable contextual explanation or discussion and debate, such as current affairs programmes and documentaries. This form of programme tends to be more open to counter-dominant interpretations of conflict than "relatively closed" forms such as news bulletins or news magazine programmes.

17 The results of visual presentation in print and online news content and broadcast news content are presented in separate tables because the units of analysis are different. In print and online news content, the still images are analysed, whereas in broadcast news content the shots of video footage are analysed.

54 *News representation*

References

Hallin, Daniel. 1989. *The "Uncensored War": The Media and Vietnam*. London: University of California Press.

Krisadawan Hongladarom and Soraj Hongladarom. 2006. วาทกรรมเกี่ยวกับภาคใต้และความรุนแรงใน สังคมไทย [Discourses Concerning the Southern Region and Violence in Thai Society]. In: Krisadawan Hongladarom and Jantima Eamanondh. eds. มองสังคมผ่านวาทกรรม *[Looking at Society through Discourses]*. Bangkok: Chulalongkorn University Press, pp. 103–134.

Picard, Robert G. and Adams, Paul D. 1991. Characterizations of Acts and Perpetrators of Political Violence in Three Elite U.S. Daily Newspapers. In: Alali, A.O. and Eke, K.K. eds. *Media Coverage of Terrorism: Methods of Diffusion*. Newbury Park, CA: Sage, pp. 11–22.

Samatcha Nilaphatama and Rungrawee Chalermsripinyorat. 2014. วาทกรรมสื่อมวลชนใน กระบวนการสันติภาพสามจังหวัดชายแดนภาคใต้ 2556 [Media discourse on peace process in Southern Thailand 2013] [online]. *Media Inside Out Group*. Available at: www.deepsouthwatch. org/sites/default/files/peaceprocessdiscourse_samatcha_rungrawee.pdf [Accessed: 20 May 2015].

Schlesinger, Philip, Murdock, Graham, and Elliot, Phillip.. 1983. *Televising 'Terrorism': Political Violence in Popular Culture*. London: Comedia Publishing Group.

Srisompob Jitpiromsri. 2010. สรุปหกปีไฟใต้: พลวัตการก่อความไม่สงบกับการสร้างจินตกรรมของการก่อความ รุนแรง [Summary of the six years of violence: The dynamics of unrest and the construction of imagined insurgency] [online]. *Deep South Watch*. Available at: www.deepsouthwatch.org/node/728 [Accessed: 14 January 2013].

3 Reporting the southern conflict

From the field to the newsroom

The previous chapter discussed the southern conflict coverage produced by four news organisations, and the results revealed that the diversity of Thai news ecology does little to produce diversified news representations of the conflict. Moreover, the prominent aspects of southern conflict in news content and the general depiction of key protagonists remain within a similar vein throughout the seven-year review period, with minor discursive shifts. Nonetheless, the different interpretations of the conflict – particularly its causes and solutions – still enable challenging discourses to arise, which signals the struggle and complexity in news ecology.

This chapter moves behind the scene of news production to examine the conditions and culture wherein Thai news workers operate, which shape the portrayal of the conflict in news contents. It deals with the journalistic practices and obstacles that journalists encounter while covering the conflict, while the subsequent chapter focuses on the dynamic and fluid relationship between journalists and their sources.

The making of southern conflict coverage

Southern conflict reports originate mostly in the three southern border provinces, namely, Pattani, Yala, and Narathiwat, and four districts of the neighbouring Songkla Province. Some stories, however, come from the capital city, where national-level politics takes place. For the incidents that occur in Bangkok, reporters of the thematic news desks at the headquarters, such as politics (including security affairs), economics, crime, social issues, and foreign affairs, are responsible for filing stories to the newsroom directly. Additional steps occur when it comes to stories from the southernmost region. Typically, Bangkok-based media outlets hire stringers who reside in the provinces to send in stories from the area. Most television stations also have a southern news centre, composed of a chief,[1] reporters, and production crews, to produce their own reports, liaise with local stringers, and edit stringers' copy before sending it to their headquarters. All stringers and regional news centres usually fall under the supervision of the regional news desk in Bangkok.

Stringers, or freelance local reporters based in provinces, are primarily responsible for filing straightforward news reports, still photos, and video footage of the incidents. The organisation's own crews are mostly tasked with producing live reports and long-form presentations such as feature stories, interview pieces, and analytical and investigative reports. Local stringers mostly work for more than one news organisation. For instance, a stringer who was interviewed for his work with *Thai PBS* also files stories to eight other news companies: five dailies and three television channels.

Journalists generally obtain information from three channels: 1) *routine*, 2) *informal*, and 3) *enterprise* (Sigal 1973).[2] The *routine* channel refers to press releases, press conferences, and scheduled events. The *informal* channel is when reporters receive information via background briefings, leaks, or reports from other news organisations. Lastly, the *enterprise* channel refers to journalists' own initiatives, such as one-on-one interviews, unprecedented events, first-hand observations, and independent research and analysis. When covering news about violent incidents in the deep South, local journalists usually receive the preliminary investigation reports sent out to news organisations by three local authorities: army, police, and the provincial data centre.[3] As will be discussed in a moment, southern journalists and stringers' safety concerns make them rely more on these official reports than going out in the field. This dependency, therefore, allows official voices to appear in news content more frequently than those of other protagonists. The stories from the field and those produced in-house are sent to desk editors in Bangkok, then screened in editorial meetings, prioritised by the editor in charge of the daily production, and edited by responsible crews before being presented on the respective media platforms. The lines of production of the southern conflict news are described in Figure 3.1.

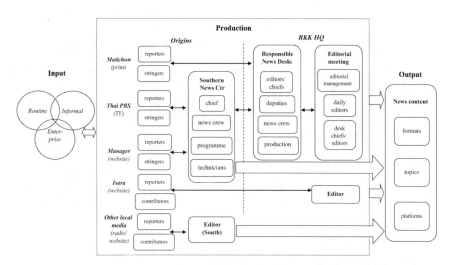

Figure 3.1 The lines of production of the southern conflict news employed by news organisations

Reporting the southern conflict 57

The coordination between the headquarters and southern reporters varies from one news organisation to another. The *Matichon* newspaper does not own a news centre in the region; therefore, their local stringers generally contact the regional news desk in Bangkok directly. Both *Thai PBS* and *Manager* have the southern news centres, but their scale of operation differs. *Thai PBS*' southern news centre comprises approximately 30 staff, including news production crews and transmission technicians, whereas the *Manager*'s southern news unit is composed of ten people who are responsible for the content on southern violence across all Manager Group media platforms: print, television, and online. Another difference between these two organisations is the interaction with the Bangkok head office. *Thai PBS* uses its regional news centre to coordinate with stringers and edit copy, but the ultimate decision on media output rests with the Bangkok desk and daily editors. Meanwhile, with the southern news website launched in February 2012, the *Manager* southern team takes its own responsibility and bypasses Bangkok in producing the online presentation itself. Like the *Matichon* daily, the two news centres still exchange story ideas and assignments with the Bangkok editorial team. Meanwhile, the *Isara* website operates with a small news production team, similar to most local alternative media. The difference is that the *Isara* editor for southern conflict news is based in Bangkok and also works as a senior reporter/editor for a national newspaper, whereas editors and managers of most local alternative media are based in the region, and some work as stringers and fixers.

While the news filtering process varies from one organisation to another, the media outlets still share one similar practice: an editor[4] has to be informed of the story ideas and the finished product. However, the degrees of verification and quality control may vary, depending on the experience and expertise of reporters who file the story. The next step after receiving the southern conflict reports from the field is similar across all media outlets. For large media operations such as *Matichon* and *Thai PBS*, the responsible editors present the stories in editorial meetings in which other reports and story ideas are also discussed. The editorial meetings are held at least twice a day and are attended by desk editors, managers, daily editors,[5] and senior journalists. At *Thai PBS*, a representative from the legal department also attends the evening editorial meeting to share expertise and ensure that the coverage does not violate any laws. Additionally, a staffer from the Civil Media Network department, which is in charge of citizen reporter training and production, partakes in the meeting to provide stories and ideas from citizen reporters based around the country, including the southern border provinces.

Generally, the regional news desk[6] becomes the "host" of the southern conflict stories because most incidents originate in the South. When authorities in Bangkok or other parts of the country speak about or react to the events that take place in the southern region, reporters from relevant news desks, such as politics, security affairs, current affairs, or special reports, are required to cover the story. Therefore, the coverage sometimes becomes a collaborative product from different news desks and production departments. Based on the information presented and discussed in the editorial meeting, the editors in charge (such as front page and daily editors) will prioritise the stories as they arrange the front page

58 *Reporting the southern conflict*

appearance or assemble the news bulletin rundown. At the same time, the meeting attendees will discuss news angles and presentation formats, make suggestions, seek coordination with other desks and departments, and give new assignments to relevant parties.

The common presentation formats are straightforward, inverted-pyramid style news reports, feature articles or TV packages, interviews, and analysis and investigative reports. The editorial meetings sometimes entail talks about presentation on the main distribution platforms. The print and online media often publish interview transcripts, studies, official reports, or speeches in their entirety, while the TV station takes advantage of its communicative features by conducting live reports, interviews, or discussion panels with involved parties. Editorial meeting participants sometimes discuss additional presentation channels for some major stories, such as live streaming via their website. But generally, the presentation of news outputs on additional platforms such as the organisations' website, online social media such as YouTube, or online social networks such as the reporters' personal or the organisation's Facebook or Twitter accounts, is carried out independently by the responsible departments or the reporters themselves.

Talks and discussions in the editorial meetings typically involve immediate tasks such as allocating news stories to daily presentation and planning the coverage for the following day and week. News managers have expressed that, ideally, the editorial meeting should be the forum where editors, producers, and senior reporters share and exchange ideas, news tips, and expertise. Nonetheless, based on some senior participants' and my observations of the *Thai PBS* editorial meetings, the gatherings are a rather passive panel where editors merely present the stories they receive from their reporters, then leave. Occasionally, there are debates about news angles and presentation formats, but in-depth discussions about the situation rarely happen.

The editorial and production process is described in Figure 3.2. The diagram may best explain the practice in large media organisations, as it shows various parties involved in the process. Nonetheless, smaller operations such as *Manager*, *Isara*, and other local media outlets also apply similar editorial procedures, although the process may not include as many participants.

Despite their different organisational principles and structures, the four selected news media organisations employ a similar news production process. At the heart of this system is the acts of screening, selecting, packaging (and re-packaging), editing, and prioritising – the clear evidence that news is not simply presented as "how it happened," but rather "how it happened as journalists see it". As to be discussed later, it is this editorial system, along with the notion of "neutrality," that news organisations and news workers consider the foundation of journalistic professionalism, and they use these characteristics to distinguish themselves from other alternative and advocacy media outlets. Nonetheless, news workers' perceptions of professionalism vary, leading to the disparate roles they have played in the conflict.

Another noteworthy point that will be brought up later is the fact that the regional news desk is tasked as the host by default of southern conflict coverage and that

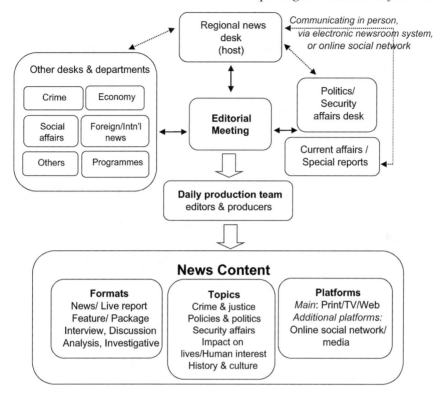

Figure 3.2 The editorial meeting and daily news production process

this newsroom arrangement becomes an obstacle in news production. McCargo criticises the Thai press's "Bangkok-centric news priorities" (2012, p.99) in reporting the southern conflict and other phenomena outside of the metropolitan areas, as it not only gives little attention to provincial news workers' potential and well-being, but also fails to explicate the complex relationships between local and national politics, economy, and other public policies (McCargo 2000, pp. 47–49, p. 177; 2012, pp. 98–100). This shortcoming contributes to the public's lack of understanding of the country's structural problems, as it severs the connection between rural and urban issues.

Journalists and the difficulties in southern conflict reporting

Journalists involved in the production of southern conflict coverage can be broadly categorised into two groups based on their locations: the southern border journalists and the Bangkok-based ones. In these two groups, journalists are divided into two camps: those working in the field and those based in the newsroom. However, as will be explained later, beat reporters in Bangkok share common culture and

60   *Reporting the southern conflict*

obstacles with newsroom staff rather than with journalists based in the South, despite not always being in the office. Therefore, in this study, "field reporting" refers to working in the southern border provinces, whereas "newsroom production" includes both editorial decisions made by the southern newsrooms and Bangkok headquarters and the work of beat reporters based in Bangkok.

News-making in a volatile environment: difficulties of reporting from the field

For Bangkok-based reporters and editors, the beat system mostly shapes the topics and people they cover. For instance, political reporters are usually stationed at major governmental agencies and shadow respective policy-makers, while security affairs reporters are attached to military offices.[7] On the contrary, reporters and stringers based in the provinces are required to cover a broad range of issues in their region of responsibility, from local politics, businesses, and crime to social problems and environmental issues. Their job description resembles that of current affairs reporters who are not attached to specific topics,[8] but the regional news reporters' tasks are more geographically oriented.

Interestingly, a number of southern stringers follow in the footsteps of their parents who were stringers by inheriting the freelance reporting business, which provides them with existing production resources as well as connections with news organisations and sources. Notwithstanding these vocational assets, most stringers are not considered the key presenters of news coverage. As a southern news centre chief puts it, being based outside the main office, regional journalists are often regarded as "second-class reporters" by those based in the headquarters because most stories from the provinces are considered trivial and not as important as ones taking place in Bangkok.[9] Nonetheless, a handful of news organisations' employees who have been reporting from the region since the beginning of the conflict earn the agencies' recognition and become their regular presenters when it comes to stories from the southern border provinces.

Three key factors influence journalists' work in the restive area, from most apparent to most obscure: 1) intimidations and threats, 2) information deficit and misinformation, and 3) personal and professional dilemmas.

Dodging bullets, bombs, and abuses: intimidations and threats towards field journalists

When violent incidents re-emerged in early 2004, reporters' newsgathering routine was affected. Despite not being a direct target, journalists were injured in several bomb attacks when reporting from the scene. Thus, field reporters stationed in the area learned to acquire a new set of skills to do their work. Both news editors and reporters point out that staying safe in the volatile region is the first qualification of covering the deep South. Reporters and stringers have to study the patterns of attacks and come up with ways to keep themselves safe in a hostile environment. They avoid travelling to unfamiliar territories and at night. Instead, other means

Reporting the southern conflict 61

of long-distance communication, mostly telephone calls, are used to gather and verify information.[10]

News management have claimed they prefer to keep reporters away from the scene rather than sending them in equipped with protective gear. As one news editor puts it, "It's not like we want them to go in and wear armoured vests. It's not that necessary."[11] While this caution corresponds with the well-known remark, "no news is worth getting killed for," it also reflects the news organisations' pre-termission of southern conflict reporting. Most Thai news outlets and professional organisations do not specifically provide hostile environment training or protective equipment for their southern reporters. Moreover, stringers are not covered by news media organisations' insurance policies.[12] With safety being the key concern and the frequency of field visits minimised, the reports might lose certain details essential to better understanding the case, and rely more on official accounts of the events.

While unprecedented attacks are the obvious danger, reporters in the far South also encounter other forms of pressure that could compromise their reporting ability, in the form of threats and intimidation. The threats range from verbal abuse to stalking. More importantly, the intimidation comes from all levels of various involved parties, be it junior officers, high-ranking authorities, local interest groups, or even villagers.

Reporters are used to snide comments and officials' requests to "tone down their reports". Army officials sometimes accuse journalists of being an "unwitting ally,"[13] or insurgent sympathisers, by reporting their attacks. Some accuse journalists of being "oxygen providers" for insurgent movements, reasoning that perpetrators might feel glorified by the reports and encouraged to instigate more violent incidents. While these remarks do not cause physical harm, they do not foster a comfortable environment for journalists to work in. Besides the subtle criticism, journalists also receive "warnings" in the forms of mysterious calls or tailings to signal that they are being watched. A former *Isara* reporter said he was warned via email of becoming a target after posting an interview with an Islamic studies professor criticising the insurgents' attacks on civilians. "Previously the gun was pointed towards state officials. But today, the aim was changed from state officials to include you, too," the former reporter, who now works as a fixer for international news organisations and the editor of a local online news agency,[14] recalled.

Two *Isara* reporters recounted stories when they faced an unwelcoming feeling of distrust from residents upon entering unfamiliar areas, especially communities where attacks had recently occurred. Raising an example of a village where a shooting just took place, they said that as they walked in, a group of villagers moved towards them slowly and started questioning them. As they became surrounded, the news crew recognised the crowd leaders as members of the insurgents' "community relation team". These leaders then loudly denounced news media for reporting inaccurately, calling in more villagers to join the circle. The crowd dispersed when a high-profile authority figure arrived at the scene.[15]

62 *Reporting the southern conflict*

While "intimidation from below" seems straightforward and comes in the form of direct violence, "intimidation from above" – meaning measures used by authorities to hinder journalists – are complex and often legal. Since 2004, three sets of security laws, namely martial law, the Emergency Decree on Public Administration in State of Emergency (or the state of emergency decree, in short), and the Internal Security Act, have been imposed together and separately in different parts of the southern border provinces.[16] Human rights advocates heavily criticise the implementation of these regulations, particularly martial law and the state of emergency decree, as they pave the way for excessive extrajudicial power.[17] Media professional organisations have also voiced concerns in several statements[18] that these regulations, especially the state of emergency decree, generate a chilling effect as they permit state authorities to scrutinise and restrict media content that is deemed a threat to national security, a disruption of social order, an instigation of social division, or an insult against the monarchy. Such actions, they feel, allow authorities to curtail freedom of speech and of the press.

However, interestingly, journalists working in the South rarely mentioned these laws or viewed them as a primary structural constraint, despite the laws' potentially critical restriction. Instead, journalists looked at authorities' less public means of intimidation, which range from monitoring news workers' movement to summoning them for interrogation. Members of local alternative media raised concerns when regional military officials "invited" one producer in for "interviews and talks" at a military camp, where he was questioned about the production process, the funding from international organisations, and the content emphasis on the sufferings of Muslims.[19] A former *Isara* reporter and fixer says international news organisations, particularly television channels, crave exclusive interviews with those involved in insurgent movements. But such a need results in him being monitored and questioned by intelligence officials on the whereabouts of the insurgents. "[TV producers] would blur the face or alter the audio [of the interview subjects]. But you did not realise that after you went back, how people in the area . . . your coordinator . . . would continue their lives here," he remarked.[20]

Another *Isara* reporter said she was tailed and the house where she lived with her husband and three small children was broken into after a story criticising the regional administrative body was broadcast on radio. "There had always been intimidations, but we didn't report them to officials. I would tell [the *Isara* editor] that we constantly faced such situations. At first we didn't think it would happen, so we didn't do anything. But later, there were a lot of things missing [from the house]. It was baffling," said the reporter.[21]

The same reporter also came across similar forms of intimidation suspected to be carried out by another local interest group. After her interview piece with a senator about his views on the special administrative models debate, part of *Isara*'s series on the issue, was posted on the *Isara* website, the reporter noticed she was followed by unknown motorcyclists. She decided to move to a "safe house," fearing for the safety of her children. Still, she found her vehicle was tampered with, and some strangers still suspiciously drove around her current

Reporting the southern conflict 63

residence. The situation even prompted her to consider purchasing a handgun for protection. The facts that this junior reporter and her spouse started out as free-lance journalists and have been working for small media organisations for less than a decade potentially deprives them of a well-known news establishment that would support their work and protect their safety, making them more vulnerable to intimidation than senior peers.

Swimming in the vortex: information deficit and misinformation

Reporters often come across situations where they cannot gain access to data, or receive information they cannot verify, as disparate players utilise several means to conceal information or disseminate the versions that best promote their cause. Stringers said the murky atmosphere following an incident when no one was will-ing to talk made their job of gathering information even more problematic.

> During the first two years [of the unrest], my job had been rather difficult, because we had no idea who the perpetrators were. Especially the first year, we didn't know what happened. We only knew there were casualties and losses, but not about who caused them. For the locals, they felt these were the state's actions. And for people working in the area like us, accessing informa-tion had been difficult. No information was released, and there were attempts to conceal it, as if those events were nothing or they were small matters.[22]

Additionally, because most incidents that reporters have to report are from the scenes of violence, getting past security officers guarding the perimeters and gleaning first-hand information from investigators and local residents becomes difficult. One local reporter raised an example where he had to negotiate with soldiers to enter the scene, saying, "Sir, I'm also working here. I have to perform my duty, and you have to do yours. I know what is appropriate or not. I am also a Thai and love my homeland. I know what to do."[23] Interestingly, this remark cor-responds with an earlier observation that state officials often see reporters as being unpatriotic. Thus, the "I'm also a Thai" defence is used to show the reporter's patriotism and that he is on the same side as the soldiers.

Another method used increasingly by protagonists is to feed journalists their side of stories. Authorities usually do so by organising press conferences, dis-seminating official statements, and seeking cooperation from the media to report "correctly". There are several occasions in which the regional Internal Security Operations Command (ISOC) issued their statements to clarify the situations and counter the news reports that were deemed to criticise or undermine the military's operation.[24] These statements were generally faxed or emailed to the journalists in charge of southern conflict news and the news organisations directly, but were not posted on the agency's official website. Meanwhile, local civil societies or even separatist groups based overseas, such as PULO, are persistent in sending out press releases criticising the Thai government and justice system to reporters in the far South and those specialising in the southern insurgency.

64 *Reporting the southern conflict*

Press conferences, news releases, and "fact-finding" trips are among the frequently used formal methods to provide journalists with their explanations of the problem, but some players in the conflict employ more subtle means, such as involving journalists in their work. For example, the regional administrative body, SBPAC, appointed several local reporters as members of its committees on southern solutions, reasoning that these reporters could share their expertise in the field with other responsible agencies. A senior journalist revealed that some intelligence agencies went as far as paying local reporters retainer fees in exchange for information they gathered.

In similar vein, local NGOs working on the southern conflict issues often forge partnerships with media organisations, especially alternative ones, in running their campaigns. For instance, *Thai PBS* established a working group, comprising local academics, civil society organisations and media workers, to consult on the southern news centre's locally produced programme production. The partnership with local NGOs brings about a reciprocal exchange of information that enables journalists to acquire the locals' underreported insights. However, this partnership does not necessarily guarantee that every player involved will be fairly represented. As a senior editor observed, civil society organisations also have their own agenda, and their press releases sometimes omit crucial information to buttress their arguments. But because of their non-profit organisation status, their messages are usually reported unchecked or without careful scrutiny.[25] This is a significant point and will be brought up again in the next chapter in discussing the complex relationships between sources and journalists, and their influences on the diverse roles journalism plays in this conflict.

Damned if I do, damned if I don't: personal and professional dilemmas

Threats, intimidation, and confusing and false information generate a challenging environment that prompts field reporters to conduct themselves with discretion in order to get the story while maintaining relationship with disparate sources and staying safe. Similar to reporting about other conflicts, journalists say the protagonists usually accuse them of supporting their adversaries. No matter how the news media reports the conflict, not every player will be pleased. A senior reporter observed that their position is similar to that of religious leaders in the area who are "being caught between the buffalo horns". This dilemma puts reporters in a precarious spot as they negotiate their stance in the conflict. "Sometimes, performing our duty as the media here is very difficult because we are amidst a lot of interests. We are attacked from every direction. And if we don't do it, sometimes villagers will say that we are gagged by state officials or whatever. But if we [criticise the state], we are attacked either way," said a TV reporter.[26]

As stated earlier, minimising travelling to unfamiliar zones could compromise the newsgathering process. At the same time, the concerns over threats from local interest groups, particularly underground crime syndicates, as well as intervention from authorities, also causes a chilling effect among local media workers, including small civic media practitioners. Media producers have resorted to

Reporting the southern conflict 65

self-censorship to prevent state interference. A community radio[27] practitioner said that the station's volunteer presenters avoid directly discussing the southern conflict and relevant problems, even in their internal workshop.[28]

Instead of tackling the conflict head-on, local media producers talk about the direct impact of violence on people's daily lives. For instance, if an attack occurs, the university radio station in Pattani would immediately devote airtime to traffic reports and safety precaution announcements rather than focusing on the investigation of the incident. According to a senior producer, such reports would keep listeners informed and calm amidst the chaos.[29] In similar vein, a civic community radio station in central Pattani focuses on boosting morale among the residents, which would be more useful to them than talking about their predicament, because that mainstream media already discusses such aspects of the unrest. "We would talk about . . . positive issues. Anything here should be positive. [. . .] We must be neutral, otherwise we can't stay. This is the thing. We have to set our position," said the community radio practitioner.[30] It is also worth noting that the community radio operator's definition of "being neutral" means not to allude to any players. Moreover, as hinted here, one reason behind this is to prevent their small operation from being interfered with by state authorities, insurgents, or interest groups.

The observation that local media producers do not want to elaborate further on violent incidents corresponds with a comment by a key member of the civic advocacy group Deep South Watch[31] who, among other work, organises a citizen reporter workshop for the locals. She pointed out that, instead of talking directly about the unrest, the deep South residents, be it Malay Muslims or other ethnic and social groups, opted for telling the world outside about their ways of living to signal their desire for violence to end.

> We trained [the locals] so that they can communicate [to the public], and we asked them to communicate from their stance. So instead of communicating about the impact of violent incidents on their lives, they chose to communicate about culture, their ways of life first. That was what they wanted to tell, under the condition that there were stories they could and could not talk about. [In the stories that] they could tell, they wanted to explain the kind of people that they are. Then, the society needs to read [between the lines] to realise what they could not talk about [because] they live in a violence-ridden area.[32]

On the surface, these "way of life" stories seem to paint an idyllic picture of the pre-violence deep South communities, as they do not openly and sufficiently question the impact of structural inequality and cultural marginalisation, particularly of Malay Muslims. McCargo asserts that this genre of "positive" reporting does little to tease out the conflict's complex political and ideological debates for the general public (2012, pp. 108–109). Nevertheless, the Deep South Watch advisor argued that stories about the southern residents' livelihood, especially from the locals' perspectives, are essential because they provide a cross-cultural learning space regarding the Malay Muslim identity for the Thai state and Thai population, who "live in the same territory but feel like being in different worlds".[33] Because

66 *Reporting the southern conflict*

of the conflict's violent nature and cultural nuances, the advocate felt it is vital to minimise the "us-*versus*-them" perception by stressing that southerners, particularly Malay Muslims, are no different from people in other parts of Thailand, and deserve equal rights, despite not discussing the ramifications of conflict and violence directly.

Other journalists cited scenarios when they were tipped off or came across crucial information, but could not report because no sources would openly verify it, or exposing these stories might bring harm to the reporters themselves. A Yala stringer pointed out, "Every reporter in the area knows what happened in each incident. They know, but sometimes we can't do anything. One, it is our safety. It's risky because there are people who hate us and people who like us. [. . .] If I go against the trend, others would attack me."[34] A number of these problematic cases involve the deaths of locals, which authorities ruled out as resulting from the unrest. Although some of these cases were known among community members as personal conflicts, no one would formally and publicly admit it because the victim's family would not earn compensation from the state from such casualties. Stories about civil servants such as teachers, police officers, and army personnel who perished in the far South usually honoured the deceased for their sacrifice. This is because, as these reporters said, using the non-glorifying narrative to report these incidents might not be supported by the newsroom or other peers. A TV reporter gave an example.

> There is this one case. A police officer had an affair with someone's wife and was shot dead. But, excuse me, every TV station made a report, honouring him, saying he made a sacrifice because he didn't want to be relocated. But do you understand, that was not the truth. [The headquarters] told me to report about this, but I didn't do it because I knew what the truth was. [. . .] They became heroes, praised for not moving away and being loved by the locals. But I don't do this. I can't do it. It goes against my will. But I don't object [the headquarters] from reporting. I don't write about it, but I let others do it. At least I'm not part of this.[35]

Another *Thai PBS* news manager raised an interesting argument concerning conflict reporting. Giving the example of citizen reporters, he remarked that, more important than reporting "the truth," journalists should also consider the implications of their exposé. His statement below brings in a new perspective in the dilemma news workers face in southern conflict reporting: peaceful resolutions.

> Somebody asked me if citizen reporters could report about soldiers slapping a villager's face. They had photos. I asked, "The question is, if you present it, what you think it would bring about? For one thing, you might be attacked. But secondly, it would definitely intensify the hatred between the locals and state officials in the area, wouldn't it?"[36]

Overall, the manufacturing of southern conflict news is not always a clear-cut process, as journalists sometimes struggle to overcome their personal and

Reporting the southern conflict   67

professional dilemmas and limitations while producing news reports. Self-censorship does not necessarily mean journalists willingly become the state's propaganda vehicle, or succumb to the forces of vested interest groups. In several cases, certain issues are not reported right away because they may bring harm to informants or incite further hatred instead of serving the public interest or facilitating non-violent resolutions.

Producing news in a competitive environment: difficulties in the newsroom

The previous section deals mainly with three problems that field journalists in the southernmost provinces come across. This section moves to present the factors influencing the works of Bangkok-based staff, mostly news managers and senior journalists. Two key factors are highlighted: 1) the diverse understandings of the southern conflict, and 2) the pressure of competition among news organisations. Similar to what happens in field reporting, the two factors here also determine how the southern conflict coverage is carried out, especially in terms of news presentation and coverage continuity.

Competing views, differing approaches: the diverse understandings of the southern conflict

Although stories are sent from the field, it is people in the newsroom who decide on the final output. Many reporters voice their concerns that the disparate comprehensions of newsroom staff could highlight some interpretations of the conflict and undermine others. A discernible example of how newsroom staff have various understandings of the conflict is their lexical choices, particularly their labels for antagonists. One senior reporter said, when reporting about violent incidents under investigation, instead of labelling the suspects "separatist," "secessionist," or "insurgent," she opted for the term "troublemaker," which, to her, seems neutral and does not implicate any parties until proven. However, the same practice was not carried out by other editors, and sometimes she conceded to allow such labelling, thinking it was too troublesome to argue with her colleagues all the time.[37]

Meanwhile, the editor of *Isara* website, who specialises in security affairs, uses "instigators" (*klum ko kwam mai sa-ngop* – literally translated as "unrest makers"), instead of "perpetrators of violence" (*klum phu ko het run raeng* – literally translated as "violent incident makers") – the term that the army has asked the media to use. Citing academic works in security affairs, he added that the use of "instigators" implies that the violent incidents are carried out with particular political motives, while "perpetrators of violence" refers to those performing random attacks without clear goals.[38] Another senior reporter agrees with this practice. He uses "separatist," "insurgent," or "Juwae" – the local Patani Malay term for militant groups[39] – when insurgent movements' involvement is proven. He added that the use of "terrorism" to label antagonists would imply that the conflict is beyond the Thai authority's control and requires international intervention and

68   *Reporting the southern conflict*

mediation – something that the Thai administration does not wish for. While not directly commenting on the question of whether the southern conflict has reached such a magnitude, the senior reporter said the Thai media's uses of disparate labels also reflect the Thai authorities' varying stances towards the southern conflict, hence, its ambivalence towards labelling the antagonists.[40]

How the newsroom crews make sense of the southern conflict also influences the coverage's continuity and approaches. Journalists who spend a long time reporting about the problem said that, as the violence becomes protracted, news editors see the southern situation as repetitive incidents that offer no new angles. This circumstance renders most newsroom staff passive, as they generally wait for a story to emerge rather than taking on a proactive role by breaking the story themselves. For instance, a desk editor said the primary source of information concerning the conflict is local stringers, saying they know best about the situation because they live in the region.[41]

Because most stories filed from stringers are events of the day, mostly attacks and clashes, the newsroom then treats most stories of southern violence as generic crime stories and presents them in a straightforward news format. Coupled with the high costs of news production, which will be discussed subsequently, the newsrooms, with their limited financial and human resources, therefore, have little interest in pursuing the stories further. Only when the cases contain prominent or serious elements, such as when they involve a significantly high number of civilian and/or official casualties, does the coverage include more contexts, which are typically presented sequentially and in various formats.

Among the three national-level mainstream media studied, only the *Thai PBS* has special sections dedicated to southern conflict issues, and it occasionally produces short documentary or discussion programmes about the problem.[42] Nonetheless, seeing the protraction of this armed conflict, a southern news centre reporter suggested that, rather than delegating the production responsibility to certain departments like typical special report assignments, the news organisation should have made this issue "the station's agenda" and established a concrete long-term policy about southern conflict reporting. A path to achieve that mission, he pointed out, is to consolidate and streamline the organisation's many news desks involved in southern conflict reporting. In doing so, the work would become less redundant, and every member of the news staff would be consistently informed of the station's news policy and direction.[43]

Fighting for audience and funding: the pressure of competition among news organisations

Newsroom staff and reporters agree that, be it commercial or non-profit, news media organisations are vying with one another for audiences. While it is clear that commercial media rely on circulation numbers, audience ratings, or page hits to generate advertising revenue, non-profit media also use similar quantitative evidence to prove to financial sponsors that their news content is worth funding.

Reporting the southern conflict   69

Therefore, the bottom line of news operation is that news workers constantly look for ways to appeal to audience.

One way to draw readership and boost sales is to use sensational language. As elaborated in the previous chapter, the most prevalent term used to describe the antagonists is "southern bandits" [*chon tai*]. Editors explain that the label becomes a norm in news presentation because it best fits with the limited headline space[44] and is direct and easily comprehensible, despite casting an undertone of criminality and being deemed offensive by the locals. The *Isara* editor noted that although he never used "southern bandits" on the website or in his own reports for his primary employment, he was not aware the term was considered derogatory and still spotted other news outlets using it. Similarly, a Pattani stringer remarked that, despite field reporters' attempt to avoid using this label in their stories, the editors would revert to the familiar title because it sells. "You may bring in editors for conferences,[45] spending some 10 million baht on a tour, the result would be the same. It is not a solution because their policy is like that. [. . .] This cannot be changed. It's business," said the stringer.[46]

Immediacy is considered the first rule of thumb of news production, and for most organisations, especially commercial broadcasters and news websites, being the first to report a story is a win. However, in reporting the southern conflict, news workers admitted that getting the story out quickly means the report is likely to lose some context. A TV reporter recalled that when she was working for a commercial station the newsroom's constant need for live reports deterred her from expanding her investigation. A *Thai PBS* news manager also conceded that the conflict's dynamic nature and the rushes of daily news production do not enhance journalists' ability to explore the southern problem further. In the end, the news media must be able to disseminate their output on the expected schedule.

> Whenever we try to do something, we would face the whirlwind sweeping us away from what we were trying to work in a long term. We attempt to have a profound knowledge of the southern problem. We want to talk more with community leaders, thinkers, academics, and army officials – the job which takes time. [. . .] But suppose there was an explosion or a shooting, the main mission of local reporters is to cover this story.[47]

Speed is not the only element of media competition. As some journalists put it, news organisations contend to be alike, yet different. They cover the same issues, but have to distinguish their news content from other media outlets by presenting with different styles, angles, or approaches. Ironically, in the case of southern conflict reporting, the fact that one local stringer works for many news outlets means the reports usually come from the same source. With the demand to meet deadlines, and in some cases insufficient understanding of the issues, newsrooms may edit the copy only slightly. Even though the end products are not identical, they nonetheless offer the same angle.

70 *Reporting the southern conflict*

Some senior reporters observed a new direction in Thai journalism: news media, particularly newspapers, are no longer keen on reporting the same issues. Instead, on slow news days, the dailies choose to go with what they think is exclusive and original content to stand out from other organisations' front page. This practice allows new issues to emerge. By the same token, the variety of new "hot" subjects could also push the long-term, recurring, and "no longer sexy" stories such as the southern conflict off media platforms, especially when there is an influx of more pressing stories emerging.

After all, the southern conflict issues must compete with other news stories to win media space. In line with the findings of the previous chapter, the frequency and variety of themes concerning the southern conflict decreased in the later years of the conflict, partly due to the national political crisis originating in the capital city in early 2006. Stringers and fixers said their income dropped significantly when the newsrooms' attention was moved to other major news stories, such as what happened during the mass political demonstrations in 2009 and 2010, or the massive flooding in central Thailand in late 2011.

The final point is the cost of southern conflict reporting. A senior correspondent called the restive area "a challenging field" because the quality news coverage comes at an expensive price. To produce quality reports and programmes, apart from recruiting experienced news crews to cover the ground, news organisations also need to consider additional costs such as accessibility to certain areas, live broadcast, safety precautions, translation, logistics, and administrative tasks. When the stories become repetitive and other crises happen, news management have to relocate their resources to cover more pressing issues. The *Isara* editor agreed, saying a number of issues, such as the prevalence of gun violence in the southern border region, require investigative and interpretative reporting so that decision-makers and the public can form an understanding of the region. However, for a small operation like his, the limited amount of manpower and budget as well as the hostile environment in the far South do not allow the agency to invest in in-depth journalism.

The changes in *Isara*'s organisational structure and sponsorship best exemplify the impact of financial deficit on news coverage. No longer acquiring a hefty budget from the National Reconciliation Commission, as it did when it was established in 2005, the Southern News Desk, now part of the Isara News Agency (see the organisation's changes in Appendix C), has a quarter share in the agency's four million baht (approximately 120,000 US dollars) funding in 2011 and 2012. Unable to afford a rental office and hire permanent staff in the south, the current editor decided to shift the website's emphasis from cultural affairs and local inputs to the analysis of and the investigation into the state's strategies, budgets, and policies, using the existing news database and limited manpower.

> It is difficult for us to investigate the local issues deeper, to seek comments from [insurgent movements'] sympathisers, or to travel to remote areas and follow up on some stories. Thus, I have changed the website's focus so that it heads in the direction which I think is right, which is to scrutinise the poli-

Reporting the southern conflict 71

cies of state agencies responsible for solving the southern problem, and to examine those working in the region – performing my duty as the media, just like professional ones. I would examine the issues that affect people's lives, and the solutions [to the problem]. If the issues don't have an impact, or are minor, there are local alternative media reporting them.[48]

The website's position shift, albeit necessary and offering critical insights into southern policies, does not allow for as many local voices and diverse views as before. More importantly, the future of their desk looks uncertain due to unstable financial support. The *Isara* news team also expressed concerns about the unsustainable state of southern conflict reporting, especially from the policy-analysis approach, because its operation has relied heavily on individual journalists rather than establishing a solid news production system and workforce.

The *Bangkok-centric mindset*[49] as the overarching framework of news production

This final factor encompasses the works of both journalists in the field and in the newsroom. Despite being called "Bangkok-centric" here, the notion refers not only to the geographically focused views, but also to the emphasis on the conventional top-down and centralised perspective, where decisions come from national-level authorities and focus on urbanites. The statement "every story ends in Bangkok," voiced by a veteran regional news reporter,[50] signals the significance of the central government, policy-makers, and news crews in the capital city in setting national agendas. This corresponds with McCargo's critique of the Thai newsroom structure, particularly the deficiency of the regional news desk, as mentioned earlier (2000, pp. 47–49, p. 177; 2012, pp. 98–100).

The *Bangkok-centric mindset* is discernible in the interactions between field reporters and the newsroom staff. Stringers said the diverse, and sometimes limited, understanding of the southern conflict among some Bangkok-based writers and editors put more pressure on them.

> Bangkok [newsroom] only makes demands and constantly pushes for answers. [. . .] They thought the situation was like what happened in Bangkok. When a person was shot, they knew [the cause] immediately. Here, no one knew who fired that shot. All of the sudden, a dead body was found. What happened before that, even officials did not know. But we had to report the story, as well as provide context as to what happened before this incident happened. It's difficult, especially when I have to file a report for radio. Reporting quickly may cause misunderstanding. If we report it, especially for TV, the villagers may be upset.[51]

A Yala stringer told how the insensitivity of a senior TV reporter from Bangkok towards conflict situations nearly put the team in danger. Accustomed to commercial TV's popular "hard question" style, the senior reporter asked villagers in an

72 *Reporting the southern conflict*

interview whether they want "to incite people". The stringer recalled, "Somebody told us, 'We give you 5 minutes to get out of here.' On our way back, some guys sprayed the road with spikes and tree trunks. [The senior reporter] shouldn't have asked like that. Sometimes it's not like that. And this makes the work of local reporters more difficult."[52]

The *Bangkok-centric mindset* also affects how stories are presented and prioritised. Because most local stringers make their living from selling stories – only a few receive monthly retainer fees from media organisations – they attempt to file as many reports as possible. Typically, a stringer's routine entails listening to police scanners for incidents, screening press releases and invitations to events, and making contact with sources and informants for news tips. Since not all stories would make news, stringers need to "read the mind" of responsible daily editors on the kinds of stories they prefer, so that the stories they file would be used and they would be paid accordingly. Considering this, stringers cannot pursue every story they come across because they have to focus on the ones that are more likely to be taken by the southern news centre and the Bangkok newsroom. Stringers said covering stories that are unlikely to be reported is not a worthy investment, and may even cause troubles with the locals. A Yala stringer said, "If [the stations] don't take [the story] or follow up on it, letting it fall out of the trend, I may be in a difficult position. If I investigate too deep, there would be criticism or attack, like, 'Why do you have to dig on this issue?'"[53]

Referring to the *Isara*'s shift of focus, a reporter expressed her slight disappointment that most stories on the website are becoming policy-oriented, which may not answer the locals' needs. While she understands the limitation of *Isara*'s news operation and the reasons behind such presentation, the reporter feels that the lack of local content makes it difficult for her to build trust with southern residents. This also means the *Bangkok-centric mindset* could silence the locals' voices. Thus, like the insurgents who resort to violent means to show their resistance, the locals needs to shout about their problems or connect with the press directly, so that their voices will be heard by the state.

> Currently, [most stories] are the analyses of strategies and policies. Before, there weren't stories about budget or policies, which seem to be the issues that are brought up by "the above" [referring to the Bangkok editor], following the [national news] trend . . . something 'the above' is interested in. But there is no attention to "the below" [referring to the locals]. . .
>
> For ordinary people, there is no way for them to become news. [. . .] They had to form a movement to make news, then everyone would be interested. They had to find an angle, such as demanding the 7.5 million baht [compensation money], making it an issue, inviting the press to cover their stories, then the state would be interested in them.[54]

While field reporters are often on the receiving end of the *Bangkok-centric mindset*, some senior journalists in Bangkok get to see first-hand how this approach works in the newsroom, for example, through the popular use of "southern

Reporting the southern conflict 73

bandits". The *Isara* editor who is also a senior reporter/editor at a daily newspaper in Bangkok raised an example, which reflects the newsroom's *Bangkok-centric mindset* and insensitivity towards the conflict. He said: "Some editors, when they were advised against using 'southern bandits', they would go, 'Well, when there was a gold shop robbery in Bangkok and we used 'city bandits,' no one protested. So from now on, can I also make an objection against the use of 'city bandits' because I'm a Bangkokian?'"[55] Another senior correspondent pointed out that most national-level news media still use "Thai Muslim" as a general reference to the Muslim population in the southern border provinces instead of "Malay Muslim," the ethnic-oriented term mostly used in academic works and international agencies' reports. The lexical choice, he explained, not only seeks to blur the differences between Malay Muslims and other Muslims in the rest of Thailand as one homogenous group, but also signals the rejection of deep-seated Malay nationalism in the far South, essentially maintaining the dominant Thai nation-state construct.[56]

The lack of understanding of Malay Muslim identity from Bangkok-based news crews, coupled with their perceived notion of "Muslim insurgency," not only takes place in the newsroom's conversation, but also manifests itself in news output. One of the most prominent and controversial cases was when a photograph of a slain suspect in the orchestrated attacks on April 28, 2004 was published on the front page of the economy/politics news-oriented daily *Krungthep Turakij* on the following day. The photograph was found to be edited, with the object lying in the dead suspect's hand (a machete cover) replaced by a double-edged sword similar to a dagger. The newspaper released its apology a day later, citing editorial negligence and comparing the original with the edited photographs. Its editorial team subsequently issued a statement explaining its mistake was caused unintentionally by a graphic designer and a member of the editorial staff, who were admonished. The Thai Journalists' Association also gave an ethical warning to media professionals to take extra care when presenting news, texts, and photographs regarding the incident.[57] While this example shows professional reflexivity at work as the newspaper promptly attempted to rectify this crucial error, it also signals how urbanites' misconception of the perpetrators in the southern insurgency is at play in news production.

The minimal communication between Bangkok-based editors and provincial stringers leads to routine and circumstantial reports that are mostly devoid of in-depth perspectives, as a senior correspondent explained. Unlike in the newsroom, where reporters can easily approach editors for guidelines and advices about news production before going into the field, editors merely let provincial stringers file in stories through the regional news centres or desk coordinators without giving clear directions first. Southern news centre *Thai PBS* reporters also pointed out a Bangkok-centric flaw inherent in the passive and centralised newsroom structure. Since the organisation was transformed from a commercial company to a public service broadcaster in 2008 (see more on this transition in Appendix C), they observed, no formal gatherings between the regional news desk staff and stringers to discuss contemporary issues in the southern provinces, as well as organisational

74 *Reporting the southern conflict*

policies in covering these stories, had been organised. The work flow routinely continued through the transition period as if there were no structural and administrative changes. A reporter remarked:

> [The organisation] regarded [stringers] as colonial people because we never improve [their potentials]. They are an original source for understanding the country, but they have never been made aware of the public service broadcaster's direction. The awareness of this concept stops at me [. . .] The only thing they know is to get their stories broadcast.[58]

Some editors and senior reporters view the mainstream media's passive coverage and minimal emphasis on southern conflict media as a problem. Seeing online news agencies such as *Isara* and Deep South Watch as main reference sources for southern conflict news, some mainstream media news managers suggested the establishment of the "southern conflict news desk" to oversee the issue directly. Regardless, a veteran correspondent who now organises media production trainings for southern civil society groups remarked that, insofar as the *Bangkok-centric mindset* is sustained in the newsroom, the issue-specific news desk does not necessarily guarantee new approaches to southern conflict reporting.[59]

Conclusion

This chapter presents an overview of Thai journalists' modus operandi in southern conflict reporting and factors that have various impacts on news production. In the beginning, the analysis and discussions demonstrate that Thai journalism seems rather homogenous, because the four studied news organisations and even local civic media producers adopt some common practices and professional values, notably the editorial and production process. However, there appear to be subtle variations in how journalists translate these abstract terms into practice, particularly when they come from dissimilar backgrounds and operate in different environments or under news organisations of different principles.

The difficulties that journalists face in producing southern conflict coverage, as demonstrated in Figure 3.3, reflect the disparate conditions inherent in the vocational conventions, the culture of the news industry, the conflict's distinct characteristics, such as hostility and fierce discursive contestation, and dominant perspectives in Thai society. These factors show that, although being shaped by the professional customs, the practices of journalists and their news outputs are not born and performed in a political and cultural vacuum. The difficulties outlined here also signal the interplay between journalism and other political players, and the impact of the overarching ideologies in the settings wherein journalists operate. Moreover, the testimonies and other empirical evidence presented here also indicate that Thai journalists sometimes reflect upon their work, question predominant views, and attempt to challenge collective, conventional practices.

After having discussed the problematic conditions that shape the news production, the following chapter will focus on a vital element of newsgathering – news

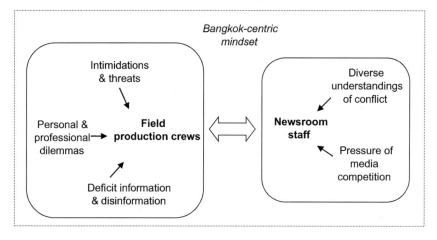

Figure 3.3 The difficulties of southern conflict reporting: in the field and in the newsroom

sources. It will look at the relationship between journalists and their sources, and how that interaction influences the coverage of the southern conflict.

Notes

1 How a news organisation appoints its regional news centre chief is rather interesting. While experience and knowledge in the region are part of the criteria, it seems, from my field observations, that the number of years the person has been with the organisation is a prominent norm. The chief's job mostly deals with administrative tasks and perhaps producing a weekly commentary piece, but the daily news production is left in the hands of reporters. This resonates with McCargo's study (2000), which states that seniority is entrenched in the newsroom structure, although it is the junior staff who actually run the show on a daily basis.
2 In Leon V. Sigal's study (1973), the difference between the *routine* and the *informal* channels is that the *routine* channel centres around governmental activities, while the *informal* channel focuses on unofficial and non-governmental sources. However, in the case of Thailand's southern conflict, the sources become more diverse and complex than those in the original study in early 1970s. In this case, a number of non-governmental sources also employ press relations strategies similar to those carried out by authority sources, such as organising events and issuing press releases. Such tactics enable the information to reach journalists via the *routine* channel. Therefore, in this study, the *routine* channel includes scheduled events and activities organised by both governmental and non-governmental sources, while the *informal* channel refers to background and confidential information. For more on Sigal's study, see Leon V. Sigal. 1973. *Reporters and Officials: The Organization and Politics of Newsmaking*. Lexington, MA: D. C. Heath and Company.
3 During the past few years, the popularity of online messaging applications for mobile devices among Thais, particularly LINE – operated by a Japan-based company – makes it even more convenient and faster for news workers to receive and disseminate such information. The application enables users to create online group chats where group members can send texts, photos, and short video clips to others via the Internet.

76 Reporting the southern conflict

Journalists and their sources, both authorities and non-officials, typically communicate through this channel and use information circulated here to file their reports.

4 In a large organisation, the desk editor, writers, and reporters will take turns during the week to perform as the "daily desk editor," whose tasks are to monitor daily occurrence, contact field reporters, edit copy, and approve the finished product.

5 In most Thai television newsrooms, the term "daily editor" refers to the senior editorial staff in charge of assembling content for a news bulletin. The term "producer" refers to senior technical staff overseeing the news programme's presentation during the broadcast.

6 The regional news desk of the news organisations studied in this book covers reports from Thailand's 76 provinces, excluding the capital city. They do not have a "metropolitan" desk to cover the capital city specifically. Issues concerning Bangkok are often assigned to thematic news beats such as social issues, crime, and politics.

7 See McCargo 2000, pp. 56–59 for discussion on parliamentary reporters, and the entire volume for more discussion on the Thai press's political news reporting culture.

8 Some news organisations, such as *Thai PBS*, set up a desk to cover current affairs and social issues that do not fall into a specific beat, or require interdisciplinary specialisation from different beats, and to produce long-form presentations such as feature stories as well as analytical and investigative reports. In some organisations, the tasks may go to the social affairs desk and the feature desk, which are two separate entities.

9 *Manager* southern news centre chief. Interview. 21 February 2012.

10 *Thai PBS* assistant news director. Interview. 8 February 2012; *Matichon* regional news desk chief. Interview. 23 February 2012; Pattani stringer 1. Interview. 18 February 2012.

11 *Matichon* regional news desk chief. Interview.

12 It cannot be inferred, based on the southern conflict case alone, that media organisations neglect the safety of their employees; however, the argument here is that the media organisations' policies concerning reporters' safety seem to vary from one case to another, depending on the level of physical threats, the magnitude of the problem, and possibly the geo-political interests. For instance, during the coverage of the antigovernment mass demonstrations in Bangkok, which turned to violence and were later suppressed by police and military during May 2010, reporters, especially broadcast journalists, were shown to be equipped with bullet-proof vests and helmets when reporting from the demonstration sites. Professional organisations also issued statements condemning threats against and assaults on media practitioners (Thai Journalists Association, 20 May 2010). Nonetheless, media and professional organisations generally do not organise training on hostile environment reporting specifically for relevant reporters and southern stringers, although other types of training courses held by professional organisations, such as investigative reporting workshops, may include a brief session on weapons and survival skills.

13 Translated from the term แนวร่วมมุมกลับ [*naew ruam moom glub*].

14 Aman News Agency editor. Interview. 18 December 2011.

15 *Isara* reporter 1 and 2. Interview. 19 February 2012.

16 Martial law was first imposed in Pattani, Yala, Narathiwat, and four districts of Songkla on January 5, 2004 by the regional military chief, following the weapon heist at the Narathiwat military base. The Thaksin Shinawatra government lifted martial law in July 2005 and replaced it with the state of emergency decree, which has been reenforced every three months ever since. However, martial law was put in effect in the region again when the military junta staged a coup against the Thaksin administration and enforced martial law nationwide in September 2006 to prohibit political activities. Although martial law was lifted in other parts of the country subsequently, it remains enacted in the southernmost region. The Internal Security Act was imposed to replace martial law and the state of emergency decree in four districts of Songkla in

Reporting the southern conflict   77

October 2009. Meanwhile, most districts in the three southernmost provinces remain under both martial law and the state of emergency decree.

17 See, for example, Kongpob Areerat. Interview with the human rights lawyer facing judicial harassment from the Army [online]. *Prachatai English*. 11 September 2014. Available at: www.prachatai.com/english/node/4335 [Accessed: 20 April 2015]; and Thailand: Army Secretly Detaining 17 Muslim Activists [online]. *Human Right Watch*. 3 April 2015. Available at: www.hrw.org/news/2015/04/03/thailand-army-secretly-detaining-17-muslim-activists [Accessed: 20 April 2015].

18 It should be noted that these statements were issued when the laws were enforced nationwide, following the national-level political crises in 2008, 2014, and 2015, not specifically addressing issues at the southernmost provinces.

19 Local media producers reported that Sahari Jeh-long, a volunteer of the Southern Peace Media Volunteer Network, was called in for questioning by military officers at a Pattani military camp for two days in July 2012. According to the articles, the authorities summoned Sahari in for interrogation because he was a former student leader who was involved in a demonstration in 2007 and was suspected to be involved in other violent incidents. Apart from being asked about his participation in Islamic students' activities, Sahari revealed that he faced queries regarding alternative media production, and was questioned about the local media's financial support and its presentation emphasis on the sufferings of Muslims. For more detail, see, *Deep South Watch*. เชิญสื่อทางเลือกสอบ เสร็จแล้วขอเก็บดีเอ็นเอ [Alternative media summoned for interrogation, DNA also collected] [online]. 26 July 2012. Available at: www. deepsouthwatch. org/node/3422 [Accessed: 14 January 2013], and *Prachatai*. ปาตานีดีไซน์ 1: สื่อทางเลือก เลือก สื่อทางยุติธรรม [Patani Design 1: Alternative media select to communicate with justice] [online]. 28 July 2012. Available at: www.prachatai.com/journal/2012/07/41768 [Accessed: 14 January 2013].

20 Aman News Agency editor. Interview.

21 *Isara* reporter 2. Interview.

22 Pattani stringer 2. Interview. 19 February 2012.

23 Yala local reporter and freelance photographer. Interview. 16 December 2011.

24 See, for example, *Manager Online Manager Online*. กอ.รมน.ภาค 4 สน." โต้ "แนวหน้า" กรณีตั้ง ศูนย์ประสานงานข่าวสารชายแดนใต้ [ISOC Region 4 refutes "Naew Na" in the southern border information collaboration centre case] [online]. 2 September 2012. Available at: www.manager.co.th/South/ViewNews.aspx?NewsID=9550000107948 [Accessed: 14 January 2013]; and *Krungthep Turakij*. ปฏิบัติการข่าวสารของ กอ.รมน. [ISOC's Information Operation] [online]. 11 December 2012. Available at: www.bangkokbiznews.com/home/detail/politics/opinion/politic-view/20121211/481533/ปฏิบัติการข่าวสารของ-กอ.รมน... html [Accessed: 17 December 2012].

25 *Isara* editor. Interview. 25 January 2012.

26 *Thai PBS* southern news centre reporter 1. Interview. 23 December 2011.

27 Civic community radio in Thailand refers to non-commercial short-wave radio operation with a transmission radius of no more than 15 kilometres (approx. 9.3 miles). Mostly situated in rural residential areas, community radio requires operation licenses from the National Broadcasting and Telecommunication Commission, the independent state regulatory agency. Funded by community members or sponsored by civil societies, most civic community radios are run by volunteering members of the community and broadcast during certain hours. Some stations allow local governmental agencies and civil advocate groups, such as public health and the army, to host programmes. For more detail on civic community radio in Thailand, see Pirongrong Ramasoota. 2013. *Community Radio in Thailand: From Media Reform to a Sustainable Regulatory Framework*. Bangkok: Heinrich Boell Stiftung and Thai Media Policy Center.

28 Pattani civic community radio practitioner. Interview. 17 February 2012.

29 Prince of Songkla University Radio news producer. Interview. 17 December 2011.

78 *Reporting the southern conflict*

30 Pattani civic community radio practitioner. Interview.
31 Deep South Watch is a non-profit advocacy group based at the Prince of Songkla University, Pattani Campus. The agency was founded in 2006 by a network of academics, medical and healthcare practitioners, and local activists to systematically study and analyse the southern conflict and violence. The group's current work focuses on peace mobilisation. For more detail, see their website at www.deepsouthwatch.org/about.
32 Deep South Watch advisor 1. Interview. 20 December 2011.
33 Deep South Watch advisor 1. Interview.
34 Yala stringer. Interview. 19 February 2012.
35 *Thai PBS* southern news centre reporter 1. Interview.
36 *Thai PBS* Civil Media Network director. Interview. 1 February 2012.
37 Senior reporter of an English-language daily newspaper. Personal conversation. 24 January 2012.
38 *Isara* editor. Interview.
39 The term "Juwae" means "fighter" in the local Malay language. Local insurgent members use the term for themselves, and many southern insurgency experts also use it in reference to the movements. According to senior journalist Don Pathan, "Juwae are organised into semi-independent cells that span the three southernmost provinces of Pattani, Yala and Narathiwat and the four Malay-speaking districts in Songkla. Juwae and the BRN-Coordinate are working towards establishing a shared command." See Don Pathan. Did Thaksin meet insurgents? [online]. *The Nation*. 9 April 2012. Available at: www.nation multimedia.com/politics/Did-Thaksin-meet-insurgents-30179611. html [Accessed: 14 January 2013])
40 Patani Forum co-founder and senior reporter of an English-language daily newspaper. Interview. 18 February 2012. Patani Forum is a Pattani-based non-profit advocacy group. Similar to Deep South Watch and Aman News Agency, the organisation collaborates with local NGOs, academics, students, and writers in publishing articles concerning the history and culture of the southern border provinces online and organises discussion forums to stimulate public debate about southern conflict.
41 *Matichon* regional news desk editor. Interview.
42 In 2011, *Thai PBS* was supported by the US-based advocacy organisation INTERNEWS in organising the on-location training for the station's journalists, including those from the Bangkok headquarters and its southern news centre, to investigate various aspects of the conflict. The end-product of this months-long training was a series of short documentaries that were aired as a special programme, titled รอยร้าวชายแดนใต้ [*Roi Rao Chai Daen Tai* – Cleavage in the Southern Provinces]. The documentaries, investigating the deficiency of governmental agencies in dealing with the southern problems, legal disputes, excessive use of forces, and authority's lack of understanding of local identity and culture, won the Sangchai Sunthornwat award, the Thai broadcast journalism's equivalence of the Pulitzer Prize, in 2012.
43 *Thai PBS* southern news centre reporter 2. Interview. 20 February 2012.
44 In Thai, the word southern bandit [โจรใต้ – *chon tai*] occupies four headline units. Other relevant terms, such as instigators [กลุ่มผู้ก่อความไม่สงบ – *klum phu ko kwam mai sa ngop*] or perpetrators of violence [กลุ่มผู้ก่อเหตุรุนแรง – *klum phu ko het run raeng*], are composed of 14 and 13 units respectively. Interestingly, the term criminals [คนร้าย – *khon rai*], which carries a less implicating undertone and comprises four and a half (4½) headline units, is typically used in news leads and content, but not as often in headlines.
45 The interviewee referred to the "fact-finding" trips and seminars in the deep South, organised by professional organisations and state agencies, which news editors, managers, and reporters from Bangkok were invited to attend. These projects were aimed at educating Bangkok-based and national-level journalists about the distinctive nature of the southern border provinces and the conflict, so that they could have a better grasp of the phenomenon, become sensitised to the matter, and produce constructive reports.

Reporting the southern conflict 79

46 Pattani stringer 1. Interview. 17 December 2011.
47 *Thai PBS* assistant news director. Interview.
48 *Isara* editor. Interview.
49 By using the term *mindset*, I do not intend to base this argument on a psychological approach. Interestingly, the expression was frequently used by many informants, so I maintain that term as such in this study. Nonetheless, to me, the use of *mindset* here refers to the prevailing beliefs entrenched in Thai newsrooms and Thai society, rather than to the way of thinking of an individual or a collective group of journalists. In line with my proposition on the discursive contention of the southern conflict, I see the *Bangkok-centric mindset* as a socially constructed perspective that determines how news workers view the problem, and, as will be elaborated further, influences the production of southern conflict news.
50 *Manager* southern news centre chief. Interview.
51 Pattani stringer 2. Interview.
52 Yala stringer. Interview
53 Ibid.
54 *Isara* reporter 1. Interview.
55 *Isara* editor. Interview.
56 Patani Forum co-founder. Interview.
57 See, for example, แมลงวันในไร่ส้ม [Malaengwan Nai Rai Som – pseudonym]. กรณี"ตัดต่อภาพ" "กรุงเทพธุรกิจ"พลาด อีกบทเรียน 28 เม.ย. [The case of "edited photograph" "Krungthep Turakij" failed. Another lesson of 28 April]. มติชนสุดสัปดาห์ [*Matichon Weekly*]. 24 (1238–7–13 May 2004); and *Manager Online*. นสพ.กรุงเทพธุรกิจ ตีพิมพ์ภาพที่ใช้เทคนิคการตัดต่อ หน้า๑ [Krungthep Turakij daily published an edited photograph on Page 1] [online]. [No date]. www.manager.co.th/politics/politicsview.asp?newsid=4733504921793 Available at: www.numtan.com/nineboard/view.php?id=1717 [Accessed: 20 August 2015].
58 *Thai PBS* southern news centre reporter 2. Interview.
59 Senior freelance journalist. Personal conversation. 18 January 2012.

References

McCargo, Duncan. 2000. *Politics and the Press in Thailand: Media Machinations*. London: Routledge.

McCargo, Duncan. 2012. *Mapping National Anxieties: Thailand's Southern Conflict*. Copenhagen: NIAS Press.

Sigal, Leon V. 1973. *Reporters and Officials: The Organization and Politics of Newsmaking*. Lexington, MA: D. C. Heath and Company.

4 News access and southern conflict reporting

Sources play an integral role in news production. They provide journalists with information needed for news reports, and that information and its delivery determine the coverage's direction. While the structural and cultural settings in which news workers operate, as described in the previous chapter, largely shape the production process, how journalists select and maintain a relationship with their sources potentially influences the meanings of news output. News workers' decisions to bring forth certain facts and comments are not solely based on the information itself, but on its presenters as well. As such, it is important to tease out theoretical discussions and debates on this subtle, yet complex, interplay between news practitioners and their informers[1] and the impact on news-making. This will be examined in the first part of this chapter. The second section will look at the frequency of source attribution in news output, and the final part will explore the interchange between news workers and their sources in southern conflict reporting.

Balancing on a tightrope: the symbiotic relationship of journalists and their sources

While there may be several protagonists vying for the media's attention, not all of them receive the same treatment from news media. As Archetti argues: "a social embedding of journalistic practices, or national journalistic culture, affects the journalists' very sense of what is news and what is newsworthy. This, again, also applies to the sources" (Archetti 2010, p. 578). News media tend to give higher rates of credibility and significance to those in the upper echelons of society than those in other groups (Hall, Critcher, Jefferson, Clarke, and Roberts 1978; Bennett 1990; McChesney 2002). When a phenomenon is typified as routine events, the groups of sources involved then earn the privileged "habitual access" (Molotch and Lester 1974, pp. 107–108), which guarantees their newsworthiness to news organisations; hence, their constant appearance in the news. In the case of Thai journalism, McCargo finds that political reporters approach only a handful of Members of Parliament (MPs) as their regular news sources due to their position, which implies they are articulate and well-informed of relevant policies (McCargo 2000, p. 61). Studies concerning the Thai media's coverage of the southern and national-level political conflicts find that broadcasters tend to favour the voices of government and politicians over academics, the civil society sector, or demonstrators when reporting demonstrations.[2] Wolfsfeld infers that the political actors with more resources and power usually make their appearance through "the front gate coverage," which endorses their legitimacy in the discursive battle. On the contrary, "the back gate coverage" is generally reserved for political and social deviants (1997, p. 42), which effectively undermines them as legitimate actors.

Nonetheless, Cottle argues that news media do not deliberately marginalise the non-elite in order to sustain the hegemonic control of the powerful; they generally follow the pre-set "culturally dominant assumptions" that shape their views of who to approach and get information from (2000, p. 431). For instance, the news desk structure, which is generally drawn up in line with the country's bureaucratic system, often places reporters at the centre of events. Such arrangements enable journalists to identify with their sources and become institutionalised by the official settings in which they are based (McCargo 2000, p. 46; Schudson 2003, p. 150). Therefore, the structure "not only provides routine access to particular sources, they also serve as means of cultural inculcation," as Wolfsfeld points out (1997, p. 42). Waisbord also observes that journalists' deference to authoritative sources is inherent even in watchdog journalism culture, which tends to investigate authority's abuse of power and questions the establishment. He argues that, when coming across any information leakage by politicians that could potentially lead to an exposé, news workers are keener in verifying the sources' credibility, the reliability of information they provide, and tangible evidence to support their claims, rather than questioning the political motive behind the leak (Waisbord 2000, p. 109). In the end, informers with better and richer resources, as well as a closer proximity to the press, gain easier access to the news media than the resource-poor groups (Schudson 2003, p. 151).

While reporters rely on their sources for soundbites and news tips, the sources also need journalists for valuable information and publicity (McCargo 2000, p. 64; Schudson 2003, p. 151); as a result, the interplay between news workers and sources, especially in political news, tends to be reciprocal and collaborative rather than confrontational (Blumler and Gurevitch 1995 cited in McCargo 2000, p. 63; Franklin 2003). Schudson explains that the symbiotic interchange between journalists and their sources is a "human relation" where each party takes turns to manipulate the other (2003, p. 144). Knowing news organisations' thirst for information, the news sources, especially those who already have "habitual access," may take this as their opportunity to feed journalists with information and organise events for them to cover. Political players, in particular, adopt the "going public" strategy (Ibid., pp. 158–159) to keep their appearance and agenda in the news (Franklin 2003; Cook 2006). Attempting to secure their place as "primary definers" (Hall et al. 1978, pp. 58–60) of the topics, some political protagonists deploy media strategies such as appointing professional public relations officers or press counsellors to liaise with journalists, to plan and arrange publicity events, or sometimes to spin the story in order to create positive feedback (McNair 1998, pp. 147–153; Schudson 2003, p. 147; Campbell 2004, pp. 88–92). The employment of such schemes further widens the gap between elite sources

82   *News access and reporting*

and resource-poor ones, as demonstrated in the case of the Gulf War, where news media were fed with information from state and military sources, leading to news coverage that underpinned the hegemonic views of the elites (Wolfsfeld 1997).

As the interaction between journalists and their sources is a human relation, the boundary between the two sides, based on the occupational ethics and objectivity principle, can sometimes be overridden by the frequent acquaintance and intimacy. For instance, Morrison and Tumber argue that reporters who travelled with the British troops on the Falklands mission became bonded with soldiers who they accompanied and inadvertently shared the troops' sentiments and agenda (1988, cited in Tumber 2004, pp. 191–194). In covering politics, Schudson cautions of the "seduction by proximity to power," in which journalists consider themselves privileged to gain access to political elite sources, and fear if they cannot achieve that goal (2003, p. 142). McCargo makes a similar observation in the case of Thai politics reporting, saying "in seeking to establish good relationships with news sources, reporters might find that their independence and integrity were compromised" (2000, p. 67). He notes that reporters often face a dilemma when the sources host complementary dinners or parties, or invite them on a "fact-finding" trip or press junket. By partaking in such events, some journalists feel they owe the host a favour or indirectly take a bribe. But to deny such invitations, news professionals risk weakening their affiliation with sources, or missing out on valuable information. By the same token, politicians will foster a connection with the selected few reporters with whom they share exclusive information and explicitly express their trust (Ibid., p. 68). As journalists are included in what appears to be their territory, they may find being taken in by the world of politics more enticing and rewarding, which can subsequently result in them inadvertently serving the politicians' agenda, or eventually showing full allegiance to the politicians. As such, McCargo argues that reporters, particularly junior ones working in the field, are "double outsiders" who do not belong completely to either the journalistic or the political world, because they hold "only peripheral or associate membership of the institutions they cover, and occupy a peripheral or marginal position within the newspaper itself" (Ibid., p. 45), since the influential work is assigned to newsroom-based senior editors and columnists.

The play of power between journalists and their sources resembles a tightrope walk. Journalists feel that it is crucial for them to strike a balance in gleaning information from the sources while preserving their accessibility and not compromising their occupational values. A slip can jeopardise either their source relations or their professional integrity, or both. Nevertheless, while concurring that news workers may constantly be "seduced" by benefits from the intimacy with their sources, journalist and researcher Jennifer Hasty argues that occupational ideology and obligations will evoke professional reflexivity and prompt journalists to scrutinise their sources despite their propinquity (2010, p. 147). Under the conditions of political conflict and violence, journalists will find themselves in an even more precarious position, as their sources will be varied, potentially at opposite ends of the socio-economic and political ideology spectrum. How news workers cultivate and select their sources is, therefore, essential in the investigation of the news media's role in political conflict.

In authority, we trust: the analysis of news sources in southern conflict reporting

This chapter continues by examining the providers of information and drawing connections between preferred sources and how the southern conflict is represented in news reports.

Police, government, and military: the trinity of sources in southern conflict reporting

The study of source attribution reveals that frequently cited informers are mostly authority figures, particularly police officers and members of the government, as shown in Table 4.1. In line with existing studies, it is apparent that the coverage of southern conflict principally relies on the authorities' accounts. While the

Table 4.1 The types of sources quoted in news content

Rank	Types of sources	Frequency (percentage – each)
1	Police	16
2	Government	14
3	Military	9
	State agencies[1]	
4	Media: Thai	7
	Parliamentarians (MPs, senators)	
5	Community members	6
6	Administrative agencies	5
7	Civil societies	4
8	Business and agriculture sectors	3
	Academics	
	Family of victims	
	Anonymous with association	
9	Independent agencies	2
	International figures/ agencies	
	Others (miscellaneous)	
	Anonymous without association	
	Media: Foreign	
10	Ministerial officials	1
	Members of Royal family and associates	
	Insurgents	
	Total ($n = 2,237$)	100

[1] State agencies refer to organisations under the government's supervision and operated by civil servants, such as educational institutions, medical and healthcare services organisations, etc., whereas administrative agencies refer specifically to national and local administrative organisations, such as the provincial governor's offices and the local administrative offices, etc. The SBPAC, for example, was considered a regional administrative agency.

84 *News access and reporting*

voices of community members are often featured, the analysis also shows that sources who are likely to challenge the state's explanations, such as independent state agencies,[3] civil societies, academics, and even insurgents, are among the minimally quoted ones. It is too premature to conclude here that the prominence of authority sources and the minimal citation of challengers indicate journalists' intention to support the *crime and conspiracy* discourse. Nevertheless, in line with the previous analysis, it can be concluded that with state authority gaining privilege in news access, the news media in effect follow the discourses proposed by political elite rather than those proposed by other groups.

Interestingly, reporters and news organisations are also among the most frequently used sources, even more often than other societal members and stakeholders. The study also shows that reporters' accounts are mostly used to describe the scene and atmosphere. While these accounts give additional information that is not mentioned by sources or shown in the photographs and video footage that accompany the stories, the frequent attribution enhances journalists' role in the southern conflict. Rather than being a mere messenger, journalists become an indispensable element of southern conflict reporting. Inherent in the news writing template, the attribution to reporters' observations as a source of information is a way to ensure that the stories meet professional standards of accuracy and objectivity. As a southern reporter put it, every account in the news article must be accompanied with source attribution to guarantee that it is not fabricated. Therefore, a story with "It was reported that. . ." would not be seen as being reliable as "Our reporter observed . . .".

Law enforcement, national security, and policies: principal perspectives in the southern conflict coverage

This study produces results that still support the *crime and conspiracy* discourse, which sees the problem as criminality and security threats. As demonstrated in Table 4.2, sources with expertise in law enforcement and crime investigation, often police officers, are quoted most, followed by those with specialisations in security and state policies. This finding is in accordance with the emphasis of coverage on policies, description and investigation of violent incidents, and security measures found in the analysis of news themes and frames. Similarly, sources offering observations, mostly personal experiences, eye-witness accounts, and journalistic descriptions, feature highly. On the contrary, those with expertise in southern affairs, history and culture, human rights, and terrorism and separatism – the subjects that are relevant to the *minority's grievance* and the *Malay nationalism and Islamism* discourses – feature far fewer. While the information these experts provide may not necessarily support the three aforementioned discourses, their minimal presence indicates that journalists treat the southern conflict like other political conflicts and unrest, and engage very little with the distinctive elements of the phenomenon. Because of this, the explanations beyond the visible impact of the conflict are rare, and their absence effectively allows the *crime and conspiracy* discourse to dominate others.

News access and reporting 85

Table 4.2 The specialisation of sources presented in news content

Rank	Sources' specialisation and contribution	Frequency (percentage – each)
1	Law enforcement and investigation	18
2	Security	14
3	National policies	12
4	Personal experience and eyewitness accounts	11
5	Journalistic observations	8
6	Administrative authority	7
7	Economy	4
	Southern affairs	
	Education	
8	Justice system	3
9	Religion (Islam)	2
	International relations/ affairs	
	History and culture	
	Human rights	
	Healthcare and medical services	
10	Others (miscellaneous)	1
	Social/community development	
	Religion (Buddhism)	
	Terrorism/ Separatism	
	Royal affairs	
	Total (*n* = 2,237)	100

When comparing the output from the four organisations, the findings show that community members and personal experience are among the most cited sources and contributions in the coverage of *Isara* and *Thai PBS*. Meanwhile, the reports by *Matichon* and *Manager* rely more on authority figures and administrative matters such as security, policy, and law enforcement and investigation. The different source emphases among these outlets suggest that political and general news-focused news agencies such as *Matichon* and *Manager* tend to depend on regular official sources to which reporters can gain routine and convenient access. Meanwhile, *Thai PBS* and *Isara*'s inclination to include opinions from community members could be shaped by their news focuses on the impact of public policy and the conflict on the southerners. The fact that stringers are major contributors in the southern conflict coverage may play a part in the inclination towards local security and law enforcement officials. As discussed in the previous chapter, stringers may have certain degree of power to push forward a news agenda, as they are often the first "gatekeepers" of the southern conflict stories. However, the ultimate decision to present any stories lies with the Bangkok newsrooms, which usually see violence as the most prominent feature of the conflict. The need to serve Bangkok's

86 *News access and reporting*

expectations, which results in their pay rise and the easy access to official daily incident reports, prompts stringers to file stories concerning the uses of force as documented by state authorities, whose report template is similar to recording other criminal cases. As such, incidents from the deep South have frequently been told in crime news narratives, with police investigators and army officers being the lead actors and perpetrators cast as the anti-heroes.

A national problem: the use of national-level sources in southern conflict reporting

The final discussion point looks at the sources' locations and bases. While the frequency of attribution of sources based in the restive region is the highest, about one third of sources are from the capital city or represent national-level politics, as seen in Table 4.3. This finding shows that the conflict is not a mere regional problem, despite originating in the far South, but is considered a significant national problem, as it receives a great deal of attention from national-level sources, mostly policy-makers.

However, the finding shows that Bangkok-based media organisations use more national-level sources than those in the region. The majority of sources appearing in the coverage of the *Isara* website are local, while attributions to national-level sources are fewer. The four agencies' news concentration and the presence in the region could play a role in source selection. The fact that *Isara*, *Thai PBS*, and *Manager* have full-time news crews stationed in the area, while *Matichon* depends mostly on stringers, could influence the organisations' frequent use of sources. At the same time, this discovery shows that the national-level mainstream media have better access to political elite sources than smaller alternative operations, and explains why alternative outlets choose to dedicate more space to local and non-elite sources as a way of distinguishing their coverage.

In line with the previous discussion on international influence, the sources based overseas are featured in news content more than those from other parts of the South or the country. This finding indicates the involvement of international figures, from Islamic countries and the neighbouring Malaysia to international watchdog agencies, in what the Thai government considers domestic affairs.

Table 4.3 The locations and bases of sources in southern conflict reporting

Bases and locations	Frequency (percentage)
Southernmost provinces	50
National level (capital city)	37
Overseas	5
Other southern provinces	4
Other parts of the country	3
Unknown location	1
Total ($n = 2,237$)	100

News access and reporting 87

In summary, the examination of source attribution agrees with the theme and news framing analysis detailed in Chapter 2: news coverage tends to favour the *crime and conspiracy* discourse over others because the majority of sources are state authorities and the political elite, and have expertise in national security, policies, and law enforcement and crime investigation.

Cultivating reciprocity: the journalist-source relationship in southern conflict reporting

The theoretical discussion and debate above provide an analytical lens in examining how journalists interact with their sources in producing southern conflict coverage. This section, divided into three parts, moves to illustrate the interplay between journalists and sources in southern conflict reporting. First, the elements involving source accessibility in general will be discussed. The second part deals with journalists' professional "craft" of maintaining the source's trust. The final part then investigates the informal interchange between journalists and their sources outside the work contexts that help stabilise their relationship, and potentially shape news output.

Initiating contact: getting access to and being approached by sources

The conflict's violent nature and complex political and cultural contexts make it difficult for journalists to gain access to a variety of sources and produce multi-perspective coverage of the issue. To earn the trust and openness of sources, particularly the locals, is not a simple task. Journalists often find that the volatile setting can prompt locals, at first, to cast doubt on and distrust reporters. As briefly discussed in the previous chapter concerning threats and intimidation against journalists, news workers are generally greeted by an unwelcoming, if not hostile, atmosphere, when entering unfamiliar ground. Southern reporters have added that some locals believe that intelligence officials sometimes pose as journalists to glean information from them, which further increases the residents' scepticism towards strangers. At the same time, news media's presence in the deep South, and their coverage, play a crucial part in setting the locals' expectations towards journalists' roles in the conflict. As a *Thai PBS* reporter put it, in the eyes of villagers, reporters resemble state authorities who are influential, and therefore responsible for solving the conflict. "Everybody feels media are a panacea [to the southern problem]. . . People have high hopes towards news media to solve problems in the three southern provinces. If [news media] fail, they are wrong," said the reporter.[4]

Under these apprehensive conditions, the characteristics of both journalists and sources, from their identities to their employers, play an important part in their interplay. A Pattani-native Muslim reporter said she occasionally finds Buddhist villagers, especially those believed to be attacked by insurgent groups, reluctant to speak to her. She raised a case in which she interviewed a family who recently lost a son, and the entire conversation, which was to be a profile piece, took place at the family's doorstep. While feeling the distrust, the reporter also

88 *News access and reporting*

thought such a reaction was also caused by grief.[5] Similarly, local Muslim reporters also observed that high-ranking military and police officials seemed more cautious around them than their fellow Buddhist or Bangkok-based reporters. By the same token, another veteran reporter said that senior Islamic religious leaders sometimes subtly expressed contempt against her, a Buddhist woman. In several incidents, including the oft-cited navy officers' hostage situation in Tanyong Limo village in 2005, Malay Muslim villagers strictly forbade members of the vernacular press from entering the scene, allowing only Thai authorities and a local Malay Muslim stringer who worked for international media. They also demanded that Malaysian reporters cover the story (see Appendix B for more detail).

Some stringers and senior correspondents are able to get in touch with insurgents and the supposed leaders of separatist groups. A stringer who connected a Bangkok-based TV news crew with a former leader of a separatist movement, stationed in Malaysia, revealed his way of negotiating access with the secretive sources. He had to explain to the sources' coordinator who he was, and offered them a chance to clarify their actions in front of an audience, so they would see the interview as "an exchange" instead of being just the news company's commodity.[6]

While not entirely disregarding journalists' personal attributes as an obstacle in newsgathering, news editors and senior reporters argue that sources' reservations might not stem from religious or cultural differences alone. The reporters' association with news organisations could also become a leverage or hindrance in accessing the sources. Being a senior reporter for a national-level daily, the *Isara* editor said that, to the sources' eye, his primary employee exudes more credibility and impact than the small alternative online news agencies. Such an impression grants journalists from large, national-level, mainstream news outlets a competitive edge in gaining access to or being approached by sources, particularly high-ranking authorities. Similarly, a *Thai PBS* reporter is recognisable among local authorities and residents thanks to her regular reports which usually feature her appearing on camera. Such a status enables her to have easier access to sources. Meanwhile, Deep South Watch editors and *Isara* reporters who are based in the far South conceded that it is difficult for junior reporters and those from smaller agencies like them to schedule interviews with top-brass officials. The reluctance may change into a more accommodating tone, however, if the Bangkok-based editor makes the contact or says the mainstream media will also cover the stories.

Nonetheless, being a reporter still has certain privileges, particularly when dealing with authoritative sources. A local stringer admitted that state official sources are more easily accessible because they see the high frequency of their coverage, particularly that which concerns the authorities' achievements, such as arrests of suspects. Thus, they are likely to approach journalists whenever they have stories to tell. In similar vein, a TV reporter added that when newly appointed authorities arrived in the region, among their priorities was to hold a meeting with local press to iron out any differences.[7]

In many cases, journalists' characters and affiliations prove to be useful with the locals, too. Villagers tend to be apprehensive towards the press at first, but

News access and reporting   89

may agree to talk to the press if people they know put in good words. Thus, being a native or speaking the local dialect enables journalists to put their sources at ease more quickly, and a personal connection is equally crucial. For sources who are unaccustomed to the press, talks on daily life can help lessen tension and distrust towards the news crew, and can often provide reporters with fresh story ideas concerning the socio-cultural conditions that can help describe the region and its characteristics. As mentioned in the previous chapter, when reporting violent incidents journalists generally rely on authorities' statements to minimise the travelling costs and the risks of entering unfamiliar territories. Regardless, if there are discrepancies among official reports or sceptical data, reporters will phone their sources in the areas, such as district chief-officers, village defence volunteers, community and religious leaders, or even acquaintances and families, to verify facts and collect unreported information. In the Tanyong Limo hostage case, a Pattani-based journalist said because of his connection with former religious school classmates, he was allowed to stay longer in the village and be able to take exclusive photos, instead of having to rush out with the authorities like other news teams. In another incident, a pair of local reporters mentioned that they earned the first and exclusive interview with survivors of a high-profile shooting case – vital testimonies concerning the event – through a relative who was a survivor's daughter-in-law. A stringer added that her advocacy work in community development and women's empowerment helps foster strong ties with sources in many villages. Essentially, the locals become the "eyes and ears," as southern journalists put it, especially in inaccessible areas. Not only do the members of communities provide reporters with invaluable information which is sometimes contradictory to the officials' accounts, but they also tip off journalists. However, reporters have to treat the information with caution, and occasionally these news tips are not reported in order to protect the sources' and the reporters' own safety.

> There were several cases where the locals phoned me, [for example] saying they were at a rubber plantation, then saw soldiers stopping their vehicle by the road and opening fire on their own vehicle. A few moments later, the radio scanner announced that soldiers were [attacked]. I was like, I knew it. Because there were no injuries [reported]. [. . .] There were many cases, but it's difficult to report.[8]

Another emerging group of sources are civil advocates and citizen media producers, who rarely get priority access to mainstream news organisations. These players generally distribute their information via online channels and public forums, which do not always guarantee a wide reach. Nonetheless, their entrance into the discursive arena catches the attention of alternative media agencies which have limited access to high-ranking official sources. Instead of following prominent and influential news-makers in order to compete with mainstream national-level organisations, small media outlets forge alliances among themselves and with southern civil society organisations so they can acquire and present information – some of which is often overlooked or hardly featured in mainstream

90 *News access and reporting*

national press. At the same time, alternative media producers can help their fellow small producers and local NGOs disseminate information and support their agendas. The public service broadcaster *Thai PBS* also joins in this collaboration via its civic networking mechanism, enabling this group to become both source and content producer for the station. This partnership, the director of *Thai PBS* Civil Network Department noted, brings down the traditional media production framework and, at the same time, decentralises the power to communicate from national-level mainstream media to other societal factions, including villagers.[9]

This mutual exchange elicits a noteworthy discussion point. As will be demonstrated later, a relationship between journalists and sources from all levels is reciprocal. By immersing themselves in the sources' domains, journalists obtain the stories and earn an "insider" status, prompting them to walk the line between professional values, particularly objectivity, and maintaining the relationship.

Building trust: the art of fostering symbiotic relationships

Senior journalists have admitted that maintaining a relationship with their sources is essential to newsgathering, a "capital," according to one seasoned reporter. Journalists have voiced that sustaining the relationship with their sources is a "craft" which requires a great deal of personality and experience as much as professional integrity. News workers learn that sources' trust cannot be built overnight. As a result, it is even more difficult for junior reporters to gain access to influential sources, let alone exclusivity, especially if they do not have advantages such as personal connections and the organisation's reputation to back them. A veteran security affairs journalist shared how he fostered his relationship with military sources.

> Trust wasn't born in a few years – it took some 10 years. Many big army officers, I have known them for more than 10 years. They have seen me working and my work presented on the screen. They are aware how I present them. The Region 4 Army [the deep southern-based military unit] officers even said, 'Whenever you come here to cover stories, brother, tell us right away. Whatever you want, however you want.' They asked for one thing; they asked for an opportunity to say what they want to present. So I told them, 'Whatever errors or incidents caused by the officers, I must report them. You cannot ask me not to cover it, alright?'[10]

The statement reflects two interesting points. The first is, notwithstanding the closeness with their sources, journalists naturally have declared that their priority is to "do their job" – that is, to report newsworthy incidents. Therefore, it is essential to set certain ground rules on what can and cannot be done in a way that will not sabotage the relationship while maintaining professional impartiality. The second point is, while seemingly accommodating, both sources and journalists exercise their power to negotiate the extent of this access, which indicates that, instead of being confrontational, journalists and sources have a rather negotiable and cooperative interplay.

Similar to how journalists initiate contact with sources, the news organisation's status can become a factor shaping the direction of relationship. As a news producer at the radio station of Prince of Songkla University at the Pattani campus explained, news workers feel they have to operate differently from other for-profit media since the station belongs to an established educational institute and upholds a public service ethos. She raised an example of how military officers usually offer to pay for fuel costs for reporters and stringers when they cover the army's organised events; her team's stance, however, is to politely turn down any offers. "It's like we have a brand to keep. If we receive anything, we are no different to others. Because we are an educational institute, we have high expectations and have to maintain credibility. This is the standard we need to sustain to distinguish ourselves from other media," said the producer.[11] This practice, she believes, not only maintains professionalism, but also subtly informs their sources of the boundary of their relationship. At the same time, the station is not afraid that such actions may offend the sources, resulting in losing them. The fact that its news policy does not compel the local public service broadcaster to compete with other media outlets for audience ratings and funding allows some flexibility in terms of news angles, delivery, and source selection.

Another element involved in the establishment of trust between reporters and sources is the constant violence in the region. The complex and volatile nature of the southern conflict puts journalists in positions where they come across sensitive information, from confidential national security intelligence to counter-state accounts that may defy predominant beliefs in Thai society. Given this circumstance, journalists admit that they have to consider if their reports will jeopardise both the safety of people involved and their relationships with these sources. The boundary between confidentiality and self-censorship is sometimes difficult to justify. Nonetheless, decisions are clear when it comes to protecting vulnerable informants such as key witnesses, victims of violence, and minors. Referring to her exclusive interview with survivors of a high-profile incident in which villagers were shot by village defence volunteers, an *Isara* reporter said that she had to seriously consider how to write the story in a way that would not endanger her sources. Like other media organisations, the reporter used both the name and photo of an elderly survivor in her story, as he allowed disclosure, but did not name or interview another surviving victim, a 15-year-old teen, until the official investigation commenced.

Maintaining trust with sources from insurgent movements also creates challenges. Due to the clandestine and complex nature of the groups, named sources in news reports are mostly the supposed leaders of separatist groups based overseas, former insurgents who were active in the 1980s, and those who were convicted and imprisoned. At the same time, because of the movements' fragmented structure, as discussed in Chapter 1, journalists who have access to these sources cannot rely solely on any particular group. A senior reporter explained that if

92 *News access and reporting*

a journalist chooses to report heavily on one movement – mostly one with rich communication resources – the reporter may lose a chance to form a relationship with others who have different goals or strategies.[12] Meanwhile, approaching and interviewing currently active field operative insurgents is difficult, due to their covert status and concerns over their safety. Therefore, these people often become anonymous tipsters rather than on-the-record sources. As mentioned briefly in the previous chapter, state authorities sometimes approach or interrogate journalists to ask for their knowledge of insurgent movements. To keep confidentiality of their sources, journalists may refuse to divulge vital information. Nonetheless, by not revealing the identity of insurgent sources and their whereabouts, journalists can still share their analyses of the situations with sources from other camps – a role that some peers criticise.

In all, apart from the personalities and organisational affiliation, journalists' experiences play an important part in gaining the trust of sources. Maintaining source anonymity is also crucial, especially when journalists have to deal with sources from opposing groups. Nonetheless, staying in the "middle" position is a challenge, particularly when news workers are closely involved with various players and developing situations.

Being insiders: between blending in and keeping a distance

To keep a close relationship, news workers and sources occasionally touch base and socialise out of work contexts. This kind of closeness enables journalists to call their sources at any time of the day for tips, verification, and responses without fear of refusal, and vice versa. Despite the propinquity with their sources from various societal sectors, journalists adamantly affirm their professional neutrality and see the close acquaintance as a leverage to gain information rather than causing partiality. Like many news workers, the *Isara* editor asserted that he is able to demonstrate his professional integrity and credibility by not exploiting the relationship. He said: "I'm close to many army officials – a lot, actually. They even ask for my advice or ask me to write this and that for them. But I don't do it. Most importantly, I never ask them for anything except their comments. Never ask them to treat me to a meal, to give me money, to fund *Isara*, nothing at all that is in my personal interest."[13]

Insisting on upholding professional independence from sources, journalists acknowledge some unacceptable and unethical practices, such as accepting or paying bribes or any forms of financial reward. Regardless, some forms of relationships bring about the "objectivity versus practicality" debate. For instance, during my observation of the *Isara* news crew in the South, the then SBPAC secretary general invited the news team to stay for two nights at the security-guarded SBPAC compound, generally reserved for the organisation's honoured guests. During the stay, not only did the SBPAC chief spend some time talking to the reporters and asking their opinions on various matters, but also invited them to dine with his aides and visitors. By doing so, the reporters were able to converse with these high-profile guests while observing and learning about the agency's future plans and the dynamic of the people involved. While the reporters expressed their unease with the invitation, they conceded to accept it in order to maintain a good connection with the high-ranking official. The Bangkok-based *Isara* editor said he had been close with the SBPAC head ever since he was the chief of a special police investigation task force, and revealed that he had been consulted on several matters since the officer assumed this post. Meanwhile, the two local reporters were appointed as members of the SBPAC's working committees – a position in which the two often expressed the dilemma of maintaining news professionalism versus being able to convey their insights and "help the locals" via official mechanisms.

In another example, a *Thai PBS* reporter was invited to attend a counter-terrorism course at the Army's prestigious Command and General College and was later invited to be a guest speaker for the course. The reporter said that, while participation enabled her to have a better grasp of the military's perspectives and rationales behind its operations, she could also share her expertise in field reporting so these officials could learn how best to utilise mass media to counter insurgency.

> [Referring to army officials' lack of knowledge on local media] Because you aren't familiar with them, you don't know how to use them. But the bandits know. They don't have to be acquainted [with the reporters], but know what types of news journalists like to do. How about you? Do you know the types of stories that reporters like? How would you twist the angle? So I taught them ways to twist the news angle. [. . .] Before you use [the news media], you must know their nature, how they are.[14]

Journalists connect not only with state official sources, but also with other social groups involved in the conflict. While establishing a relationship with army authorities, the same reporter also forms a network of locals as she spends most of her time covering the southern region. When available, the reporter will visit her informants and accept invitations to attend their social functions so she can strengthen the bond. This kind of practice is common among other local journalists. Another reporter uses her connection with state officials to stabilise her relationship with villagers, indicating that it is a way to expedite the state's assistance for these locals.

These examples show that a diverse source pool and claiming non-partisanship is crucial in newsgathering, not simply because the professional principle of impartiality requires journalists to do so, but because it is also a production necessity. It is vital for journalists to generate a vast array of sources at every level to produce more extensive news coverage than their competitors. Moreover, as shown in the recent remark, a connection with one group could advance the relationship with another. While it may take some time for individual journalists to establish a wide range of sources of their own, a large news organisation comprising various news beats and specialist journalists could benefit from such diversity, generating a broad network of sources.

94　*News access and reporting*

Despite the potential benefits of journalists' dual status, some news workers remain sceptical of this practice. A TV reporter voiced concern that by joining the governmental committees, news practitioners are incorporated into the state mechanism. He observed: "[News media] have become a part of benefits and values [from the conflict] because media workers are closely pulled into serving as a state's tool. [. . .] Of the several hundred billions baht allocated, have you ever seen any serious examinations of budget spending or the ways it was used from any media? Rarely."[15] However, not many media professionals criticise such acts, and seem to condone them. This practice, he noted, not only compromises the news media's watchdog role against the powers-that-be, but also signals the deficiency, if not lack, of self-monitoring and reflexivity in the culture of Thai journalism.

Overall, the discussion in this chapter shows that sources are vital to newsgathering, but getting access to and strengthening the connection with sources can be a complex process. Junior reporters and small alternative news organisations often find it difficult to reach and be approached by influential sources, making it hard for them to produce in-depth or investigative reports that require input from the authorities on their own. For seasoned journalists, getting access to high-powered sources might not be a problem, but they might be more inclined towards the sources' perspectives due to years of acquaintance.

To make up for their lack of opportunity with elite sources, alternative media seek new sets of informers who are easier to access, who sometimes offer under-reported, even challenging, insights and analyses. These emerging sources include marginalised local voices, such as southern residents, academics, activists, and those related to the insurgents. Some of these sources are considered unconventional by mainstream media, and, if allowed to emerge, usually enter media space via "the back gate coverage". By providing them with "the front gate coverage," local alternative news outlets add to the diversity and dynamic of the source pool in the ecology of southern conflict reporting.

The diversity of sources also happens in the same news organisation. Members of a news outlet do not necessarily hold similar views towards the conflict and the roles of journalism. For instance, at *Thai PBS*, journalists with extensive experience and source association in this large news corporation could contribute to a wide array of sources who present disparate interpretations of the conflict. By the same token, these journalists' dissimilar expertise, inclinations towards certain groups of sources, experience in the field, and, ultimately, understandings of the southern conflict, could also give rise to power plays in news production. As briefly mentioned in the previous chapter, in the editorial meeting, news managers and senior journalists sometimes discuss and argue about the news angles that they believe could best represent the problem. Therefore, even within one organisation, the discursive contention manifests itself, although news workers with more experience or higher administrative positions tend to win. This leads to a majority of coverage supporting dominant elite views, particularly the military's national security perspectives. As shown in a study of peace talk coverage in 2013,

News access and reporting 95

mainstream media maintained sceptical stance towards the dialogue and adopted "military doctrine" terms in their reports because news organisations' primary presenters of the coverage are senior correspondents who have an expertise in security affairs (Samatcha and Rungrawee 2014, p. 94, pp. 134–135).

Another noteworthy point is that the journalist-source interchange is often fluid and dynamic. Both parties are seemingly close to and trusting of each other, but at the same time, they maintain some distance and professional autonomy. Journalists do not openly pledge their alliance with any particular camp in order to claim professionalism, particularly impartiality and objectivity, while attempting to expand their connection with every involved party. While it is a professional value for journalists to be non-partisan, becoming acquainted with disparate players involved in the conflict can also become leverage in newsgathering.

The final discussion point here is that the journalist-source relationship is a symbiotic and reciprocal one. It is often a subtle, mutual exchange between journalists and sources, no matter at what level. Journalists acquire information for their news production, and in the process, earn a certain social status, such as an advisor to state officials and NGOs working on particular issues, ad-hoc intermediary in conflict situation, or coordinator between villagers and responsible officials. By the same token, apart from getting their messages across, sources can earn publicity, authority over the issues, or prompt assistance. In the end, despite some struggle in access, these relationships are cooperative rather than confrontational; journalists get stories and sources get closer to their goals.

Conclusion

This chapter discusses an indispensable component of news production – the interchange between journalists and their sources – and demonstrates the complexity of their relationships at various levels. The study of news content shows how authoritative and elite sources specialising in national security, law enforcement, and national policy, dominate the coverage. On the contrary, sources who could provide counter-dominant interpretations of the conflict, such as locals, civil society organisations, or even insurgents themselves, are minimally featured. The customs of news production and the violent aspect of the conflict, as discussed in Chapter 3, may play important parts in source selection. Nonetheless, this chapter argues that the journalist-source relationship is complex and involves multifaceted factors, from an individual's personal touch to the structural and cultural mechanisms that enable journalists to enter the "inner circle" hosted by sources, be it the powers-that-be or at the grassroots. At the same time, fostering and maintaining relationships is not a simple and clear-cut practice. Negotiation, compromise, and struggle are parts of the process, with professional values, personal beliefs, and political ideologies at play. As will be discussed in the subsequent chapter, these factors not only contend to define the journalist-source interplays, but also how news workers place themselves in the southern conflict.

96 *News access and reporting*

Notes

1 Sources in this chapter mostly refer to individuals and institutions they represent, along the line of discussions on the journalist-source relationship in McNair's sociology of sources (1998, pp. 143–161) and Cottle's news access (2000). For more on journalists' access to documentary resources, see Waisbord's discussion (2000, pp. 93–118).
2 See, for example, Kanlayanee 2004; Media Monitor 2005, 2007a, 2007b, 2008a, 2008b.
3 Most independent state agencies are regulatory bodies that were established following the constitutional mandates and organic laws with the mission to scrutinise the actions of elected officials and state employees. These agencies are empowered with judicial authority and autonomy to prevent the government's interference. Among the prominent independent agencies are the Election Commission, the State Audit Commission, the Administrative Court, and the National Human Rights Commissions. In the case of the southern conflict, the National Reconciliation Commission was an ad-hoc independent agency which was set up according to the Prime Minister's 2005 directive to investigate the conflict and propose solutions.
4 *Thai PBS* southern news centre reporter 1. Interview. 23 December 2011.
5 *Isara* reporter 3. Interview. 19 February 2012.
6 Pattani stringer 2. Interview. 19 February 2012.
7 *Thai PBS* southern news centre reporter 1. Interview.
8 Yala Stringer. Interview. 19 February 2012.
9 *Thai PBS* Civil Media Network director. Interview. 1 February 2012.
10 *Thai PBS* senior reporter. Interview. 1 February 2012.
11 Prince of Songkla University radio producer. Interview. 17 December 2011.
12 Patani Forum co-founder. Interview. 18 February 2012.
13 *Isara* editor. Interview. 25 January 2012.
14 *Thai PBS* southern news centre reporter 1. Interview.
15 *Thai PBS* southern news centre reporter 2. Interview. 20 February 2012.

References

Archetti, Christina. 2010. Comparing international coverage of 9/11: Towards an interdisciplinary explanation of the construction of news. *Journalism* 11(5), pp. 567–588.

Bennett, W. Lance. 1990. Toward a theory of press-state relations in the U.S. *Journal of Communication* 40(2), pp. 103–125.

Campbell, Vincent. 2004. *Information Age Journalism: Journalism in an International Context*. London: Arnold.

Cook, Timothy E. 2006. The news media as a political institution: Looking backward and looking forward. *Political Communication* 23(2), pp. 159–171.

Cottle, Simon. 2000. Rethinking news access. *Journalism Studies* 1(3), pp. 427–448.

Franklin, Bob. 2003. A Good Day to Bury Bad News?: Journalists, Sources and the Packaging of Politics. In: Cottle, S. ed. *News, Public Relations and Power*. London: Sage, pp. 45–61.

Hall, Stuart, Critcher, Chas, Jefferson, Tony, Clarke, John, and Roberts, Brian. 1978. *Policing the Crisis: Mugging, the State, and Law and Order*. London: University of California Press.

Hasty, Jennifer. 2010. Journalism as Fieldwork: Propaganda, Complicity, and the Ethics of Anthropology. In: Bird, S.E. ed. *The Anthropology of News & Journalism: Global Perspectives*. Bloomington, IN: Indiana University Press, pp. 132–148.

Kanlayanee Kanchanatanee. 2004. *การรายงานข่าวโทรทัศน์เหตุการณ์ปล้นคลังอาวุธหน่วยทักษิณพัฒนา ระหว่างวันที่ 28 เมษายน- 5 พฤษภาคม 2546 [Television News Reporting of Southern Development Unit's*

Amory Robbery Between 28th April–5th May 2003]. MA Thesis, Chulalongkorn University.

McCargo, Duncan. 2000. *Politics and the Press in Thailand: Media Machinations*. London: Routledge.

McChesney, Robert. 2002. The Structural Limitations of US Journalism. In: Zelizer, B. and Allan, S. eds. *Journalism After September* 11. London and New York: Routledge, pp. 91–100.

McNair, Brian. 1998. *The Sociology of Journalism*. London: Arnold.

Media Monitor. 2005. รายงานผลการศึกษารอบที่ 2: ภาพตัวแทนและความสมดุลในรายการข่าวโทรทัศน์กับบทบาทใน การสร้างความสมานฉันท์ในสังคมไทย (ช่อง 3, 5, 7, 9, 11 และ iTV เดือนกันยายน-ตุลาคม 2548) [Report of the second round of study: Representation and balance in television news programmes and the role in reconciliation building in Thai society (Channel 3, 5, 7, 9, 11, and iTV September to October 2005)] [online]. Available at: www.mediamonitor.in.th/main/research/docman.html?start=50 [Accessed: 15 January 2013].

Media Monitor. 2007a. รายงานผลการศึกษารอบที่ 15: ความเป็นละครในข่าวการเลือกตั้ง (ฟรีทีวีช่อง 3, 5, 7, 9 และ TITV 18 ตุลาคม – 19 พฤศจิกายน 2550) [Report of the 15th round of study: The drama in election news (free TV channel 3, 5, 7, 9, 11 and TITV 18 October–19 November 2007)] [online]. Available at: www.mediamonitor.in.th/main/research/docman.html?start =30 [Accessed: 15 January 2013].

Media Monitor. 2007b. รายงานผลการศึกษารอบที่ 16: สื่อมวลชนกับบทบาทการนำเสนอเนื้อหาการเลือกตั้ง (ในฟรีทีวี ช่อง 3, 5, 7, 9, 11 และ TITV 21–28 พฤศจิกายน 2550) [Report of the 16th round of study: Mass media and the role in election news presentation (in free TV channel 3, 5, 7, 9, 11, and TITV 21–28 November 2007)] [online]. Available at: www.mediamonitor.in.th/main/research/docman.html? start=30 [Accessed: 15 January 2013].

Media Monitor. 2008a. รายงานผลการศึกษารอบที่ 22: ฟรีทีวีกับการรายงานข่าวการชุมนุมทางการเมือง 31 พฤษภาคม – 1 มิถุนายน 2551 [Report of the 22nd round of study: Free TV and the news coverage of political demonstration 31 May–1 June 2008] [online]. Available at: www.mediamonitor.in.th/main/research/docman.html?start=30 [Accessed: 15 January 2013].

Media Monitor. 2008b. รายงานผลการศึกษารอบที่ 26: การรายงานข่าวเหตุการณ์ชุมนุมทางการเมืองในฟรีทีวี (ช่อง 3, 5, 7, 9, NBT และ TPBS 26–27 สิงหาคม และ 2 กันยายน 2551) [Report of the 26th round of study: The coverage of political demonstrations in free TV (channel 3, 5, 7, 9, NBT and TPBS, 26–27 August and 2 September 2008)] [online]. Available at: www.mediamonitor.in.th/main/research/docman.html?start=20 [Accessed: 15 January 2013].

Molotch, Harvey and Lester, Marilyn. 1974. News as purposive behavior: On the strategic use of routine events, accidents, and scandals. *American Sociological Review* 39(1), pp. 101–112.

Samatcha Nilaphatama and Rungrawee Chalermsripinyorat. 2014. วาทกรรมสื่อมวลชนใน กระบวนการสันติภาพสามจังหวัดชายแดนภาคใต้ 2556 [Media discourse on peace process in Southern Thailand 2013] [online]. *Media Inside Out Group*. Available at: www.deepsouthwatch. org/sites/default/files/peaceprocessdiscourse_samatcha_rungrawee.pdf [Accessed: 20 May 2015].

Schudson, Michael. 2003. *The Sociology of News*. New York: W.W. Norton.

Tumber, Howard. 2004. Prisoners of News Values? Journalists, Professionalism, and Identification in Times of War. In: Allan, S. and Zelizer, B. eds. *Reporting War: Journalism in Wartime*. Oxon: Routledge, pp. 190–205.

Waisbord, Silvio. 2000. *Watchdog Journalism in South America: News, Accountability, and Democracy*. New York: Columbia University Press.

Wolfsfeld, Gadi. 1997. *Media and Political Conflict: News from the Middle East*. Cambridge: Cambridge University Press.

5 Disparate roles of journalism in the southern conflict

With the previous chapters detailing the conditions that shape the production of southern conflict coverage, this chapter brings the discussion back to journalists and their roles in the conflict. It will first explore journalists' disparate comprehension and interpretations of the phenomenon, and draw connections between news workers' understanding of the conflict, their practices, and news representations of the southern conflict. The chapter will then conclude with what journalists see as their desirable roles in this conflict, and how they carry these out.

Diverse understandings, different portrayals of the conflict

The observations of news production teams and interviews with journalists reflect how news workers from different organisations and with a variety of expertise understand the southern conflict in different ways. My personal conversations with two journalists epitomise their different, if not opposite, stances on the issue. In the first situation, after speaking about the far South's many natural and cultural treasures, a senior reporter ended his comment with a rhetorical question: "So, can we just cede [the deep South] to them?" – the "them" referring to the insurgent movements. In another incident, a news manager jokingly remarked, "I'm supporting separatism," after explaining his department's work with local NGOs advocating the special administrative system in the southernmost provinces. It is even more interesting that both journalists have served as the editor of the same alternative news agency at different periods. Their contrasting views reflect not only the diverse perspectives among news workers, but also the shifts in news organisations' directions, especially when they change hands.

While the aforementioned instances clearly demonstrate the speakers' positions, most interviewees did not reveal such discernible stances. Because the unrest has gone on for more than a decade and has been at the centre of many public debates, journalists involved in southern conflict reporting have become familiar with the common rhetoric used to describe the phenomenon. Therefore, they tend to adopt similar views towards the conflict: it is a political struggle caused by insurgents who are an ethnic minority in Thailand. These insurgents use force to fight for a number of causes, ranging from basic rights, justice, and cultural recognition

Disparate roles of journalism   99

to self-administration and separatism. Reporters generally cite the state's lack of understanding of the region's cultural and religious distinctiveness as well as mistreatment and injustice against the Malay Muslims as contributing factors. News workers anticipate a peaceful resolution of the conflict via dialogue, local participation, and public policy. This remedy, however, is difficult to achieve because the complex networks of vested interest groups, including underground crime syndicates, local and national-level politicians, and military and state authorities, continue to fight in order to maintain their status. Some journalists also view the southern conflict as a lucrative enterprise in which many stakeholders contend for financial sponsorship and authority over the issue.[1] Military and local administrative agencies vie for the hefty state budget. Residents demand compensation for their losses, while local non-profit organisations, including the mushrooming alternative news outlets, strive for funding, mostly from international sponsors. As a result, a number of journalists eye these advocacy organisations sceptically and do not believe their causes are genuine.

Despite their nearly conforming answers, news reporters and producers approach the conflict dissimilarly and focus on the aspects of conflict that they deem to be most detrimental and deserving of immediate attention. As mentioned by a reporter, even in the same news organisation, people do not share the same outlooks on the conflict. Three main emphases are used to explain the southern conflict and propose solutions: 1) security-oriented, 2) socio-cultural, and 3) ideology-oriented emphases.

The security-oriented emphasis

In general, journalists cite the continuing unrest and the impact of violence on the locals' livelihood – the warfare dimension of the conflict – as primary problems. While not completely ruling out insurgent groups as principal perpetrators, many veteran journalists and local reporters point to other interest groups, such as narcotics and illegal oil traders, or even state officials, as the instigators of violence. This interpretation is in line with the military's "additional threats" theory, which explains that underground crime syndicates keep the region in disorder, and potentially fund the insurgents to maintain their interests. One stringer remarked: "I don't think it's much of the separatist movement. If you put [separatist movement] in percentage, it is only a little. At the moment, it's about illegal oil trade, contraband, drugs. Simply put, it's about interests. There is a lot of conflict of interests."[2] Another local news editor agreed:

> If [the unrest] happened because of the state and [separatist] movements, it would end easily. But the unrest in the three southern border provinces isn't caused by only two parties. It also comes from drugs cartels, human trafficking, corruption, local influential groups, local politics, personal reasons . . . all mixed up. It's difficult to solve, and difficult to end, as long as there are a lot of weaponry involved, a lot of budget.[3]

100 *Disparate roles of journalism*

This emphasis also focuses on the ramifications of violence such as the suffering of people involved, as well as unjust treatment and human rights violations faced by locals, victims of violence, and detained suspects and convicts. Some local reporters, being at the heart of the conflict, have raised concerns about local social problems in the region, such as the prevalence of narcotic drugs among youths, the deficiency of standardised and religious education systems, and corruption in local administrations. Believing that these problems are as equally crucial as the unrest, journalists expect the government and military to set out clear security maintenance strategies in the region, along with policies that facilitate rehabilitation, justice, social improvement, and local participation.

The socio-cultural emphasis

This emphasis sets out to recognise the histories of political struggles as the underlying cause of the current conflict. Therefore, while concurring that maintaining the region's safety is paramount, this emphasis focuses on the fact that the recognition and promotion of local identity in the region, such as the Patani Malay language or Muslim customs, should be key elements in easing the tension. At the same time, any unjust treatment, such as legal actions prejudiced against the Malay Muslim way of living, should be rectified. Additionally, it sees the need to empower the locals in public participation and engage every stakeholder in dialogue as a way to solve problems. A TV reporter explained:

> [The first cause of conflict] is injustice. The second is the differences between our ideas and [insurgents']. We don't try to learn about them, but we want them to learn from us as much as they can. Meanwhile, some of them don't try to learn about us either. [. . .] I'm not talking about religious [difference] here, because previously, the Buddhists and Muslims, we could still attend one another's [religious events]. But we think differently.[4]

Another TV producer concurred. He pointed out that the conflict stems from the lack of understanding of local culture, particularly among state authorities stationed in the region. "When [the officials] are off duty and wind down after working hours, they still use the term *Ai Khaek*[5], calling them this and that [to refer to the Malay Muslims]. If they don't actually have a positive attitude about the local Muslims in their heart, the problems cannot be solved."[6]

The ideology-oriented emphasis

The third emphasis sees the root cause of the conflict as the Thai state's internal colonialism in the far South. To those who agree with this emphasis, the lack of understanding of local culture and customs, mistreatment of southerners, many forms of violent retaliation, and minimal trust in state authorities are the repercussions of the Thai state's long-term marginalisation of Malay Muslim identity. While the problem diagnosis and prognosis are seemingly similar to the socio-cultural

Disparate roles of journalism 101

emphasis, the ideology-oriented emphasis focuses more on the structural changes that would encourage the remainder of Thai population both to acknowledge and become more culturally aware of differences. In this way, the Malay Muslims would not be regarded as a minority group and would be guaranteed the rights they are entitled to despite their dissimilar ethnic identity. Therefore, it is essential to stimulate public dialogue and debate to enable Malay Muslim narratives to co-exist with Thai accounts and pave the way for a better understanding of their unique and dynamic culture; hence, tackling the conflict at its root. The *Thai PBS* Civil Media Network director remarked:

> If we realize that the problem is simply not a daily incident, we need to find the root cause – what is an actual cause of this? Hatred? We need to think . . . If you ask experts in the region, they would say the problem happens because of three conditions: the Patani State, Malayu identity, and Islam. These three parts are intertwined and cause the conflict. The Patani State [explanation], for one, does not have any space [in public discussion] because it entails historical accounts that the region had been crushed by the Thai state. The hatred remains [in the region] and has constantly been passed down [to next generations].[7]

In a similar vein, a senior reporter and co-founder of the Patani Forum also explained that the locals' needs and beliefs must be elicited and discussed in political and cultural communicative arenas in order to establish a "comfort zone" in which the Malay Muslim identity is not marginalised or suppressed. "I believe [the people] here would agree to stay under the Thai sovereignty, but it has to be under their conditions, not the conditions from Bangkok. And their conditions would be based on their identity, history, and culture," said the senior journalist.[8]

This stance also agrees with civil advocates campaigning for decentralisation and self-determination in the southern border provinces as a key solution, concurring that certain autonomous administrative models should be established to ensure and enhance the residents' political rights and participation. However, this goal is greeted with scepticism and doubt, often by people who do not trust the unstable Thai representative politics and bureaucracy. Instead of alleviating the tension, autonomous governance may give rise to a tug of war among national-level politicians, local political elites, and influential cliques in the region.

This section lays out different aspects of the southern armed conflict which journalists believe to be of paramount concern and requiring solutions. Similar to the argument made earlier with regard to journalists' various expertise and source pools, this section shows that news workers' understandings are not homogenous, although the study does not find a conclusive correlation between journalists' personal backgrounds, their affiliations, and their standpoints on the conflict. Deep South-based journalists do not necessarily have a deeper understanding of the conflict's discursive explanations than their peers in Bangkok. As mentioned in Chapter 1, some Malay Muslim reporters tend to associate with the *crime and conspiracy* and *minority's grievance* discourses, not the *Malay nationalism and Islamism*.[9] From my

102 *Disparate roles of journalism*

observation, those who lean towards the *Malay nationalism and Islamism* discourse are civil advocates and academics who work on conflict resolution and peace processes, as well as senior reporters who see the southern conflict as a social inequality issue. Many of these people are not residents of the southern border provinces and are from Bangkok. Meanwhile, experienced news practitioners do not always lean towards an ideological interpretation more than their junior colleagues. On the contrary, veteran beat reporters' in-depth knowledge and long-time affiliation with sources in their specialisation, particularly governance and security affairs, propel them to adopt their sources' perspectives. Also, as discussed earlier in the chapter, news workers in the same organisation do not share similar views. The different stances among news workers reflect the discursive contestation and the constant power struggle at work in news production, prompting journalists to perform differently in the conflict. This will be discussed in the following section.

No single definition of news practices: the disparate roles of Thai journalism in the southern conflict

This final part concludes with discussion on the reporters' understanding on their desired roles, and how they perform such roles in the conflict. These views reflect the shared values concerning occupational obligations of news media and variations as to how such functions are carried out. They also demonstrate the diverse perspectives towards "unconventional" positions that journalists take on, or that are entrusted to them in resolving conflict. These roles are: 1) *journalism as a presenter of truth*, 2) *journalism as a forum for every party*, and 3) *journalism as a supporter in conflict resolution*.

Journalism as a presenter of truth: *investigating and maintaining neutrality*

Many news workers believe the fundamental role for journalists in the southern conflict is to perform their core occupational requirements: monitoring the dynamic situations, examining and investigating every protagonist's actions and claims, and supplying the public with accurate information. They are adamant that the media merely facilitates the conflict resolution processes initiated by responsible stakeholders, and that they are not part of the problem-solving mechanism itself. The *Thai PBS* assistant news director remarked on this view: "The media have to solve the problem? No! The government does. And the media report about it. The media are not the one to solve the problem, but the media are an important cogwheel to move the content and issues that lead to solutions of the problem."[10] The organisation's deputy director of news and programmes also pointed out that, in reporting conflict, news media have responsibility to present facts; nevertheless, they must verify the materials and not settle only for one set of information. "The principle of making news that I tell the younger generation is, our duty is to be a messenger; don't believe in what your eyes see. [. . .] The constant attempt to investigate and find the facts is an important

Disparate roles of journalism 103

principle in news reporting. Don't be entrapped in your own 'Hey, this is right!' thinking," said the deputy director.[11]

The *Isara* editor concurred that investigating, examining, and presenting facts to ensure every involved party's transparency are the crux of conflict reporting. He also criticised the argument raised by some stakeholders and news workers that news media should perform other tasks to solve the conflict and partake in conflict resolution processes, believing such a move would turn news practitioners into a part of interest groups. He reasoned that every protagonist in the conflict has their own agenda and did not take it lightly when the press present opposite views.

> I won't 'build the atmosphere of talks and negotiation' because that [atmosphere] doesn't exist. I have gone to work [in the deep South] and I know it doesn't exist. So I don't play that role. [. . .] There are forums [for discussions], but do people really speak the truth? Or do they accept it if the truth is spoken? [. . .] To build the atmosphere where every party speaks out, I don't think it will lead to peace. Like the issue of the special administrative zone, I did the stories and my junior colleagues were threatened. Like this, it is not peaceful.[12]

To carry out this role, journalists emphasise that it is crucial to produce impartial and well-rounded reports, comprising opinions and analytical views from every stakeholder in every aspect possible. In essence, the multi-perspective news contents would affirm the journalistic values of non-partisanship and objectivity. Two *Thai PBS* staff proposed similar means to achieve this end and admitted the road is not easy. The deputy director of news and programmes stressed the importance of "balanced content," saying, "Every time there is a political conflict involving [different] political beliefs, it is impossible that you will be free from criticism."[13] Similarly, a field reporter observed, "The thing that shields us from being stabbed by the 'buffalo horns' is that, what we say must be the truth from both sides. Although [the protagonists] aren't pleased with the reports, they can't reprimand us for reporting the contents. The most they could do is to say their [quotation] is shorter or longer, but they cannot criticise our contents because they are factual."[14]

For some local media practitioners, the purpose of neutrality is to earn trust from and access to insurgents, enabling journalists to report from all sides. Interestingly, Al-Jazeera, which often presents the counter-Western perspective, is considered the epitome of professional objectivity and ideal news practices.

> [Al-Jazeera] is neutral. It is the idol [for southern reporters] because . . . why has this media organisation gained acceptance from Al Qaeda or Hezbollah? Why can the channel approach these groups? There must be something right about it. Similar to what happens in this area, if there is a media outlet which the insurgents can reach . . . when they have some information, they will want this organisation to report [about it] because they have confidence in that media organisation.[15]

104 *Disparate roles of journalism*

The reporter's idea corresponds with Iskandar and El-Nawawy's notion of "contextual objectivity" exercised by Al-Jazeera (2004, pp. 319–323). In their study of the Qatari news organisation, Iskandar and El-Nawawy find how the satellite television station strives to maintain balance between upholding journalistic integrity and presenting regional perspectives to their Arab and global audiences in the Western-dominated discursive environment. Despite being praised for unveiling underrepresented perspectives from the Arab world to audiences elsewhere, the broadcaster still faced accusation from US officials of disseminating the then-Iraqi government's propaganda when their reports depicted the deaths of Iraqi civilians. Such a precarious position makes it difficult for Al-Jazeera to receive universal recognition as a "fair and balanced" news organisation, even from its western counterparts (Samuel-Azran 2010). Still, Iskandar and El-Nawawy argue that the presence of Al-Jazeera and the like, as well as the use of "contextual objectivity," is crucial in conflicts where the representation of certain protagonists is inadequate. Likewise, this *Isara* reporter feels strongly that every party, particularly insurgents, should have their voices heard so the public can have informed discussions and debates about their rationale and actions.

This duty of journalism is translated into some organisations' news concentration and presentation. The birth of the *Isara* website, despite its shortcomings as discussed in existing studies (Supopohn 2006; McCargo 2006; Witchayawanee 2009), marks a pivotal point in Thai journalism. Since its inception in 2006, the agency has established itself as one of the primary sources on the southern conflict by committing to reporting about the region. More importantly, in the beginning, this peace journalism initiative also attempted to challenge conventional news production system and practice by focusing on socio-cultural aspects of the region and the ramifications of violence. In several instances, the website broke crucial stories that gave rise to public debate and state investigations, such as the exclusive coverage of the Tanyong Limo hostage situation from inside the village, which will be discussed later in this chapter,[16] and the probe into the explosive detector GT200.[17] As discussed in Chapter 2 and again in Chapter 4, the distinction of *Isara*'s coverage of the conflict during the reviewed period is its emphasis on views from the far South. Being a news outlet that is known among fellow media practitioners and relevant decision-makers, it has provided a space where residents from various ethnic backgrounds and social groups, as well as state officials based in the region, have shared their experiences and voiced their concerns to the general public – contrary to other mainstream national-level media, who mainly relied on national-level sources. Nonetheless, as studies point out, the news agency's ambiguous objectives since its start, as well as its constantly changing structure and financial support, which will be elaborated upon later, make it difficult for the organisation fully to achieve the ambitious goal of implementing innovative practices (Supapohn 2006; McCargo 2012, pp. 100–107). Therefore, despite its merits, the forms and news angles of *Isara*'s general news output remain similar to those of other studied media outlets.

While *Isara*'s position and small operation allow the agency to focus its coverage on the deep South, other larger news organisations cannot do so because they

Disparate roles of journalism 105

have to serve a broad audience base or follow different organisational principles. Nonetheless, seeing the significance of the southern conflict issues, they set aside space for reports concerning the region. For instance, the *Manager* website has launched the Southern Region page, which is dedicated to 14 provinces in the South. Although the coverage of the deep South armed conflict does not always take centre stage, and the rationale behind this operation is merely financial, the page allows stories of the southern conflict to last longer on the dynamic news website. As for *Thai PBS*, with its public service principle to recognise different identities and promote cultural diversity, the organisation allocates fixed segments in the station's primetime news bulletin and programming for content concerning the southern conflict and the far South, including those produced and contributed to by civic media and citizen reporters. During the reviewed period, the station's Sunday primetime news bulletin at 7 p.m. featured a five-minute segment called *"Reung Lao Jak Plai Dam Kwan* [Stories from the tip of axe handle]," presenting reports from southern news centre reporters.[18] Since 2010, the station has aired three 30-minute weekly news magazine shows with original content from its regional centres' programme production crew in the South, North, and Northeast, and the southern news centre was in charge of producing *"Di Selantan Na Dan Tai* [In the South]".[19] Meanwhile, the introduction, discussion, and debate on the southern conflict and relevant issues, such as political and military policies, the justice system, Malay Muslim identity, and Islam, were constantly brought up in the station's news discussion shows, investigative news presentations, and documentary programmes. Additionally, the varied expertise of the station's reporters, from those based in the South to experienced politics and security affairs journalists, as well as programme producers, contributes to the variety of news contents and formats.

Other practices that make *Thai PBS* stands out from other news organisations are the organisation's formal codes of ethics and conduct (Thai Public Broadcasting Service 2009), as along with other monitoring mechanisms such as the Audience Council and the public complaint sub-committee (see Appendix C for more detail on the organisation structure), which ensure that the content is in compliance with organisational principles and professional ethics. The code of conduct also stipulates guidelines in reporting conflict, demonstration, terrorism, and war (Ibid., pp. 138–145). For instance, the code states that its employees should not label antagonists with judgemental or partisan terms such as terrorist, extremist, or fanatic, but they should use the labels these antagonists use to call themselves (Ibid., pp. 139–140). During my newsroom observation, a chief editor[20] told me that the station was developing news reporting and writing guidelines to translate the codes of ethics and conduct into practice. For example, in a murder case, the guidelines suggest the use of the terms "the injured or affected person" instead of "victim," and "perpetrator" instead of "criminal".[21] When asked about concerns and difficulties in southern conflict reporting, a deputy editor of the regional news desk said working at *Thai PBS* is "more stressful" compared to her time at another commercial station. She said she has to be more careful and make sure that the news scripts and footage comply with the organisation's codes.

106 *Disparate roles of journalism*

In the case of *Isara*, struggling to maintain what he believes to be "professionalism" under financial and human resources limitations, the editor has re-positioned the online news agency by focusing less on local occurrences and more on scrutinising government, state offices, and the military – their policies, spending, and actions. By doing so, the agency can optimise its existing archive and convenient access to government information without investing much in field reporting. To him, despite the news centre's minimal presence in the southern border provinces, the coverage still offers significant insights that most mainstream media rarely report. "Our position is not a local news centre, not a news centre for people in the region, and not an Islamic news centre. So, I can work on this [news orientation] even without getting paid," said the editor.[22]

This statement, from a veteran investigative journalist, summarises what news workers generally consider to be news professionalism. While welcoming the expansion of small alternative media outlets, he believes that the role of journalism is primarily reporting, investigating, and questioning political and social players. He remarked:

> [The online alternative news agencies] should become another channel to balance [news contents]. There should be a lot more [of these agencies]. But they need to be trustworthy and professional, not nonsensical. They have to have credibility, some processes, professionalism, and clear ethics – a complete set. These websites may not have a lot of viewers, but if there is diversity, people can select the information they want.[23]

Journalism as a forum for every party: *levelling the playing field*

Some news media practitioners argue that journalism should do more than simply presenting "the truth" from every angle; it should amplify often-silenced or marginalised voices. Seeing news and public forums as unequal fields of discursive contention, some journalists believe the media arena should become a level playing field for all stakeholders involved, particularly the resource-poor and those that present counter-dominant views. By doing so, every societal member will be able to convey their messages and gain access to useful information. A local news editor said that it is crucial that the general audiences comprehend the region in many aspects, so they "understand why people here need to struggle and fight, and are called 'rebels',"[24] instead of simply seeing the uprisings as violent acts. The *Thai PBS* Civil Media Network director noted:

> The duty of the media is to introduce new players, to open up the space for new groups, new issues, in hopes that there will be new players entering, and help minimise the space occupied by violence. This may reduce the number of players on the other side – the military and those who are armed.[25]

The news content analysis findings discussed in Chapter 2 and 4 illustrated how the studied news organisations did not particularly perform this role, because

Disparate roles of journalism 107

their news frames and sources primarily focused on familiar state authorities or public figures. Nonetheless, *Isara*'s source selection is discernibly different from others, as it enables local voices to emerge rather than sticking with the political bigwigs. Other mainstream news organisations and workers carry out this role differently. Some reporters and stringers file "off-the-beaten-path" stories, such as those concerning women's empowerment projects and the student's peace initiative movement, and receive a positive response from the Bangkok-based editors. A *Matichon* stringer in Pattani who also serves as an advisor to local advocacy group Deep South Watch supplies the daily paper with stories written by the group's junior reporters. Calling this the "spinning" strategy because stories are circulated among media outlets with a wider reach, he explained that the practice enables stories that are not initiated and shaped by the Bangkok newsroom, but by the locals and southern civil society sector, to emerge in national media.[26] This practice not only gives presence to alternative narratives and opinions regarding the conflict in mainstream media, but also enables local talents to gain access to national media arenas. This corresponds with Cottle's explanation of interactions among news media outlets in conflict and global crisis reporting. As global news ecology expands and diversifies, large news corporations may pick up on stories that individuals and small media operations produce, some of which may generate cross-over production, or even contra-flows against hegemonic viewpoints (Cottle 2006, p. 51; 2008, p. 18).

Meanwhile, local commercial and non-profit media focus on immediate matters and provide information necessary for current living situations. Restrained by their proximity to violence, as mentioned in Chapter 4, local media feel compelled to circumvent sensitive and controversial subjects in order to avoid clashing with opposing views in their neighbourhoods, or to evade intimidation and interference. Instead of rigorously investigating authorities, insurgent movements, or local interest groups, southern media produce content deemed useful for the residents' daily activities. A news producer at the Prince of Songkla University radio station pointed out how the continuing coverage of local incidents and its direct impact on people's daily lives, such as traffic information and incident alerts, is crucial: "The media must help build up the atmosphere of confidence, the feeling that the state mechanism really works and can solve the problem. But we will need to nudge the state as well."[27] Similarly, community radio practitioners feel the need to provide listeners with knowledge of laws and regulations that affect their lives, which helps villagers become aware of their rights. These reports may be considered elementary forms of journalism, as they neither require a sophisticated production process nor tackle dominant establishments head-on. Nonetheless, as a radio producer put it, this type of presentation helps "nudging" stakeholders and responsible authorities to become aware of the conflict's direct impact on people's lives, which could eventually give rise to discussions on structural problems and solutions to the conflict.

As for local alternative news organisations who have proximity with the region as their advantage, they become platforms for southerners to speak out to the wider public. Because small alternative news agencies' operations are

108 *Disparate roles of journalism*

facilitated by affordable media technology and platforms, producers are able to create content with minimal cost and disseminate their output via websites, online social media, and social networks. As such, despite the lack of hefty funding and the wide terrestrial footprint that most mainstream news corporations have, small local media are able to expand their audience base, interact with their supporters, and develop a network of media producers, advocates, and followers via these online channels. A community radio practitioner voiced her optimism towards advocacy group projects that enable local women to communicate through local media. "I'm glad to see women become braver to express themselves, because, previously, they didn't have a channel to communicate. Now there is the Civic Network for Women.[28] There is a forum for them to express their feelings and sufferings, to inspire them to fight and demand, to strengthen their hearts and get them through this crisis," said the local community radio producer.[29]

Notwithstanding their growing presence, the local alternative media's momentum alone may appear inadequate to push the issues further, due to their being in a stage of infancy, having a limited audience, and often being overlooked by state authorities, as mentioned in the journalists-sources relationship section. As discussed briefly in Chapter 3, according to a senior southern news editor, "Every issue ends in Bangkok." Such a remark is a clear example of the impact of a centralised administrative structure. Even with the "off-the-beaten-path" stories filed from local reporters, if the national media do not pick up the stories, it is unlikely for national-level political elite and the general public to pay attention to them. As a way to promote people's communication rights, *Thai PBS* established a mechanism that links localised media production with its national-level platforms through its civic engagement projects. Thanks to its extensive civil society and citizen reporter networks, the public service broadcaster then optimises the organisation's technical capacity and manpower to produce reports and programmes from the perspectives of locals and the many advocacy organisations based in the region. Collaborating with one another, *Thai PBS* and small non-profit media work to reach a larger audience, including policy-makers, while informing deep South residents and encouraging them to partake in deliberative resolution processes. An advisor to Deep South Watch observed:

> Two important issues that community media or 'horizontal media' together push forward are to communicate about the Patani City model and we want to use decentralisation as a solution in the region. From community radio, local radio, personal media, public forum, to various alternative media and social media, we all push for these issues. This is the role of local alternative media that is inconsistent with *TV Thai* [former name of *Thai PBS*]. So we try to explain that if every party joins hands, we can create a forum. We started this so it can empower the civic media network, and open up spaces [for them] so the state and security authorities see the collaboration among civic media can communicate in a positive way.[30]

Disparate roles of journalism 109

In all, this role enhances the voices and views of overlooked sectors and neglected minority groups, as well as presenting different, if not challenging, narratives in news coverage. By focusing on ordinary citizens and protagonists with alternative views in local political and social scenes, news media can break away from the traditional, centralised news reporting template that emphasises actions of state authorities and major business owners. As such, this kind of coverage not only shows discussion and debate on decentralisation, but also demonstrates "decentralised journalistic practice". The news practices and product stemming from this role also resemble what Fink and Schudson (2013) call "contextual reporting," a tendency of American political journalism in the latter half of the twentieth century. As they observe, this change in American newspapers allows news coverage to become "more critical of established power, [. . .] longer (and presumably deeper), [. . .] less government and electoral politics centred, [. . .] and more contextual" (Ibid., p. 3). In a way, this finding signals a slight shift in Thai journalism in that news workers, who themselves become a diverse group of people, take note of shortcomings in conventional news production culture and seek to perform differently.

Journalism as a supporter in conflict resolution: *juggling dual roles*

While journalists seemingly agree that the two roles discussed above remain within the bounds of journalistic professionalism, their opinions are markedly divided when it comes to the third role news workers perform in the southern conflict. Considering their work as media professionals insufficient to solve the conflict, a number of journalists take on or are entrusted with various tasks outside their employment, from independently producing media content to lending their expertise in governmental and private sector projects concerning conflict resolution. This subsection lays out two main roles journalists perform in the southern conflict: 1) coordinator and arbitrator and 2) advocate and political player, and the debate regarding the influences of these positions on news production.

Coordinator and arbitrator

As mentioned in Chapter 4, regarding the journalist-source relationship, journalists occasionally use their connection with high-power sources to gain trust with local people. While admitting their reluctance to explicitly advertise their association with authorities, reporters reckon that they can help expedite the assistance that these affected residents rightfully deserve. An *Isara* reporter, a local herself, pointed out: "We can use our journalist status to coordinate with state agencies to help [the locals], and this makes us widely known by the locals. Because we are reporters and it is easy to connect [with responsible state agencies]. The villagers don't know how they can contact [the agencies]."[31]

Another TV reporter said she would rather see a dispute between state officials and villagers settled before airing the report about it. Instead of ambushing the

110 *Disparate roles of journalism*

involved parties and demanding solutions on-screen, she said she would reach out to them and ask both sides to confer first and see if the problem could be resolved. Some off-screen dialogues also are involved in news making.

> People stand in their corner, like they are boxers about to fight. If it is most media, they would perform as a referee. But for me, I would rather be the coach for both sides. It is already a conflict. [. . .] When the media act like, 'Ready? Fight!', isn't that more fun? Of course. Viewers around the country would see and enjoy it, this pair [of rivals]. But for me, this is not the case. We only generate more blood, increase more vengeance. But if we act like a trainer, telling them to talk and open their minds . . . because the media are positioned in the middle. The state officials believe in us. The locals rely on us. The media are the best mediator.[32]

Nevertheless, performing as an arbitrator or coordinator could cause professional dilemmas. Being a Malay Muslim and recognised by villagers, a former *Isara* reporter was asked to contact the Malaysian television station who hired him as a fixer to report about a high-profile hostage situation in which villagers refused to grant access to Thai press. Despite being able to satisfy the residents' demand, the journalist faced concerns from another international media corporation he freelanced for about his involvement in the incident.

> [The organisation's name] was concerned and wondered what role I took there, why I had to be one of the coordinators, because this made them . . . uncomfortable. Then [the news organisation's headquarters] called me and I had to report to them in detail about what happened, why I had to get involved. [. . .] In hindsight, well, I should not have had got involved. If [the hostage takers] wanted to kill us, they would be able to do so right there. I should not have had put my life at risk.[33]

Advocate and political player

While being a coordinator and arbitrator tends to be individually based, the role of an advocate and political player is more institutionalised, and it questions the extent of the news media's involvement in the civic movement and politics as a whole. As mentioned earlier, journalists' socialisation and formal ties with their informants potentially lead news workers to view the conflict with perspectives similar to their sources and agree with their conflict resolution methods. Recognising the media's impact in distributing information and enhancing locals' communication rights, many journalists team up with civil advocates or form their own civic advocacy units using media to communicate to the public, as in the case of Deep South Watch, the Civic Women Network, and Patani Forum.

This line of work, however, prompts some of their peers to raise questions about professionalism, particularly the ideas of objectivity and impartiality. Believing that these civil society-operated media promote their own agendas, many

Disparate roles of journalism 111

journalists find that they lack objectivity; hence, they are disqualified from being professional journalists. This similar view also occurs when employees of news organisations appear to be inclined towards the civic movement. For some news workers, to endorse civil society organisations effectively means supporting interest group.

> We see that if we become an NGO, there is some hidden agenda. Some people don't like NGO. They would say this reporter is definitely not neutral. Like a security affairs reporter, they would surely be inclined towards [the military]. As for me, I gave a hard thought on the offer that [the SBPAC secretary general] invited us to use [the space at the SBPAC premises]. We really thought about it, because he said we could still report news, and for the safety in our career. But we saw that, that was us reaping benefits from him. What would happen to our news works? Definitely partial. No credibility left.[34]

This statement raises a noteworthy point. In journalists' view, civil society organisations are also considered interest groups, akin to state authorities. Therefore, being associated with an advocacy group also implies partisanship – a breach of journalistic professionalism. Interestingly, journalists' engagement in governmental or private sector projects does not receive a similar extent of debate and discussion. As mentioned earlier, some journalists consider their appointment to state administrations' working committees or charitable enterprises a proper way to contribute to problem-solving processes.

In summary, this section identifies three prominent roles journalists perform in the southern conflict, and each role receives different degrees of support and debate. For most journalists, *a presenter of truth* is considered the principal role of journalism, and the professional values of scrutinising the powers-that-be and interest groups while maintaining neutrality are essential to conflict resolution. The second role of providing *a forum for every party* emphasises the significance of information diversity, which could enhance every involved party's access and capacity to partake in the problem-solving and conflict resolution processes, while attempting to form the equilibrium of participation. The last role, *a supporter of conflict resolution*, brings about mixed reactions among news workers, as it prompts journalists to step outside what they consider the realm of news professionalism by becoming partisan. Regardless, this role raises interesting questions of whether the existing attributes and activities believed to be quality journalism do not suffice in solving this protracted and complex conflict.

Conclusion

In all, Chapter 3, 4, and 5 have delineated significant aspects of news production culture, from the volatility of violence and dynamic political and cultural settings, and the fluid and complex relationships between news workers and sources, to organisational influences such as principles, practices, and market competition.

112 *Disparate roles of journalism*

Figure 5.1 Factors influencing news production in southern conflict reporting

The contribution of these factors and the roles of journalism can be conceptualised as shown in Figure 5.1.

This chapter summarises news workers' disparate understandings of the southern conflict by laying out three emphases used by journalists to explain this complex phenomenon: security-oriented, socio-cultural, and ideology-oriented. Focusing on different dimensions of the conflict, journalists approach the problem differently, and cast different views on what they regard as appropriate roles of journalism in the southern conflict. At the same time, this dissimilarity reflects the discursive contention and power plays among news workers, showing that journalism is not always a homogenous and monolithic culture.

The second part of this chapter discusses three roles that journalists see themselves performing and consider desirable roles of journalism. News workers consider being *a presenter of truth* to be the core professional duty in order to keep the public well informed. To carry out such a role, journalists have to scrutinise and investigate the situation from every angle, while maintaining neutrality. However, seeing how the first role remains focused on political and social elites' outlooks, despite occasionally questioning them, journalists feel news media should adjust the equilibrium of public debates and enhance participatory discussions. Thus,

Disparate roles of journalism 113

second on the list is for journalism to be *a forum for every party*, which means to facilitate and encourage every stakeholder and societal faction to gain news access and partake in problem solution processes. The last role, which gives rise to debate and criticism, is to serve as *a supporter of conflict resolution*, as it requires journalists to engage in the involved stakeholders' movement. While these roles reveal the diversity and complexity in Thai journalism, they also indicate professional reflexivity at work, as journalists analyse and assess their performance in the conflict.

Notes

1 See, for example, Supara Janchidfah. 2009. บทรำพึงถึงชายแดนใต้: บันทึกใต้พรม 5 ปีไฟใต้ [Solioquy to the southern border: The hidden memoir of 5 years of southern fire]. *ฟ้าเดียวกัน [Fah Diew Kan].* January–March 2009, pp. 88–104.
2 Yala stringer. Interview. 19 February 2012.
3 Aman News Agency editor. Interview. 18 December 2011.
4 *Thai PBS* southern news centre reporter 2. Interview. 20 February 2012.
5 The term is composed of two words that offend Malay Muslims as people and as Muslims. In Thai parlance, the "*Ai*" title is considered a foul language. Although the prefix is a casual word commonly used in everyday speaking, it reflects contempt or disrespect towards the party mentioned. "*Khaek*" is an informal term used in reference to people of South Asian ethnicity and Muslims, which are not necessarily the same. Despite being widely used, the term is deemed impolite and scornful by South Asian ethnics and Muslims.
6 *Thai PBS* programme producer. Interview. 20 February 2012.
7 *Thai PBS* Civil Media Network director. Interview. 1 February 2012.
8 Patani Forum co-founder. Interview. 18 February 2012.
9 Interestingly, these Malay Muslim reporters identify themselves as "Muslim," but not "Malay Muslim". I also notice that, while the term "Malay Muslim" is prevalent in academic literature and reports from civil society and international organisations (see more discussion on the implication of this term in Chapter 1, footnote 4), it rarely appears in the Thai vernacular media.
10 *Thai PBS* assistant news director. Interview. 8 February 2012.
11 *Thai PBS* news and programmes deputy director. Interview. 22 February 2012.
12 *Isara* editor. Interview.
13 *Thai PBS* news and programmes deputy director. Interview.
14 *Thai PBS* southern news centre reporter 1. Interview. 23 December 2011.
15 *Isara* reporter 2. Interview. 19 February 2012.
16 see Appendix B for more detail of the event, or McCargo 2006 for discussion of the implications of the Tanyong Limo incident for Thai media and *Isara*.
17 The GT200, produced and distributed by UK-based companies, was advertised to be a "remote substance detector" that could discover bombs and drugs. The equipment was used in many countries' military forces, including Thailand, for explosive detection. However, a 2010 BBC Newsnight investigative report showed the device was "incapable of detecting explosives or anything else," amidst concerns that they failed to prevent casualties from bomb attacks (see more in C. Hawley and M. Jones. UK warns world about useless 'bomb detectors' [online]. *BBC Newsnight.* 27 January 2010. Available at: http://news.bbc.co.uk/2/hi/programmes/newsnight/8481774.stm [Accessed: 4 May 2015]). The *Isara* website followed up on this report by examining how the device was used by Thai military in the deep South and having scientists test the device, which proved its defectiveness. The exposé led to official investigations into the device and its procurement, and later the termination of its use.

114 *Disparate roles of journalism*

18 The shape of Thailand's map resembles that of an axe; therefore, "the Golden Axe" becomes a metaphor referring to the kingdom. Following that notion, the segment's title refers to the southern border provinces as "the end of axe handle".

19 The three "*TV Phumipak* [Regional TV]" shows stopped broadcasting in January 2015, as *Thai PBS* announced its plan to revamp the programmes. The organisation stated that the shows will be back on-air in early 2016.

20 According to a manager in charge of the news department's strategic planning, the "chief editor" position was established to oversee the production of every news bulletin during the entire day. Senior news editors are appointed and take turns to perform this role. Focusing on the station's overall news presentation, chief editors are expected to project news trends and come up with angles that would differentiate the station's coverage from others'.

21 *Thai PBS*'s unpublished internal document.

22 *Isara* editor. Interview.

23 Isara Institute director. Interview. 8 December 2011.

24 Aman News Agency editor. Interview.

25 *Thai PBS* Civil Media Network director. Interview.

26 Deep South Watch advisor 2. Interview. 20 December 2011.

27 Prince of Songkla University radio producer. Interview. 17 December 2011.

28 Currently named "The Network of Civic Women for Peace," this civil society organisation has been advocating women's rights and women empowerment in the three southern border provinces. Their projects include providing communication skills training and media channels for women affected by the conflict and facilitating women's participation in conflict resolution processes. For more detail, see their website at http://civicwomen.com/.

29 Pattani civic community radio practitioner. Interview. 17 February 2012.

30 Deep South Watch advisor. Interview. 20 December 2011.

31 *Isara* reporter 1. Interview. 19 February 2012.

32 *Thai PBS* southern news centre reporter 1. Interview. 23 December 2011.

33 Aman News Agency editor. Interview.

34 *Isara* reporter 2. Interview.

References

Cottle, Simon. 2006. *Mediatized Conflict*. Maidenhead: Open University Press.

Cottle, Simon. 2008. *Global Crisis Reporting: Journalism in the Global Age*. Issues in Cultural and Media Studies. Maidenhead: Open University Press.

Fink, Katherine and Schudson, Michael. 2013. The rise of contextual journalism [pdf], 1950s–2000s. *Journalism* 0(0), pp. 1–18. Available at: http://jou.sagepub.com/content/early/2013/02/14/1464884913479015 [Accessed: 20 May 2015]

Iskandar, Adel and El-Nawawy, Mohammed. 2004. Al-Jazeera and War Coverage in Iraq: The Media's Quest for Contextual Objectivity. In: Allan, S. and Zelizer, B. eds. *Reporting War: Journalism in Wartime*. Oxon: Routledge, pp. 315–332.

McCargo, Duncan. 2006. Communicating Thailand's southern conflict. *The Journal of International Communication* 12(2), pp. 19–34.

McCargo, Duncan. 2012. *Mapping National Anxieties: Thailand's Southern Conflict*. Copenhagen: NIAS Press.

Samuel-Azran, Tal. 2010. *Al-Jazeera and US War Coverage*. New York: Peter Lang.

Supapohn Kanwerayotin. 2006. *Peace Journalism in Thailand: A Case Study of Issara News Centre of the Thai Journalists Association*. MA Thesis, Chulalongkorn University.

Thai Public Broadcasting Service. 2009. *Thai Public Broadcasting Service (TPBS)*. Bangkok: Thai Public Broadcasting Service.

Witchayawanee Choonui. 2009. บทบาทของโต๊ะข่าวภาคใต้ สถาบันอิศรากับการเป็นสื่อเพื่อสันติภาพ กรณี เหตุการณ์ความไม่สงบในสามจังหวัดชายแดนภาคใต้ *[The Role of the Southern News Desk, Issara Institute as Peace Journalism: In the Case of Insurgency in the Three Southernmost Provinces]*. MA Thesis, Chulalongkorn University.

6 Conclusion

"How will this conflict be resolved?" Many continue to raise this question, which has been asked ever since the re-emergence of violence in Thailand's southern border provinces over a decade ago. The responses to the above question have become varied throughout the past ten years; nevertheless, the answers to what causes this conflict remain discernibly less prevalent, yet limited and repetitive, in public discussions. Evidence supporting this observation can be found in Chapter 2 of this book, which illustrates the minimal presence and declining trend in news coverage when it comes to the conflict's causal explanations. At the same time, the debates on unjust treatment and prosecution, ethnic marginalisation, and self-determination are often undermined by violence and counter-insurgency strategies, with state authorities being the "primary definers" who shape public debate. Journalists' disparate understandings, described in Chapter 5, also signal how, right up to the present time, news workers' opinions are divided on the southern conflict's roots and ramifications; hence, their various interpretations of desirable roles of journalism in this conflict.

While examining news output and production practices to identify the roles that Thai journalism plays in this civil conflict, the study also finds that news operations do not take place in a political and socio-cultural vacuum. The conflict's hostility, journalists' association with their sources, and the directions of public debate and discussion concerning the conflict – particularly among political and social elites – largely shape journalists' understandings of the problem and their professional performance. Concurrently, the volatility of Thailand's politics and media market demands also determines the salience and frequency of the southern conflict in news coverage. All in all, this study shows the multifaceted factors influencing the Thai news production culture, and that these elements should be considered when examining the relationship between journalism and political conflict.

Highlighting crime and conspiracy: the news representation of the southern conflict

Before exploring how the southern conflict is represented in news coverage, the study identifies three prominent discourses concerning the conflict in the southernmost provinces: *crime and conspiracy*, *minority's grievance*, and *Malay*

Conclusion 117

nationalism and Islamism. Approaching this conflict from different analytical grounds, these discourses interpret its causes dissimilarly, emphasise different aspects of the problem, and, thus, prescribe different remedies for the conflict. These contending discourses are played out in news reports, but their frequency and salience are unequal.

Chapter 2 shows that the news coverage during the first seven years of the conflict tended to support the *crime and conspiracy* discourse by highlighting the violent aspect of the conflict and the preservation of public order. Concurrently, the news reports had a tendency to present a variety of solutions to the problem without further investigating the complex contributing factors and their impact on involved parties. Additionally, the depiction of state officials as heroic and protective and the portrayal of the affected locals as vulnerable and powerless also endorsed the state's status as the rescuer and supported the legitimacy of its actions. Such emphases in news coverage eclipsed the influence of the *minority's grievance* and *Malay nationalism and Islamism* discourses, because the reports rarely teased out the underpinning historical, political, socio-cultural, and ideological contexts of this conflict that these two discourses propose.

The examination of labels used to describe this conflict and the insurgents produces results that are in line with the authorities' characterisations of the events and the perpetrators. By labelling the conflict with the metaphorical "southern fire," or more broadly, "southern problem," the news media downplay the nuances of political and cultural struggle in this conflict, casting the situation as mere violence and disruption of public order. In similar vein, the use of labels with criminological undertones for insurgents, and the at times inflammatory and dehumanising descriptions, should not be taken for granted. While the criminological terms such as "bandit" seem socially prevailing and journalistically practical, as they fit with, for example, the limited headline space, these expressions effectively connote that the perpetrators' actions are unlawful and unacceptable. Together with the minimal presence of insurgents' voices in the news coverage, the conflict is reported principally in terms of regional unrest committed by clandestine militia with equivocal and impractical goals and demands. On the other hand, the state, particularly the military, is deemed the party solely for solving this problem. Such representations also keep the conflict at a distance from the general public, as the problem seems restricted to the southernmost region and does not present significant geo-political interest to the majority population.

As one veteran journalist put it, the use of criminological labels not only reflects the Thai authorities' ambiguous stances towards the insurgent groups, particularly the idea of having dialogue with them, but also signals how news workers regard the insurgents. Apart from being described as obscure and aimless, perpetrators are generally cast as despicable criminals. Therefore, it would be objectionable for the state to officially and publicly negotiate with the lawbreakers, similar to government's typical adversarial stance on terrorism (Walzer 1992 cited in Nossek 2007, p. 271). Before 2013, the minimal coverage of talks between Thai authorities and insurgent leaders, mostly long after the events took

118   *Conclusion*

place, was partly because the meetings were often done behind closed doors, and perhaps because of changes in the Thai administration and its mixed stances on these talks (Liow and Pathan 2010; Pathan 2012, pp. 4–6). At the same time, the clandestine and complex structure of the insurgent movement, a "liminal lattice" as described by McCargo (2008, p. 181), also makes organising dialogue with them difficult (Melvin 2007; Liow and Pathan 2010). Nonetheless, by characterising the assailants as ruthless and obscure criminals, news reports undermine other explanations of the backgrounds and motives of these insurgents. Additionally, the coverage tends to emphasise the security- and law enforcement-oriented solutions, while downplaying other means, such as peace dialogue, political reform, and public participation in peaceful conflict resolution.

The diversity of the Thai news ecology does little to make discursive contention fair and balanced. Despite the differences in their organisational and journalistic natures, the four news organisations in this study report the southern conflict in broadly similar ways. The analysis of the coverage's trajectories shows the news media's waning interest in the conflict, because the situation is considered repetitive. Nonetheless, as discussed in Chapter 2, there are a few discrepancies in their interpretations of the conflicts' causes and solutions, which enables underreported discourses to secure at least some public presentation. The subtle dynamic and diversity of news frames also indicate that journalists have dissimilar views on the conflict.

While the news content is seemingly homogenous, the analysis shows the subtle fluidity and discursive shifts of news coverage, resulting in part from the changes in political debate – one of the factors shaping political news. Coverage of the southern conflict tends to follow elitist political players' outlooks on the conflict, which, in this case, vary very little, yet remain predominant during the seven-year review period. The most frequently used frames involve aggressive actions, while some frames emerge only when political opportunities strike. For instance, the frequency of the *reconciliation and local identity* solutions frame became prominent when the National Reconciliation Commission was active in 2006, but subsided after the agency was dissolved. The discussion on autonomy and special administrative models did not emerge until 2007, when policy-makers started proposing, debating, and even discrediting the ideas. These examples also indicate how news reports would mirror the political elites' consensus and disagreements on the subject. Similar to the discussion concerning Hallin's *spheres of consensus, legitimate controversy and deviance* (1989, pp. 116–118) in Chapter 2, *Malay nationalism and Islamism* was considered within the *sphere of deviance*, hence receiving little media attention in the beginning of the conflict. Dealing with oft-marginalised and unconventional concepts such as Malay Muslim identity, Islam, separatist movements, and autonomy, the discourse initially had been undermined by political elites and in public arenas, as it challenges deep-seated beliefs in Thai society, particularly the notion of "nation, religion, king" that presents Thailand as a unitary state (McCargo 2012, pp. 123–124). Much later, when academic and civil society sectors had

Conclusion 119

continued to stimulate discussions and debates on the subjects, and political elites started to have divided views on these issues, the discourse moved into the *sphere of legitimate controversy*, where news media further explored these ideas and possibilities.

Having said this, the study does not suggest that the news coverage is all simply pro-state authority. A number of reports are framed in ways that scrutinise and criticise the government and state agencies for their inefficiency and failed attempts in pacifying the conflict. A handful of reports raise questions about mistreatment that the southern residents and suspected insurgents receive, and touch upon "terrorism from above" issues such as the repercussions of the Kru-Ze Mosque attack and the Tak Bai demonstration clampdown – testaments to state authorities' excessive uses of force. Nonetheless, such scrutiny and criticism are mostly crime- and security-oriented, and grounded in existing political and socio-cultural structures. This approach is more in line with the *crime and conspiracy* discourse than the *minority's grievance* and *Malay nationalism and Islamism* discourses, which challenge the dominant political establishments and hegemonic beliefs in Thai society. Therefore, the state's authority and legitimacy remain intact despite being critiqued.

It should be noted once again, as discussed in Chapter 1, that because these three discourses are socially available and among the most prominent interpretations of the southern conflict, they are used in this study to examine how news workers make sense of the conflict and how these understandings are played out in news outputs. Still, these discourses may not provide sufficient analysis of this complex and dynamic phenomenon. Thus, while this limitation reflects the intricate discursive contention in this conflict, it also indicates the inconsistency of Thai journalism, which does not enable news workers, stakeholders, and the general public fully to comprehend the various explanations concerning the southern conflict as the problem continues.

Overall, the examination of news content demonstrates deficiencies in news coverage that could hinder healthy and participatory debate about this complex and discursively contentious conflict. Nevertheless, the study does not imply that the news media deliberately promote or avoid reporting about certain aspects of the conflict. It would be premature simply to conclude that journalists purposely serve as any stakeholders' propaganda vehicle. As stated above, the dynamic, or at times static, political settings largely contribute to the coverage's frequency and emphases. Moreover, as the sociology of journalism framework suggests, news production practices are contoured by disparate forces from different levels. Therefore, it could be argued that the production of southern conflict news is also shaped by the interplay with sources, the conflict's volatile nature, and professional conventions. Furthermore, despite the seemingly homogenous news content, the study finds that news workers have diverse views about the conflict and the desirable roles of journalism in this problematic situation. This finding signals the complexity and power struggle within the Thai news ecology, which will be discussed in detail shortly.

120   *Conclusion*

Fostering the reciprocal journalist-source relationship: news access and southern conflict reporting

As shown in Chapter 4, the most attributed sources in the southern conflict coverage are members of the government, police and military forces, and politicians. In similar vein, sources with expertise in law enforcement and crime investigation, security, and national policies are also cited more than others. These findings correspond with the most-reported theme – security and public order. They also reflect the news media's known disposition towards authority figures, who are generally resourced more richly than other stakeholders in this conflict. Having louder voices than other parties, these authorities and political elite sources essentially become the "primary definers" of the southern conflict.

In line with the argument regarding the preferred theme and news frames, the frequent appearance of authorities and elite sources does not, however, always mean that journalists deliberately perform as these sources' propaganda tool. Journalists' favour to certain groups of sources could also result from the proximity and accessibility of these sources, the bonds that reporters and their informants forge during the newsgathering process, or the organisations' principles and news directions.

The analysis of journalist-source relationship is taken into account to explain the complexity of news access. Chapter 4 identified three steps of the relationship-forming process: 1) initiating contact, 2) building trust, and 3) being the insiders. In each step, reporters and news organisations do not receive the same treatment from various groups of sources. News workers need to demonstrate their ability to negotiate power and provide mutual exchanges with their sources, so that they can earn the source's information and trust. Therefore, the journalist-source relationship in the southern conflict can be described as symbiotic and reciprocal rather than confrontational.

Similar to Tuchman (1972)'s argument that journalists display professional objectivity through source attribution in their reports, this study suggests that news organisations' and journalists' diverse source pool is not only an occupational necessity to garner multi-perspectival information that contributes to impartial and objective news content, but also a proof of their non-partisanship. With a wide array of sources on their contact list, journalists can use this source variety as leverage to assert their credibility and earn access to other sources. Nevertheless, for senior reporters who have been rooted in one beat for a long time, the sources and their specialisation become more issue-specific. This concise, although exclusive, list could result in the news workers' insular and single-approach perspectives on the conflict.

The hostile nature of the conflict also affects journalists' relationship with and dependence on sources. As discussed in Chapter 3, one reason why the authorities' accounts are cited most frequently in news reports is that local reporters tend to rely on the notifications and investigation summaries released by relevant state agencies in order to minimise the risks of entering a perilous zone.

Conclusion 121

In similar vein, the frequent tribute-style reports about the devotion and sacrifice of soldiers, teachers, police officers, and medical staff based in the southern border provinces are produced, in part, from the shared experiences of working in the volatile area, as well as the socially prevailing outlooks on these occupations. Meanwhile, the minimal presence of insurgents and perpetrators, or counter-state explanations, is due to the inaccessibility of these active insurgents or promises of confidentiality to protect the safety of these sources, as well as journalists themselves.

The study also shows that being associated with larger news corporations facilitates access to elite sources, leading to the news media's tendency to adopt what Schlesinger, Murdock, and Elliott call the *official perspective* (1983, p. 2) and minimise opportunities for *alternative*, or even *oppositional perspectives,* (Ibid., pp. 16–17, 28–31) to emerge. As a result, proponents of these perspectives need to generate events to galvanise support or seek other channels to publicise their causes. Meanwhile, to make up for the lack of high-powered sources, smaller alternative media producers team up with advocacy groups, who often provide them with underreported information and analyses. This type of partnership, including the public service broadcaster's collaboration with civic media producers, opens up "the front gate coverage" (Wolfsfeld 1997, p. 42) for sources who generally do not appear in mainstream media reports, enabling them to express their counter-hegemonic views. Regardless, some news workers consider civil society organisations another vested interest group in the conflict, and question whether the partnership would bring about partisanship rather than balance.

Therefore, this study argues that the complexity of journalist-source relationship in the southern conflict largely influences how the problem is reported. The findings present reasons behind the prevalence of authority and elite sources in news content, from professional conventions and human relations in the conflict situation, to the predominant views of certain social factions in the newsroom and society in general. The study proposes that the investigation into news content and journalistic customs is integral to the study of journalism and political conflict. Nonetheless, political conflict reporting cannot be analysed using the media-centric approach alone, because the interactions between news workers and political players also prove to shape how the southern conflict is portrayed.

Struggling to counter the mainstream: news production practices in southern conflict reporting

As shown in Chapter 2, the portrayal of the southern conflict in the news coverage varies slightly among the studied four news organisations. Despite their different scales of operation, organisational structures, and journalistic principles, the studied media outlets employ similar editorial and production systems, which they believe to be the foundation of professional journalism. News workers regard the ideas of neutrality and objectivity, as well as the editorial process, as the core of

122 Conclusion

news professionalism. Thus, they tend to use these qualifications as the benchmark to reflect on their performance, as well as evaluating that of their peers and other social players who produce media. However, the views on professional values and practices are neither universal nor static.[1] Also, as elaborated in Chapter 5, Thai journalists also express disparate opinions about the southern conflict and their roles in the situation. Notwithstanding the similar news output, news workers' disparate and dynamic perspectives about the conflict and their professional obligations illustrate the diversity in news production culture. This variation also suggests that there are some contestation and power struggles involved in news production culture (Dickinson 2007, p. 193), although in the end, hegemonic news content generally prevails.

Chapter 3 discussed news practices and identified various difficulties in southern conflict reporting at different levels. In line with Reese's *hierarchy-of-influences* model (2001), journalists' personal backgrounds, such as religion, upbringing, and belief are at work, particularly when it comes to subjects that are closer to home or challenge their views. Meanwhile, the news beat and news prioritisation systems are largely geo-political, rather than subject-oriented, as the stories from the southernmost provinces are primarily delegated to the regional news desk. These stories are simply reported as repetitive violent incidents. The matters will be investigated or analysed further with inter-departmental collaboration only when they have massive or widespread impact: generating a lot of casualties, causing controversy, being initiated by high-profile protagonists, or being associated with national security at large.

The conflict's hostility also creates an intimidating and life-threatening working environment that deters journalists from searching for counter-hegemonic accounts. Concurrently, the country's volatile political settings and security-oriented policy also lead to information deficit, media manipulation, and media censorship.[2] Such circumstances cast a chilling effect on small media producers, making them resort to self-censorship, as shown in Chapter 3 of this book. Under these conditions, the state's preferred discourse is persistently kept in the dominant position.

Lastly, Chapter 3 identified the *Bangkok-centric mindset*, referring to the centralised administration and archetypal perspectives prevalent in news organisations and political institutions, as a crucial obstacle in southern conflict reporting. Rather than being a mere psychological framework that works on individual level, the *Bangkok-centric mindset* is the overarching paradigm that governs news operation. The term also reflects the hegemonic perspectives in Thai society, such as the general support for the devoted civil servants in the restive region and the ideas of the Thai nation-state constructs. The histories of the southern border region, certain explanations about the conflict, and some proposed solutions, do not resonate with the predominant beliefs and legitimacy of influential establishments in Thai society.[3] Thus, for news media to present the counter-hegemonic views could be considered partisan and unprofessional, even unpatriotic, in the eyes of the authorities, advertisers, news sources, and audience.

Having laid out the conditions and constraints that shape the news production practices, as summarised in Figure 6.1, three roles of Thai journalism in the

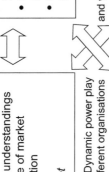

Figure 6.1 The Thai news production culture and the roles of journalism in the southern conflict

124 *Conclusion*

southern conflict were explicated in Chapter 5. These roles are: 1) *journalism as a presenter of truth*: investigating and maintaining neutrality, 2) *journalism as a forum for every party*: levelling the playing field, and 3) *journalism as a supporter in conflict resolution*: juggling dual roles. Journalists seemingly agree that the first role is within the bound of news professionalism, perhaps the core of conflict reporting. The second and third roles, however, prompt debates about professional identity and ideology, as journalists seem to step out of their domain and engage with other political players in the conflict, be it the powerful establishments or those with *alternative* or *oppositional perspectives*. At the same time, these roles indicate that journalism is "an element of politics," as Schudson proposes (2003, p. 166); therefore, complete detachment from political and social institutions would be impossible. Contrary to McCargo's observation on politics reporting – that reporters, especially junior ones, are "double outsiders" who hold a marginal status in the news organisations and the institutions they are assigned to (2000, p. 45) – this study argues whether it is possible for journalists in the southern conflict to be the "double insiders" who attempt to belong to both worlds in order to facilitate conflict resolution.

Lastly, this study argues that, although these conditions and constraints contribute to the production of less than desirable news content, disparate journalistic principles and practices could potentially bring about diversity and constructive changes in the Thai news ecology, in line with the complex contemporary "media sphere" in global conflict meditaziation that Cottle proposes (2006a, p. 51; 2008, p. 18), as conceptualised in Figure 6.2. *Thai PBS*'s collaborative projects with local media makers and civic movements move towards a "decentralised journalism practice," similar to Wolfsfeld's idea of *shared media* (2004, p. 230), which enables underreported content and underrepresented societal sectors to reach a larger audience. Concurrently, the introduction and experiment on peace journalism (Supapohn 2006; Walakka-mol 2007; Witchayawanee 2009), as well as the burgeoning alternative and civic media operation and the active civil society sector in the southern border provinces (Don 2012; Muhammad Ayup, Kasama, Ramadan, and Fareeda 2012; Samatcha and Rungrawee 2014), suggest that news workers sometimes reflect on their performance, leading to more discussion and debate about conflict reporting and the desirable roles of journalism in this volatile political situation, as discussed earlier. In addition, some forms of "thick" journalism (Cottle 2005, 2006b), such as *Thai PBS*'s short documentary and feature programmes, as well as citizen media content, *Isara*'s interpretative and investigative reports on security policy and expenditure, and the subtle display of *media reflexivity* (Cottle 2005, p. 119–120) through online social network and public discussion forums, can enable underrepresented protagonists and their discourses to emerge. Despite the optimistic outlook, these movements have yet to generate a strong momentum in the Thai news ecology and the public domain, or the "contra-flows" of information, as the predominant discourses and political structures remain unwavering.

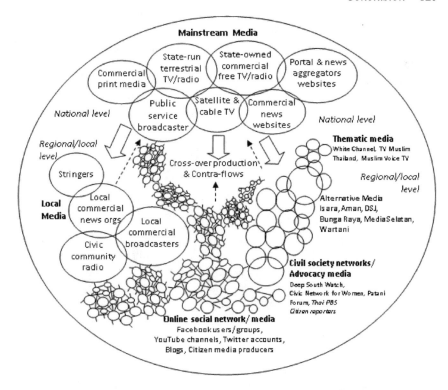

Figure 6.2 The diversity and complexity of news ecology in southern conflict reporting

Future research avenues in news media and the southern conflict

While this book's aim is to map out the complexity of Thai news ecology in southern conflict reporting, it may not provide an analysis extensive enough to keep up with the dynamic changes in the conflict and Thai politics, as well as the fast expansion of the Thai media landscape.[4] Moreover, with its focus on the vernacular media, this book may overlook the roles of those producing news and programmes in other languages, such as English, Patani Malay, and Malay. The English-language dailies target elite readers who have a considerable degree of English proficiency,[5] as well as a global audience and foreign press agencies. Meanwhile, the increasing number of locally produced Patani Malay/Malay-language programmes and the launch of the state-run Malay-speaking satellite television channel[6] signal how the local vernacular, previously considered "the language of rebels," is now recognised as a significant tool to communicate with Malay Muslim residents in the southernmost provinces and neighbouring Malaysia. The analysis of their roles in the conflict may offer noteworthy findings in the studies of news media and political conflict/violence.

126 *Conclusion*

The study of alternative, community, and advocacy media which focus on the southern conflict, southern residents, and Muslim communities can elaborate on the roles of these non-mainstream outlets in conflict mediatization (see Appendix E for examples of civil society organisations and non-profit media whose works deal primarily with the southern conflict). This book touches upon this subject briefly, but does not provide the analysis of their news content to fully support the argument. Although *Isara* is considered a non-profit media outlet, it was established and is operated by institutionalised journalists who may carry sets of practices similar to those in national-level mainstream organisations. The interviews with local alternative and advocacy media operators suggest that these producers aim to challenge conventional practices and narratives. Therefore, a full examination into their operation or comparative research of mainstream and alternative media, similar to Samatcha and Rungrawee's study of media discourse in the 2013 peace talks coverage (2014), may offer noteworthy insights, and determine whether they in fact present the counter-hegemonic perspectives and become the "contra-flows" of information in southern conflict mediatization. In similar vein, the production models pioneered by the public service broadcaster *Thai PBS*, which initiate the collaboration between institutionalised journalists and the civil sector, are worth exploring because they facilitate media access to the grassroots and endorse their legitimacy in a news production process previously reserved for "the professionals". For journalism studies scholars, it will be interesting to see how these models negotiate the boundary between news professionalism and civic engagement.

Another interesting research avenue is to explore other forms of "thick" journalism that showcase marginalised views and indicate professional reflexivity. These include television feature and discussion programmes, documentary films, magazine feature articles, and thematic publications that report the southern conflict at length. Some senior journalists write articles and books about the insurgency and its impact on the southerners based on in-depth research. Additionally, reporters who worked or are currently in the restive region have recounted their experiences and obstacles in pocket books, articles, discussion programmes, and public seminars. These programmes and publications are worth exploring in order to reveal the diversity of, and debate about, news professionalism (see Appendix F for the list of selected publications on the southern conflict written and contributed by Thai journalists).

The study of the southern conflict coverage produced by international press agencies and news outlets can also offer interesting outlooks, given the southern conflict's Malay Muslim minority and religious nuances. Therefore, investigation into foreign news organisations' reports on the subject could help explain how this conflict is communicated in the global forum, and stimulate academic discussions in the field of international journalism and political conflict mediatization.

Conclusion

This book demonstrates that there are deficiencies in journalistic content and practices that hinder news media from serving as an arena for healthy and rational democratic debate on the discursive-contentious political conflict, where

Conclusion 127

stakeholders can equally speak their minds without being curtailed. The findings indicate that the constraints of news production practices cause limitations, such as in the relatively closed presentation forms that barely allow journalists to contextualise the conflict, the competition among news media to be first and exclusive so news workers are unable to invest more time and resources to explore complex issues, and the newsroom's structural arrangement, which prioritises national-level occurrences and favours the political and social elite over ordinary people's voices. By the same token, the book highlights how the conflict's violent nature and contention among vested interest groups lead to journalists facing intimidation as well as being manipulated by misinformation or lack of information. At the same time, the notion of Thailand as a unitary state – central governance with the majority Buddhist population under constitutional monarchy – becomes a cultural and conceptual framework under which news organisations operate. Thus, matters concerning the conflict that do not fall into this dominant narrative are cast aside, unless they are debated among influential public figures. As such, the study argues the political climate and socio-cultural conditions in which journalists operate also shape news practices and contribute to these shortcomings.

Considering the news media as a part of politics, the study further points out that, rather than being a powerful proponent of predominant discourses, or a propaganda vehicle for any protagonists, news media are, in fact, a crucial facilitator of public discussion about the conflict, and not simply a passive mediator. Shaped by professional ideology and association with other political players in one way or another, news workers are not a homogenous group; they form disparate understandings of the conflict and their desirable roles in alleviating the problem. These outlooks and practices are carried out through various forms of news outputs and practices, as well as journalists' diverse interplay with stakeholders in the conflict and the general public. This variation shows that journalists "mediatize" the conflict differently; they do not simply report or "mediate" the conflict, but intentionally or indirectly become engaged in the phenomenon.

Even though the inadequacies in Thai journalism help amplify hegemonic discourses and keep them in the dominant position, the study argues that journalists' disparate stances, the subtle discursive shifts manifested in the news coverage, and the prevalence of alternative news outlets signal that Thai journalism is not always monolithic and static. Such indications suggest that the diversity and complexity in news ecology, as well as the exercise of debates and reflexivity in order to rethink the notion of "professionalism," can provide opportunities for marginalised voices to surface, insofar as these underreported sectors can offer journalists certain reciprocity, such as worthy information and connection. Nonetheless, the diversity and complexity in news ecology may yet contribute to fairer and more balanced forums that can generate healthier democratic debates. Being part of politics, the conflict "mediatization" of Thai news media largely depends on political and socio-cultural conditions. These settings will need to be conducive to generating such debates, so that mainstream organisations are not to repeat the forms of reporting and elite deference, as illustrated in this study, and small

128 *Conclusion*

media operations are equipped to become an influential source of information and a stimulating discussion arena.

Notes

1 See, for example, Iskandar and El-Nawawy 2004; Ryfe 2009; Waisbord 2013.
2 After the 2014 military coup that deposed the Yingluck Shinawatra administration, the National Council of Peace and Order issued an announcement to suspend the operation of "unlicensed" community radio broadcasters and satellite television broadcasters due to their political content. At that time, the licensing process of civic community radio and local commercial radio stations, many of which did not produce political content, was delayed by the broadcasting regulator. While the number of closed stations was not reported, civil right advocacy group iLaw noted that there were around 7,000 stations operating before the coup, and some 5,300 submitted permission to re-open. There were also reports that law enforcement and security officers seized equipment from several stations. Later, around 3,000 stations were allowed to re-open after they signed an agreement not to present content deemed contradictory to the NCPO's announcements. In the southernmost provinces, the operation of community radio was also suspended, while alternative media producers were monitored. Under this circumstance, critics expressed concerns that southerners no longer had public arenas for discussions of peace and self-determination. For more detail, see *iLaw*. 2014 Situation Summary Report 5/5: Self-censorship, restricted access to online media, and the shutdown of community radio before and after the coup [online]. 22 April 2015. Available at: http://freedom. ilaw.or.th/en/blog/2014-situation-summary-report-55-self-censorship-restricted-access-online-media-and-shutdown-co [Accessed: 22 May 2015]; and *iLaw*. 364 days after the coup: Reporter on situation of freedom of expression in Thailand [online]. 20 May 2015. Available at: http://freedom.ilaw.or.th/en/blog/364-days-after-coup-report-situation-freedom-expression-thailand [Accessed: 22 May 2015].
3 See, for example, Thanet 2007; Chaiwat 2007, 2008; McCargo 2008, 2012.
4 In 2014, there were 80 national-level newspapers, 257 provincial newspapers, 524 state-owned radio stations, nearly 7,000 civic and commercial community radio stations, 250 satellite television channels, two national-level cable subscription television channels, and more than 900 provincial cable subscription television channels in Thailand. In addition, the country's broadcast and telecom regulator recently auctioned licenses to various media producers to operate 24 digital terrestrial television channels. The number of Internet and social media users in the country is also skyrocketing. Out 66 million, there are 25 million Internet users, 18 million social media users, and more than 20 million accounts on the mobile chat application LINE. See, for example, Friedrich Ebert Stiftung. *Asian Media Barometer: Thailand 2014*. forthcoming).
5 Thailand's official and working language is Thai. English is not formally stated as a second language, although the subject is included in the compulsory education curriculum and regarded as one of the necessary qualifications in job recruitment. Nonetheless, English-language proficiency among the native population is considered rudimentary. According to the UK-based EF English Proficiency Index (EF EPI) which surveys and assesses the average adult English skill level in 54 countries worldwide, Thailand was in the "very low proficiency" category in 2012.
6 In January 2013, the Southern Border Provinces Administrative Centre (SBPAC) announced the launch of a Malay-language satellite television channel catering to the southern residents and the general public. Starting from the daily broadcast of 30 minutes a day at 8 to 8.30 p.m., the channel will be on-air 24 hours by the end of 2013. Additionally, the state agency runs a 24-hour radio channel, which also presents programmes produced by local producers. Prior to the launch of the new enterprise,

Conclusion   129

two state-run, free-to-air terrestrial TV stations already broadcast Malay language programmes for three hours a day, but the programmes are not widely received in the southernmost region.

References

Chaiwat Satha-Anand. 2007. The Silence of the Bullet Monument': Violence and "Truth" Management, Dusun-nyor 1948, and Kru-Ze 2004. In: McCargo, D. ed. *Rethinking Thailand's Southern Violence*. Singapore: NUS Press, pp. 11–34.

Chaiwat Satha-Anand. 2008. *ความรุนแรงกับการจัดการ "ความจริง": ปัตตานีในรอบกึ่งทศวรรษ [Violence and "Truth" Management: Pattani in Half-Century]*. Bangkok: Thammasart University Press.

Cottle, Simon. 2005. In Defence of 'Thick' Journalism; or How Television Journalism Can be Good for Us. In: Allan, S. ed. *Journalism: Critical Issues*. Berkshire: Open University Press, pp. 109–124.

Cottle, Simon. 2006a. Mediatized Conflict. Maidenhead: Open University Press.

Cottle, Simon. 2006b. Mediatizing the Global War on Terror: Television's Public Eye. In: Kavoori, A. and Fraley, T. eds. *Media, Terrorism, and Theory: A Reader*. Oxford: Rowman & Littlefield Publishers, pp. 19–48.

Cottle, Simon. 2008. *Global Crisis Reporting: Journalism in the Global Age*. Issues in Cultural and Media Studies. Maidenhead: Open University Press.

Dickinson, Roger. 2007. Accomplishing journalism: Towards a revived sociology of a media occupation. *Cultural Sociology* 1(2), pp. 189–208.

Don Pathan. 2012. *Conflict Management and Resolution in Asia: The Role of Civil Societies in Thailand's Deep South* [online]. *Paper Presented at the 25th Asia-Pacific Roundtable program* on October 2012 at The Asia Foundation, Kuala Lumpur. Available at: http://asiafoundation.org /publications/pdf/1148 [Accessed: 29 January 2013].

Hallin, Daniel. 1989. *The "Uncensored War": The Media and Vietnam*. London: University of California Press.

Liow, Joseph C. and Don Pathan. 2010. *Confronting Ghosts*. New South Wales: Longueville Media.

McCargo, Duncan. 2000. *Politics and the Press in Thailand: Media Machinations*. London: Routledge.

McCargo, Duncan. 2008. *Tearing Apart the Land: Islam and Legitimacy in Southern Thailand*. Ithaca, New York: Cornell University Press.

McCargo, Duncan. 2012. *Mapping National Anxieties: Thailand's Southern Conflict*. Copenhagen: NIAS Press.

Melvin, Neil J. 2007. *Conflict in Southern Thailand: Islamism, Violence and the State in the Patani Insurgency* [online]. Stockholm: Stockholm International Peace Research Institute. Available at: http://books.sipri.org/files/PP/SIPRIPP20.pdf [Accessed: 29 January 2013].

Muhammad Ayup Pathan, Kasama Jitpiromsri, Ramadan Panjor, and Fareeda Kajadmarn. 2012. ประชาสังคมกับกระบวนการสันติภาพ (ตอน 4): พลวัต บทบาท และศักยภาพของ CSOs ชายแดนใต้ [Civil society and peace process (Part 4): Dynamics, roles, and potentials of CSOs in the southern border] [online]. *Deep South Watch*. Available at: www.deepsouthwatch.org/node/3479 [Accessed: 29 January 2013].

Nossek, Hillel. 2007. Terrorism and the Media: Does the Weapon Matter to the Coverage. In: Nossek, H., Sreberny, A., and Sonwalkar, P. eds. *Media and Political Violence*. Cresskill, NJ: Hampton Press, pp. 269–303.

130   Conclusion

Reese, Stephen D. 2001. Understanding the global journalist: A hierarchy-of-influences approach. *Journalism Studies* 2(2), pp. 173–187.

Samatcha Nilaphatama and Rungrawee Chalermsripinyorat. 2014. วาทกรรมสื่อมวลชนในกระบวนการสันติภาพสามจังหวัดชายแดนภาคใต้ 2556 [Media discourse on peace process in Southern Thailand 2013] [online]. *Media Inside Out Group.* Available at: www.deepsouthwatch.org/sites/default/files/peaceprocessdiscourse_samatcha_rungrawee.pdf [Accessed: 20 May 2015].

Schlesinger, Philip, Murdock, Graham, and Elliott, Philip. 1983. *Televising 'Terrorism': Political Violence in Popular Culture.* London: Comedia Publishing Group.

Schudson, Michael. 2003. *The Sociology of News.* New York: W.W. Norton.

Supapohn Kanwerayotin. 2006. *Peace Journalism in Thailand: A Case Study of Issara News Centre of the Thai Journalists Association.* MA Thesis, Chulalongkorn University.

Thanet Aphornsuvan. 2007. *Rebellion in Southern Thailand: Contending Histories.* Washington, D.C.: East-West Center Washington.

Tuchman, Gaye. 1972. Objectivity as strategic ritual: An examination of newsmen's notions of objectivity. *The American Journal of Sociology* 77(4), pp. 660–679.

Walakkamol Changkamol. 2007. สื่อสันติภาพ: จริยธรรม การจัดการ และข้อเสนอแนะเพื่อการพัฒนา *[Peace Journalism: Ethics, Management and Suggestions for Development].* Pattani: Prince of Songkhla University, Pattani campus.

Witchayawanee Choonui. 2009. บทบาทของโต๊ะข่าวภาคใต้ สถาบันอิศรากับการเป็นสื่อเพื่อสันติภาพ กรณีเหตุการณ์ความไม่สงบในสามจังหวัดชายแดนภาคใต้ *[The Role of the Southern News Desk, Issara Institute as Peace Journalism: In the Case of insurgency in the Three Southernmost Provinces].* MA Thesis, Chulalongkorn University.

Wolfsfeld, Gadi. 1997. *Media and Political Conflict: News from the Middle East.* Cambridge: Cambridge University Press.

Wolfsfeld, Gadi. 2004. *Media and the Path to Peace.* Cambridge: Cambridge University Press.

Appendix A

Towards a new paradigm and practices: recommendations for southern conflict reporting

Similar to McCargo's proposals for the reform of the Thai press's political news coverage (McCargo 2000, p. 177), I propose some key points derived from this study's findings and discussion that may enhance more collaborative, cross-disciplinary, diverse, and decentralised approaches to reporting the southern conflict and other political struggles.

1. Structural change in national-level newsrooms

- *Thematic focus*: A newsroom should have a southern conflict-oriented news desk or production unit, and permanent segments to follow the conflict's development and provide regular reports. A similar model can be applied to the coverage of other interdisciplinary issues.
- *Decentralised content*: Each news desk and production unit should have a "regional liaison" editor to coordinate the newsrooms, regional news centres, and stringers, as well as to incorporate regional perspectives into their reports, particularly those with nation-wide impact.
- *(Public) engagement and participation*: More mechanisms to enhance collaboration among news outlets, professional organisations, civic media producers, civil society organisations, research think-tanks, academics, and audiences are essential to understand the conflict and produce reports that present in-depth analysis and multi-perspectival outlooks.

2. Paradigm shift in news production framework

- *Not just crimes and clashes*: News organisations and journalists should not focus solely on visible violence and its ramifications; they should examine less discernible implications of the conflict, including structural and socio-cultural causes and impact.
- *Diverse means of storytelling*: More media genres and formats that allow an extended production time, as well as long- and open-form presentation, are needed to thoroughly and variously explicate the complexity of southern conflict, including investigative reports, features, and visual presentations, as well as discussions, public arenas, and documentary programmes.

132   *Appendix A*

- *Innovative journalism*: News organisations and journalists should explore discussion and debate concerning "alternative" approaches in conflict reporting, such as peace journalism and advocacy journalism, and experiment with how these approaches can be applied in their current contexts.

3. News organisations' policies to improve quality of reporting

- *"Embedding"*: Instead of simply sending journalists on "fact-finding" trips organised by other parties, news organisations should sponsor and encourage Bangkok-based news production crews from all levels, including management, to spend time with various sectors in the far South to familiarise themselves with the region.
- *Knowledge and practice*: News organisations and professional organisations should organise workshops and training or provide sufficient opportunities for news production crews at all levels, both employees and stringers, to seek empirical and analytical knowledge in relevant subjects, as well as advanced skills necessary to cover conflicts, such as hostile environment training, investigative reporting, data journalism, and conflict resolution and peace building.
- *Pragmatic codes and standards*: News organisations and professional organisations should implement codes and practical guidelines for conflict coverage.
- *Comprehensive welfare policy*: News organisations and professional organisations should exercise comprehensive and effective welfare policies that cover health and risk insurance, compensation for death and injury in the line of duty, rehabilitation, and legal advice and assistance for news workers. These policies should be extended to temporary staff and stringers.
- *Professional reflexivity*: News organisations and professional organisations should arrange workshops, seminars, or forums for journalists to reflect on previous performance in order to understand their changing roles and find ways to improve their practices.

4. Working in tandem with other sectors

- *Media policy*: Policy-makers and regulators should facilitate the diversity of quality news content, as well as the plurality of media producers, in order to ensure a healthy participatory discussion and debate concerning the conflict.
- *Media regulation*: Media industry and regulators should adopt effective self- and co-regulatory systems that offer incentives for news organisations to adhere to regulations, prevent state interference, enhance deliberative democratic processes, empower consumers, and adapt to the dynamic media landscape.
- *Media monitoring*: Academics, the civil society sector, members of the public, and news workers themselves should critically examine and assess media coverage and practices, as well as the roles of other players in conflict

mediatization, while encouraging news organisations to scrutinise and evaluate one another.

Reference

McCargo, Duncan. 2000. *Politics and the Press in Thailand: Media Machinations*. London: Routledge.

Appendix B
Key moments in the southern conflict, Thai politics and media (2001–2014)

This chronological list was compiled from academic literature, reports, and media coverage of the events, some of which are listed in the bibliography.

2001–2003

6 January 2001

Thai Rak Thai party, led by Thaksin Shinawatra, won a landslide election victory and became a majority in the coalition government. Thaksin took office as the 23rd prime minister.

2 December 2001

Five police officers and one village defence volunteer were shot dead in coordinated attacks on five police posts in Pattani, Yala, and Narathiwat.

12–15 and 23–24 March 2002

Five police officers were killed in gunfire attacks on police booths and checkpoints in the three provinces.

1 May 2002

The Thaksin government disbanded the Southern Border Provinces Administrative Centre (hereafter SBPAC), and the Civil-Police-Military 43 joint command (hereafter CPM 43). The agencies' tasks were delegated to the judicial offices, provincial governors, and police who took charge of Southern security.

29 October 2002

Five public schools in Songkla, the neighbouring province of the three southern border provinces, were torched. Insurgents also bombed a Buddhist temple and a Chinese shrine in Pattani.

26 April 2003

An angry mob in a Narathiwat village accused two border patrol police intelligence officers of being members of a criminal camp. The officers were reportedly taken hostage, tortured, and killed.

28 April 2003

Five marines were killed and five rifles were stolen in attacks on marine bases in Yala and Narathiwat.

3 July 2003

Five police officers and one civilian were killed in coordinated attacks at three Pattani checkpoints

Appendix B   135

2004

4 January

Around 100 insurgents raided a weaponry depot of the Army Region 4 in Joh Ai Rong District of Narathiwat Province. Four soldiers were killed in the attack. Four hundred thirteen light infantry weapons and 2,000 rounds of ammunition were stolen. Twenty public schools in Yala were torched. Escape routes were lined with burned rubber tires and fake explosives as a diversion.

22, 24 January

The first time Buddhist monks became the assault targets. Three monks were murdered, one in each of the three southern border provinces, while two others were injured.

12 March

High-profile Muslim human rights lawyer Somchai Neelaphaijit was reported missing. His disappearance led to the years-long investigation in which a group of police officers was alleged to have abducted him to delay the judicial process concerning suspected insurgents that he represented.

19 March

The prime minister ordered the transfer of the Army Region 4 chief, along with the National Police commander, to inactive posts, as a reprimand for their failure to curb violence in the southern provinces.

27 March

The first attack where civilians were targeted began with an explosion in front of a hotel and nightclub at the border village of Su-ngai Golok, Narathiwat. Analysts looked at this incident as a smaller-scale imitation of the Bali, Indonesia bombing in 2002.

28–30 March

Thirty-nine government buildings in Pattani, Songkla, and Yala were set on fire in coordinated attacks. Another large-scale explosives heist took place at a Yala depot.

28 April

Some 200 Malay Muslims used machetes as weapon in massive, orchestrated attacks on police and military posts in Pattani, Yala, and Songkla. The incident culminated in the clampdown on suspects who retreated to Kru-Ze Mosque, a sacred religious heritage site in Pattani. Five security officials and one civilian were killed, while the number of casualties on the suspected insurgent side remained unclear, ranging from 105 to 107 deaths, including 32 who were shot dead in the Kru-Ze Mosque storm. Most victims were in their youth.

24 May

Exiled BERSATU chief Dr Wan Kadir Che Man suggested his organisation would concede its demand for complete independence and called on the Thai government for talks on peace and autonomy in the deep South.

136   *Appendix B*

3 June

Muslim politician Najmuddin Umar, who was a ruling Thai Rak Thai MP representing Narathiwat, reported to police after facing 10 charges, including treason, for his alleged involvement in the January 4 weapon heist incident. He was acquitted in December 2005.

September

Relevant agencies commenced the Queen's initiatives: the "Village Security Volunteers" project, and the "Sufficiency Economy Village and Model Farming" project.

17 September

In Pattani, a judge was killed – the first high-ranking official victim of suspected insurgents.

10 October

The government established the Southern Border Provinces Peace-building Command (SBPPC) and appointed the deputy supreme military commander as its chief. Operated under the supervision of the Internal Security Operations Command (hereafter ISOC) and the Military Supreme Commander, the agency was to maintain security in the deep South while facilitating other government peace-enhancing policies.

25 October

The clampdown on protestors in Tak Bai, Narathiwat marked another epitomic case in the history of resurgent insurgency. The crowds gathered in front of the district police station, demanding the release of six locals. Seven people were killed when police fired guns into the demonstrators. Later, 1,300 protestors were apprehended, and 78 died. Autopsy reports indicated the cause of death was suffocation during transportation in crowded trucks from the protest site to an army camp in Pattani.

26 November

Prime Minister Thaksin announced he would only partially attend the 2004 Association of Southeast Asian Nations (ASEAN) summit if the Tak Bai incident was to be discussed, stating that the incident was a domestic issue, not ASEAN's concern.

2005

6 February

Thai Rak Thai scored the second election win, but the party lost all its seats in the three southernmost provinces, most of which became the opposition Democrat's.

17 February

A car-bomb attack, the first in Thailand, killed six people and injured around 50 others in front of a hotel that was also a target of the March 27, 2004 attack in Su-ngai Golok, Narathiwat.

Appendix B 137

18–19 February

The Thai Journalists Association (TJA) and the Thai Broadcast Journalists Association (TBJA) conducted a fact-finding trip to the deep South for Bangkok-based senior reporters and editors.

28 March

The government established the National Reconciliation Commission (hereafter NRC), as proposed by academics and human rights campaigners, to initiate a peace process in the troubled region.

3 April

Three bombing attacks were launched at the Hat Yai International Airport and a supermarket in Songkla.

1 June

Former Narathiwat doctor Waemahadi Waedao and three associates were acquitted of treason charges due to lack of evidence. The four were accused of coordinating with a Singaporean JI member in plotting to bomb five embassies in Bangkok. Following the trial, Dr Waemahadi ran for a senator seat in a Narathiwat constituency and won. After his term was abruptly ended by the 2006 coup, he entered the province's MP campaign the following year and won.

20 June

Three Islamic religious teachers were killed while praying in a Pattani mosque.

June–July:

Violence escalated, with the number of people being decapitated by suspected insurgents rising to nine in two months, compared with three during the previous 17 months.

14 July

A series of synchronised bombings and torchings were launched in multiple areas in Yala, causing power blackouts and chaos.

16 July

The Government issued and enforced the newly passed State of Emergency Decree in the South and lifted the previously imposed martial law.

27 July

The TJA was set to launch "Peace Media: The Southern News Desk Project," later dubbed as "Isara News Centre," as another news outlet for stories concerning the southern conflict and other aspects of situation in the region.

30–31 August

Around 100 villagers in Su-ngai Padi District of Narathiwat gathered in front of their village to block police from accessing the crime scene where their religious leader was killed, believing officials were responsible for his death. The incident was followed by the exodus of 131 locals to neighbouring Malaysia.

138   *Appendix B*

20–21 September

Two marines accused of killing two of Narathiwat's Tanyong Limo villagers were taken hostage and later beaten to death by the village's members. The villagers also blocked the authorities' attempts to rescue the captives by gathering in front of the village, where they denied any calls for negotiations.

5 October

A television reporter and team members were wounded after a bomb was thrown into an eatery in Narathiwat. The team was assigned to report the prime minister's southern trip.

16 October

An elderly Buddhist monk and two temple boys were brutally murdered, and their residence, Phromprasit Temple in Pattani Province, was torched.

26 October

Synchronised attacks took place in 63 locations in the deep South between 7 and 8 p.m. Insurgents derailed a train, killed four people, and stole firearms from members of village security teams.

16 November

A Muslim family of nine, including a toddler, was shot dead when their house in Narathiwat was ambushed by unidentified attackers.

24 November

In the new round of Provincial Islamic Council elections, the Narathiwat president lost his seat, while the Pattani was challenged.

18 December

In two separate incidents in Narathiwat, two school-teachers were held hostage by villagers who demanded the release of two villagers in police detention.

2006

January

The anti-Thaksin demonstrations led by the People's Alliance for Democracy (hereafter PAD), which began in late 2005, escalated in Bangkok and several provinces. Displaying their united goal to drive out Thaksin and protect the monarchy, the demonstrators wore yellow tops, the symbolic colour of King Bhumibol; hence, the title "yellow shirt".

In the far South, 40 mobile phone transmission posts were set on fire. A policeman was killed, while two teachers and three soldiers were injured in other attacks.

6 March

Insurgents launched attacks on two villages late at night, killing five. Such actions were seen as a possible shift of violent patterns from point-blank assassination to targeting Buddhist civilians.

Appendix B 139

2 April

The Thaksin administration dissolved parliament and declared a snap election.

19 May

Villagers of Gujing Luepa in Narathiwat demanded the release of two members who were previously arrested for their suspected involvement with insurgent movements. They also took two female Buddhist teachers hostage before beating them. One teacher, Juling Ponganmun, died from severe injuries in January 2007, while another teacher was in a critical condition.

5 June

The NRC published its first report on the southern conflict and presented its recommendations to remedy the troubled situation.

June–August

Simultaneous bombs targeted governmental offices, banks, and police outposts.

August

A group of NGOs, media and journalists, public health professionals, and educators and academics working in conflict resolution fields, based both in and outside of the region, formed a networked independent organisation called "Deep South Watch".

16 September

A string of six simultaneous explosions took place in Hat Yai, Songkla's business centre, killing five people, including a Canadian – the first foreign victim of the violence – and injuring about 60 others.

19 September

The Thaksin government was toppled by a military coup led by Army Commander General Sonthi Boonyaratglin. The prime minister was deposed, and the 1997 constitution was abolished.

1 October

Privy Councillor Surayud Chulanont was nominated as prime minister by the coup leaders. The junta-installed civilian government also revived the SBPAC and the CPM 43.

2 October

Two reporters were injured while covering the police's investigation at an explosion site in Narathiwat as insurgents detonated a second bomb.

3 November:

The newly appointed prime minister visited the far South, and, in a groundbreaking gesture, apologised for the state's mistreatment of demonstrators in the Tak Bai incident. A few days later, a new round of arson attacks was launched, resulting in six people being killed and four schools torched. Forty-nine schools were closed for several weeks. Some 100 Buddhist residents of Yala's three villages also fled from their homes and sought refuge at a temple in a nearby district.

140   *Appendix B*

27 November

The honorary consul at the Thai Consulate in Malaysia revealed the "Langkawi Process," in which former Malaysian Prime Minister Mahathir Mohamad served as the facilitator in the talks between Thai security officials and representatives of separatist groups.

31 December

Explosions rocked Bangkok on New Year's Eve, killing three people and injured 38 others.

2007

1 January

Investigations into the New Year's Eve explosions in Bangkok were carried out. Speculations on the incident being connected to deposed Prime Minister Thaksin Shinawatra were widespread.

16 January

An improvised explosive device (IED) was detonated near an arson attack site in Narathiwat while police officers were investigating the scene. The blast killed the deputy village headman and injured two local reporters.

February 17–19

A string of bomb and arson attacks took place during the Chinese New Year festival, attended mainly by the Chinese-descended population in Songkla's Hat Yai District.

March–May

A series of violent incidents, ranging from a point-blank shooting, a *pondok* raid, an attack on mosques, and roadside bombings, took the lives of Muslim and Buddhist civilians and soldiers. Border rangers were accused of killing Muslim civilians. Insurgents were believed to launch attacks on Buddhist residents and soldiers as retaliation.

22 May

Twelve reporters, including an Australian national photographer for TIME magazine, were wounded in a blast in Yala. In a usual pattern, insurgents triggered the bomb when police were investigating a crime scene and reporters were taken in tow to cover the story.

28 May

Seven explosions were detonated in Songkla's commercial district of Hat Yai and a crowded market in its Saba Yoi District, injuring 13 people.

30 May

The former ruling Thai Rak Thai party was disbanded by the Tribunal Court for violating election laws in 2006.

Appendix B 141

15 July

Insurgents planted two bombs in front of the Yala train station, and detonated one when the bomb squad arrived at the scene. One officer was killed by the blast and another 20 people were injured, including four television and print journalists.

23 July

Anti-coup demonstrators, led by the United Front for Democracy against Dictatorship (hereafter UDD), clashed with police in front of the residence of the Privy Councillor President General Prem Tinnasulanon. The UDD was led by former Thai Rak Thai MPs and wore red tops to symbolise their political stance; hence, the title "red shirt".

19 August

Thailand's first ever referendum resulted in the passing of a new constitution, which was drafted by an assembly appointed by the military-installed civilian government.

24 November

The new Press Registration Act was enacted, replacing the draconian Press Act, which allowed authorities to close publishing houses and pre-censor publication content.

20 December

The National Legislative Assembly passed the Internal Security Act (ISA).

23 December

The general election was held, and the Thai Rak Thai's reincarnated People's Power party (hereafter PPP) won a majority and finally led a six-party coalition. A month later, PPP leader Samak Sundaravej became the country's 25th prime minister.

2008

15 January

The commercial TITV (originally iTV) station was transformed into the country's first public service broadcaster, *Thai PBS*. The commercial media organisation was found to have breached its concession agreement, prompting the government to reclaim the station and rename it *Thai PBS* on February 1.

February

Newly appointed Interior Minister Chalerm Yoobamroong faced severe criticism after proposing that the southernmost region be declared a special administrative zone.

15 March

An explosion at the CS Pattani Hotel led to two deaths and 14 injuries.

142 *Appendix B*

25 March

Authorities started an investigation into the death of an Islamic religious teacher, suspected of involvement with insurgency, while in military detention.

26 May

The PAD launched its second round of anti-government rallies, which led to a mass demonstration that lasted for nearly seven months.

20 June

The PAD demonstrators seized the Government House.

17 July

Army TV Channel 5 aired the pre-recorded ceasefire declaration made by three unnamed men who claimed to oversee insurgent groups in the southernmost provinces. However, senior military officials and analysts viewed the statement as mere political posturing, while the known separatist movements PULO and BRN denied their cooperation in the ceasefire.

21 August

A car bomb explosion in Narathiwat killed a senior reporter from the popular daily newspaper and injured another TV reporter.

September

The Constitution Court terminated Samak Sundaravej's premiership after finding him violating the law by maintaining his status as a TV production company employee while serving as prime minister. The PPP executives later nominated Thaksin's brother-in-law, Somchai Wongsawat, as its new chief, and he subsequently became the 26th prime minister.

6–7 October

Police fired tear gas grenades into the PAD demonstrators who gathered in front of Parliament Building to prevent the house meeting. During the clash, two protesters died, while 381 protesters and 11 police officers were injured.

17 November

Insurgents carried out car- and motorcycle-bomb attacks in Sukirin District of Narathiwat, wounding 73 people, including village headmen and security volunteers.

26 November

PAD demonstrators took control of the Suvarnabhumi Airport, the country's main international air hub, reinforcing their demand for the prime minister to resign.

2 December

The Constitution Court ruled that executives of three coalition member parties, including the PPP, committed electoral fraud, and disbanded the parties. The decision abruptly terminated the Somchai government. The PAD declared victory and ended their months-long rally.

Appendix B   143

15 December

Abhisit Vejjajiva, the leader of the opposition Democrat party, was nominated by MPs to be the new prime minister and began forming government.

2009

18 January

Newly MP-elected Prime Minister Abhisit Vejjajiva went on his first visit to the southern border region and announced a plan to establish a "Southern Cabinet," a special panel of ministers to oversee the southern problems.

23–27 March

A string of attacks was launched during this week, coinciding with the inaugural anniversary of the BRN. Security officers retaliated by launching intensive searches in many areas of Pattani, including a tense 30-hour mission to locate the shooter who killed a soldier.

26 March

The UDD's mass demonstration commenced, with around 20,000 people taking to Bangkok's main streets, demanding the Democrat prime minister step down.

10–14 April

UDD demonstrators blocked Bangkok's main streets, raided the ASEAN summit site in the resort town of Pattaya, and attacked the prime minister's motorcade at a governmental compound. The government enforced the Emergency Decree in the capital city and its peripheral provinces. UDD leaders claimed up to six demonstrators were killed as security officers attempted to disperse the crowd, contradicting the government's initial figure of 120 injuries and no deaths.

18 May

Muslim lawyer Somchai Neelapaijit, who disappeared in early 2004, was declared legally missing.

27 May

Attackers torched and planted car-bombs in nine spots in Yala's business district, halting economic transactions in the province. No casualties were reported.

8 June

Attackers opened fire and threw grenades into Ai-Payer Village's Mosque in the Joh Ai-rong District of Narathiwat during prayer hours, killing 12 people and wounding 11.

August 15

A new political party, Matubhum, made its debut in Narathiwat. The party's key members included the Southern Muslim Wadah faction, who moved from

144   *Appendix B*

the dissolved PPP, with former coup chief General Sonthi Boonyaratglin, also a Muslim, serving as the party chief.

October

News media started investigations into the deficiency of explosive detector GT200, widely used by security officials in the deep South, following several explosions in which the device failed to discover the bombs.

November

Opposition Phuea Thai party chairman Chavalit Yongjaiyudh proposed the "Pattani City" model, suggesting the establishment of the three southernmost provinces as an autonomous region in a bid to end the unrest.

9 December

The Thai prime minister and Malaysian Prime Minister Najib Razak visited the far South together.

15 December

Malaysian police in Kelantan apprehended three Malay Muslim men near the Malaysian-Thai border. The men were suspected of making IEDs and supplying the bombs to the insurgent movement in the deep South.

2010

January–March

The government and army carried out formal investigations into the remote substance detector GT200 and the surveillance airships. After the probe revealed that both had deficiencies, authorities scrapped all standing purchase orders for the devices.

26 February

The Supreme Court ruled that former Prime Minister Thaksin Shinawatra hid his assets and exploited his power during his premiership.

12 March

A Yala police superintendent, Police Colonel Sompien Eksomya, was killed in a bomb attack. His death led to an investigation into the unfair treatment of his transfer request.

In Bangkok, UDD "red-shirt" protestors gathered and held rallies around the city. They claimed the Abhisit administration was illegitimate, and demanded that he dissolve parliament and declare an election.

29–30 March

The prime minister and government representatives held talks with UDD leaders, an event aired live via the state's broadcasters. At first, Abhisit agreed to organise an election in six months, but later withdrew his proposal because the demonstration continued.

Appendix B   145

April–May

Demonstrators camped out on streets in Bangkok's main shopping district. Claiming some demonstrators had weapons, the army took charge and dispersed the crowds, while the government enforced a night curfew in Bangkok and 23 other provinces. Violence erupted again when authorities eventually used force to remove demonstrators from the Bangkok protest sites on 19 May, and some demonstrators were reported to have set fire to commercial buildings near protest sites in retaliation. In the end, 89 people were killed, including two foreign journalists, and more than 1,800 injured in the violence.

11 July

Academics and volunteers started travelling on foot from the capital city to Kru-Ze Mosque in Pattani to signify the need for peaceful solutions to end the southern conflict.

19 September

Four elderly members of a Buddhist family were shot dead and their house was set on fire in the Bajoh District of Narathiwat. The case prompted Buddhist villagers to call for protection in the restive zone.

October

Fifteen Pakistani men were arrested for illegal entry into the country and money laundering. They were also suspected to be involved with the regional radical Islamic movement, Jemaah Isalamiyaah, but the authorities presented no evidence to support that claim.

10 November

Parliament passed the Southern Border Provinces Administration Act, which became effective on December 30.

November

Many rural areas in the southern border provinces and the business centre in Hat Yai were affected by major floods.

25 December

The deputy interior minister in charge of southern conflict solutions proposed the instalment of Sharia Court in the southernmost region to help facilitate the resolution of civil disputes among Muslim residents.

29 December

The government lifted the state of emergency in Mae Lan District of Pattani, the first area in the far South to be free from the contingency law. The district was, however, still under the Internal Security Act.

146 *Appendix B*

2011

January–February

An explosion rocked a market in Narathiwat, killing two officers. Yala's business area faced at least two car-bomb attacks, killing one civilian and wounding more than 30 others. The Panarae District of Pattani also saw a series of shootings targeting civilians. A group of insurgents launched an attack on an army camp in Narathiwat, killing four soldiers and seizing weapons from the base.

February

Thai and Cambodian soldiers exchanged fire in the two countries' disputed border area near the ancient Khmer-architecture Phra Viharn or Preah Vihear Temple. The skirmishes gave rise to a new round of legal disputes over territory ownership between the two countries, which had begun in 2008, and was then brought into public discussions by the PAD. The International Court of Justice later ruled that both countries cease fire and withdraw troops from the disputed zone, and then decided in 2013 to award the territory to Cambodia.

23 February

A group of southern border province MPs from the Democrat Party expressed concerns over the rising number of car-bomb attacks. They criticised the Democrat-led government for inefficiency in solving the southern conflict and called for the change of responsible agencies, including then-Army Commander Prayut Chan-ocha. A deputy prime minister, however, deflected the criticism by reprimanding the party's MPs.

13 March

The first "Southern Border Alternative Media Day" event was organised by a civil society network in Pattani. The network was composed of civil society organisations, local civic media producers, and academics. The event was set up as an arena for those working on the southern conflict issues to share and exchange information as well as ideas on how to communicate to the public about the conflict, while empowering the civil society sector in negotiating with other stakeholders in the conflict.

10 May

Prime Minister Abhisit dissolved parliament and declared the election to be held on July 3.

July

Former Prime Minister Thaksin Shinawatra, who lived in exile in Dubai, gave an interview to *Thai PBS*' flagship news talk programme following sister Yingluck Shinawatra's landslide win in the July 3 general election. For the first time, he admitted to using excessive force in his iron-fist policies on the southern conflict, and publicly apologised for his actions. The episode was at first banned from broadcast, but was eventually aired after widespread public debate.

Appendix B 147

5 August

Yingluck Shinawatra, Thaksin's sister and the chief of the Pheu Thai (For the Thai) Party, became the 28th prime minister following a landslide win in the general election. She was criticised for being Thaksin's proxy and for her lack of political experience, given that she was named the party's first party-list MP candidate a few months before the election.

October

A series of synchronised explosions shook the southern provinces. The first was in central Yala, where 24 bombings killed four people and injured 49 others. The second round took place in two major grocery shops in Narathiwat, killing seven people and injuring eight more. The third round was spread across eight districts in Narathiwat; no casualties were reported.

October–November

Thailand faced its most severe flooding in 70 years. Many parts of Bangkok, along with agricultural and industrial areas in central Thailand, were under water for weeks. The southern border provinces were unaffected.

15 December

Prominent Narathiwat politician Muktar Kila, 43, was shot dead at his home. He founded the Prachatham Party to contend in the July 3 general election, advertising it as the true Malay's party, which would solve the southern conflict by local people. Regardless of this, his party's candidates, including himself, did not garner enough votes to win any seats.

Year summary

Despite the frequency of reports on violent incidents, the regional ISOC announced the number of incidents in the first six months of 2011 dropped more than 18 percent compared with the same period of the year before. Nonetheless, security analysts found the number of vehicle-borne IEDs, time-delay secondary bombs, and massive attacks and weapon heists on military camps sharply increased – these methods subsided in 2013.

There were also reports and analyses about shortcomings in the judicial system, as the majority of criminal cases were dismissed in court due to insufficient evidence and mistreatment of suspects while in custody. Analysts expressed concerns that the small number of investigators and their minimal experience caused flaws in the investigation. Meanwhile, human rights advocates pointed out that although the cases were later dismissed, suspects were still detained for 28 days without charge under the emergency decree.

2012

January 29

In Baan Num Dum Village of the Puloh Puyo Subdistrict in Pattani, four villagers were killed and four others wounded when a group of paramilitary officers

148   *Appendix B*

fired on them as they were driving. The paramilitary officers reportedly testified they thought the victims were involved in an attack on a base nearby, injuring one member of staff. Investigation into the incident was launched and its result indicated that the villagers were not involved in the paramilitary base shootout.

31 March

Three orchestrated bombings, including one at a department store/hotel in Songkla's commercial district, Hat Yai, killed at least three people and injured dozens of others.

24 April

The Cabinet agreed to compensate four groups of people affected by the southern unrest with "healing" payments. The four groups were: 1) civilian fatalities and injuries, 2) deceased and wounded civil servants, 3) people mistreated by authorities or perpetrators of violence, including in the Kru-Ze Mosque and Tak Bai clampdowns, and 4) those detained for or charged with national security violation without temporary release, and people whose charge was later acquitted or dismissed.

31 July

The CS Pattani Hotel came under another car-bomb attack, wounding five people and causing damage to property.

August

The prime minister set up an integrated command centre to solve the southern unrest, with the ISOC as the host. Three deputy ministers were appointed to oversee the centre, including the outspoken veteran politician Chalerm Yoobamroong, who reportedly stated that he did not need to visit the region to solve this problem.

18 November

US President Barack Obama, who had recently won his second term in office, visited Thailand, where he received a royal audience with King Bhumibol and held a joint press conference with Thai PM Yingluck Shinawatra. He later visited Burma, where he met the country's president and democratic leader, Aung San Suu Kyi, and attended the East Asia Summit in Cambodia.

November

The Southern Teachers Federation temporarily closed primary schools in Pattani after a series of fatal attacks on schoolteachers, including a female principal. They also called for authorities to provide safety for teachers in volatile areas.

2013

February

Sixteen insurgents were killed in a firefight with soldiers when they attacked a military camp in Narathiwat on February 14. Among the deceased was

Appendix B 149

Marosoh Chantrawadee, a prime suspect in several high-profile cases. Shortly after, local advocacy website Patani Forum interviewed Marosoh's mother and widow about his life and the reason he joined the insurgent movement. The piece was then re-published in several alternative news websites, as well as popular online portals and discussion sites. Later, mainstream media organisations followed suit by interviewing his mother and widow, presenting information other than his long criminal record.

In a separate incident, public service broadcaster *Thai PBS* was criticised for its report implying university students in the far South were recruited by BRN-Coordinate on campus. Student activists and critics said the report was unfounded and biased against southern youths.

February–August

Thailand's National Security Council officials met with representatives from the BRN in three peace dialogues held in and facilitated by Malaysia. These were the first public meetings to resolve the armed conflict between the two sides. However, critics voiced scepticism as to whether the BRN's lead delegate, Ustadz Hasan Taib, had influenced the militant movement because violence remained unabated, particularly during Ramadan. The process came to a halt in August, following the release of a YouTube video of supposed BRN members who announced the group's suspension from participating in the dialogue because Thailand had not responded to the group's conditions for peace talks and ceasefire.

November–December

Demonstrators gathered in various spots around Bangkok to oppose the parliament's attempt to amend the constitution, particularly the proposal to grant impunity to those convicted or allegedly involved in political movements since 2004. While politicians claimed the amendment was to reconcile political differences among various parties and bridge social rifts, protestors argued the change might absolve former Prime Minister Thaksin of his corruption convictions. The demonstrators, who came from different political movement factions, later formed a network and called themselves the People's Democratic Reform Committee (hereafter PDRC). The demonstration was led by Suthep Tuagsuban, a former high-profile Democrat MP and deputy prime minister in the Abhisit government.

9 December

Prime Minister Yingluck Shinawatra declared parliament's dissolution and a snap election on February 2, 2014. PDRC continued its mass demonstration and rejected the upcoming election, while demanding for political reform through the establishment of "People's Council".

Year summary

Although the open peace dialogues to resolve the southern conflict had set a crucial milestone, violence continued, with the number of incidents ranked among the highest in ten years. The number of insurgent arrests and casualties also rose from the previous year.

150 *Appendix B*

This year also saw civil society networks actively organising public debates on various solutions to the conflict, including the discussions of autonomy and self-determination, as well as the reference to *merdeka* (independence), a Malay term used by insurgent movements, previously considered taboo in the public forum.

2014

January–May

The PDRC and its allies continued their demonstrations, occupying governmental facilities and organising mass rallies on major routes around Bangkok. Clashes between protesters and officers, and, in certain incidents, unknown armed parties, were reported. Casualties in the demonstrations and clashes included eight deaths, more than 800 injuries, and 11 arrests.

2 February

Following the PDRC's heavy "Reform before Election" and "No Vote" election boycott campaigns, the unofficial voter turnout was reported at around 45 percent. Election officers were absent in some polling stations, forcing the stations to close without prior notice. In several ballot centres, demonstrators blocked voters from entering the premises – a few incidents led to clashes between demonstrators and voters. The election commissioners announced catch-up elections to be held on March 1–2 for the constituencies where polling did not take place.

21 March

The Constitutional Court ruled the February 2 election unconstitutional because the election commissioners failed to organise the general election nationwide on the same day. The ruling effectively invalidated the polling results.

May

The Constitutional Court ruled that Yingluck and nine cabinet members were guilty of power abuse in high-ranking officials' relocation and appointment. The court also ordered the caretaker prime minister to step down. Later, the National Counter Corruption Commission filed a criminal case against Yingluck, accusing her of corruption in the government's rice subsidy scheme because some million farmers who joined the programme had yet to receive their payment.

20 May

Army Commander General Prayut Chan-ocha declared martial law nationwide.

22 May

The National Council for Peace and Order (hereafter NCPO) staged a military coup against the Yingluck Shinawatra administration, which effectively abolished the 2007 constitution. The group was led by the army chief and comprised of military and police commanders. The NCPO later set up the National Legislative Assembly (NLA) and appointed its members to work on legisla-

Appendix B 151

tive matters in absence of the elected MPs and senators. The PDRC ended its demonstration. Following the coup, a number of political movement leaders, outspoken academics, journalists, and activists were summoned – some briefly detained – by the NCPO, to "adjust their attitude".

25 May

Half of Pattani's Muang District faced a black-out after a high voltage pylon explosion, followed by a string of bombings. No casualties were reported.

23 June

The NCPO announced a constitutional drafting process to replace the 2007 version, with the National Reform Council (NRC) overseeing a constitutional drafting committee and the charter drafting process. Selected by screening committees set up by the NCPO, the NRC's 250 members had expertise in areas such as politics, economics, education, national security, social affairs, and mass media.

21 July

The NCPO set up a steering committee to resolve the southern conflict, headed by the deputy army commander and NCPO's secretary general. The team largely comprised military, national security and intelligence officials.

22 July

A temporary charter was enforced.

25 August

NCPO leader and army commander Prayut took office as prime minister. Most military chiefs and bureaucrats were appointed deputy PMs and ministers in the cabinet.

November

Media professional organisations called for the revision or revocation of two NCPO edicts, stating they curbed freedom of expression and freedom of the press. This movement came after incidents in which media organisations were inspected and journalists were intimidated, and in some cases suspended, because their lines of questions and reports were deemed to instigate social disorder and conflict.

5 November

The internal security law remained in effect for another year in five districts of Songkla, while the three southernmost provinces were under the emergency decree and martial law.

1 December

Following the Thai Prime Minister's visit to Kuala Lumpur, both Thai and Malaysian premiers agreed that the suspended peace dialogue to solve the southern conflict should be resumed, with Malaysia reprising its role as facilitator. The

152   *Appendix B*

announcement came after Prime Minister Prayut's sporadic remarks about restarting peace talks and the peace process since he took office in August.

Year summary

The number of women and children who were victims of violence increased, particularly children under 15 years old – some of which were killed or injured in the authorities' actions. The number of car-bomb attacks also rose. Meanwhile, Freedom House changed Thailand's freedom status from "Partly Free" in 2014, to "Not Free" in 2015 because the exercising of political and civil rights, as well as freedom of expression and academic freedom, became highly restricted under martial law.

Appendix C
Profiles of the four media organisations in this study

This section was first published in the author's doctoral thesis: Phansasiri Kularb. 2013. *Mediating Political Dissent: A study of Thai news organisations and southern conflict reporting.* Cardiff University, UK.

Matichon Daily

The *Matichon Daily* newspaper is under the management of Matichon plc, a print media company that also publishes a mass-circulation tabloid-style newspaper, a semi-weekly business newspaper, and four magazines, and owns a publishing house. The company was established in 1978, and its founders were considered to be among the progressive political writers in the country at the time. The company became a listed company in 1989.

In late 2005, GMM Media, part of the entertainment conglomerate GMM Grammy plc, attempted a hostile takeover of the company. However, the bid was viewed as political interference with the media because of the GMM Grammy owner's connection with then-Prime Minister Thaksin Shinawatra. After facing

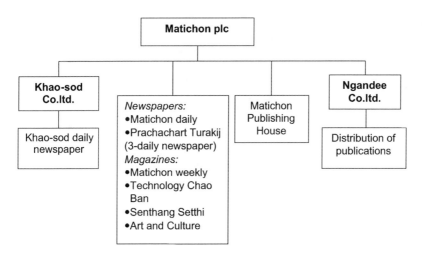

Figure B.1 Matichon plc's business structure

Source: Matichon plc's annual report 2004. Available at: http://info.matichon.co.th/report/2547/config.php?nfile=businessstrueng.txt&a=1 [Accessed 21 January 2013]

154   *Appendix C*

public outcry and continuing protests from journalists, academics, and the civil society sector, the entertainment corporation retracted its initial offer, but still acquired 32.23 percent shares of Matichon in the end.

Thai PBS

This television station was founded in 1995 as a result of the media reform movement, which aimed at liberating broadcast media from the state's ownership and control. This public campaign began after the political crisis in May 1992, when broadcast media were manipulated and their content censored by state authorities. Despite being under the care of the Office of the Prime Minister, the new television station was designed to operate independently by the concessionaire to prevent censorship and interference from authority. Additionally, to create an informed citizenry, the concession contract of the new station stipulated an emphasis on quality programme content, particularly news and current affairs, which differed from the prevalence of entertainment programmes in other commercial media. A holding company, with one of the country's major banks and a news-oriented media company, the Nation Multimedia Group, as key stakeholders, won the 30-year concession to run the station, and named it Independent Television (iTV). In its early years, iTV became widely known for its quality news programmes and investigative reports. However, with its concentration on news and current affairs, the station failed to generate ample profit and started accumulating losses during the financial crisis in 1997. In 2000, the station was sold to Shin Corporation, the communication conglomerate owned by telecom tycoon Thaksin Shinawatra, who became prime minister in 2001.

When Thaksin took office, the station reportedly encountered editorial direction to downplay its criticism against the government, and 21 news workers were fired when they resisted management (the group, dubbed the "iTV rebels" by the press, later won a legal action for unfair treatment and received back pay). In 2004, an arbitration panel allowed the station to change the news-to-entertainment ratio from 70:30, as stated in the initial concession contract, to 50:50. Moreover, the annual licensing fee was also reduced from 1 billion (approximately 29 million US dollars) to 230 million baht (approximately 6.8 million US dollars).

However, in 2006, following the military coup that overthrew then-Prime Minister Thaksin, the Central Administrative Court ruled that iTV violated its concession contract by implementing the aforementioned changes, and ordered management to pay hefty fines. When management failed to pay the fines, the concession was revoked and the frequency reverted to the Office of the Prime Minister. The interim coup-installed civilian government later appointed a new executive board and renamed the station Thai Independent Television (TITV) in early 2007.

To maintain media independence and prevent interference from political and financial powers in the long run, the interim government, media professionals, academics, and civil advocates carried out studies and organised discussions for the station's future. The general opinion was divided into two camps: 1) to make

Appendix C 155

the station an independent free-to-air commercial station, similar to the initial iTV, or 2) to reinvent it as the country's first public service broadcaster, following the models of public service broadcasters such as the BBC, NHK, or PBS. In 2008, the interim government eventually passed a law to establish a public service broadcaster. TITV was ordered to cease its transmission, and the property was transferred to the new organisation.

Operated under the Public Broadcasting Act of 2008 and with an annual budget of 2 billion baht (approximately 59 million US dollars), taken from excise tax, the Thai Public Broadcasting Service (*Thai PBS*) was established. To ensure its independence and accountability, the organisation is managed by the Board of Governors – whose members represent various civic sectors to oversee its general policy – as well as the Executive Board and the Managing Director, who manage the station's operation, as illustrated in Figure B.2. Apart from the news and programme production departments similar to most broadcasters, *Thai PBS* also has the Audience Council, composed of representatives from disparate civic and consumer groups, to ensure public participation and the organisation's social responsibility.

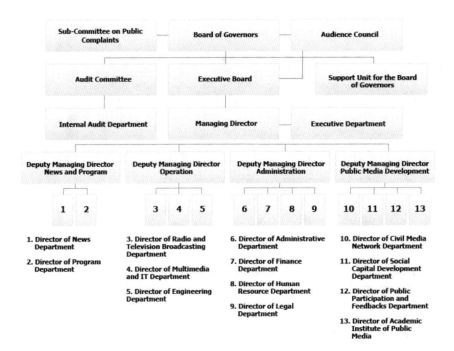

Figure B.2 Thai PBS' organisation structure

Source: Thai PBS website. Available at: www2.thaipbs.or.th/about_organization_structure.php [Accessed: 21 January 2013]

Appendix C

Figure B.3 Thai PBS' news department structure

* "Strategic news" desk generally produces in-depth current affairs reports, for example, environment news or youth development stories.

** "Social agenda" programmes include the production of two daily news and current affairs programmes (*Morning News* and *Tee Nee Thai PBS* [*Here is Thai PBS*]) and a discussion panel programme (*Way Tee Satarana* [*Public Forum*]).

Source: The author's observation and personal conversations' note

When the station was launched, a number of new staffers were hired for its news and programme production departments, as explained in Figure B.3. While some employees from the iTV/TITV continued their work with the organisation, many high-profile news anchors and reporters were offered positions at other commercial broadcasters. The audience ratings of the station's news and current affairs programmes still trail behind other channels (as of 2015). However, the station's continuous coverage of the major flooding in 2011 was highly praised and helped increase the audience ratings during the crisis.

ASTV Manager Online

The ASTV Manager Online news website is operated by ASTV Manager Co. Ltd., a media company that also publishes a political and business news-oriented daily newspaper and four magazines, and runs a satellite television, ASTV. Initially named Manager Media Group, the company was founded by media mogul Sondhi Limthongkul in 1990 and started with a daily broadsheet. The newspaper became widely recognised for its coverage of the anti-government mass demonstration in May 1992 despite state censorship of broadcast media and some print media outlets. During the financial crisis in 1997, the company encountered a major fiscal problem. Its founder filed for bankruptcy, and the company was streamlined to maintain its newspaper business. In early 2004, recuperating from financial

Appendix C 157

problems, the company launched their satellite television operation, with ASTV News 1 being the primary news channel. Later in 2005, the Manager Media Group founder started to heavily criticise the then Thaksin-led coalition and propelled the anti-government movement, which later became the People's Alliance for Democracy (PAD). The group's media outlets then served as the PAD's political mouthpiece in order to galvanise public support.

Due to heavy debts, the Manager Media Group faced bankruptcy in 2008. A new company was founded to replace the defunct enterprise, and, as a result, the titles of its publications and outlets were changed to "ASTV Manager" up to present (as of 2015). The company's anti-Thaksin stance has brought about several defamation lawsuits against its news presenters and editorial team. Regardless, the ASTV Manager Online website remains among the most popular sources for online news. Several factors contribute to its popularity, from the speed of its coverage and its gossip-style entertainment news columns, to its harsh criticism of government and support from PAD empathisers.

Isara News Agency's Southern News Desk

The operation was initially founded as The Southern News Desk Peace Media Project, commonly known as the Isara News Centre, on July 11, 2005 by the Thai Journalists Association (TJA). Aimed at pacifying the conflict and appeasing violence, the project produced stories that promoted the southernmost provinces' ethnic and cultural diversity, along with the concept of peaceful conflict resolution. Following the project's inception, an editorial team was set up, using a space at the Prince of Songkla University's Pattani campus as its office. TJA member organisations, both national and local, cooperated by sending a group of volunteer reporters to stay at the centre and report from the region.

On August 25, 2005, the Isara News Centre website was launched. Stories were posted on the website, and occasionally used by the national media whose reporters were working for the project. In the beginning, the centre was co-supervised by two news editors: one a senior reporter from Bangkok and the other a local stringer, so that they could combine their expertise in editorial process and local knowledge. The website concentrated on stories about local culture and way of life. Later on, the centre forged alliance with local scholars and advocates. As a result, apart from news and feature stories, the website also presented articles from research studies and seminars organised by partner organisations.

In 2006, the centre underwent a shake-up and was reinvented as the Isara News Institute. The new agency was under the supervision of three professional organisations: the TJA, the Press Council of Thailand, and the Thai Press Development Foundation. However, the decrease of funding in late 2006 compelled the agency to be streamlined. The duo-editor system was halted, leaving one Bangkok-based editor in charge. At the same time, fewer volunteer journalists from Bangkok were able to stay in the far South. Therefore, the newsgathering depended on local junior reporters. With declining financial sponsorship and the change of editors in the following year, the agency struggled to maintain its operation. The

Table B.1 The development of the Isara News Agency's Southern News Desk

Phases / Characteristics	Phase 1 (2005–2006)	Phase 2 (late 2006 –early 2008)	Phase 3 (2008 – present)
Supervising organisation	TJA	Isara Institute, Thai Press Development Foundation	Isara Institute
Title	The Peace Media Project: The Southern News Desk/ Isara News Centre	Isara Institute	Isara Institute's Southern News Desk/ Isara News Agency's Southern News Desk
Objectives	Focusing on the principle of peace media/ peace journalism, and the mutual learning and exchange between Bangkok and local press	Focusing on demanding for justice for the affected people, in line with the peace journalism principle	Continuing the peace journalism principle and being a hub of news and information about the three southern border provinces
Staff*	• Two co-editors, one from Bangkok and one from the area • Journalists from Bangkok • Journalists from the area • Four reporters, one in each southernmost province (all reporters were on loan from member organisations)	• One Bangkok-based editor • Five to six reporters in the area; one appointed as the centre chief (all staffers were hired as the centre's reporter) • Four reporters, one in each southernmost province (on loan from member organisations)	• One Bangkok-based editor • Five reporters in the area (paid by piece) • Contributors (stringers and academics)
An office in the South	Yes	Yes	No
Content emphasis	• Stories about non-violent events • Way of life, local culture, living situations in culturally diverse environments • Investigative reports • Feedbacks from southern residents and grassroots people who were affected by the conflict/violence	• Analytical reports about daily violent incidents • Investigation into justice system and cases of unjust treatment/abuse • Military perspectives • Summary of incidents every fortnight, including statistics of casualties and analysis of violent patterns	• Fewer reports about daily incidents • Stories related to current national trends • Analytical reports on government and military strategies • Court cases, including impact on orphans and widows • Unusual/success stories

Appendix C   159

Characteristics \ Phases	Phase 1 (2005–2006)	Phase 2 (late 2006 –early 2008)	Phase 3 (2008 – present)
Target audience	• General public (people outside the southernmost provinces) • Mainstream media • Civil society network • Local media	• The locals and general public • Civil society network • Local media • Alternative media • Foreign press agencies	• The locals and general public • Alternative media • Local media • Civil society network • Foreign press agencies

Source: Adapted from Witchayawanee 2009 and updated by the author

office at the Prince of Songkla University's Pattani campus was later closed, and the initial Isara News Centre webpage was subsumed under the Isara News Agency's site and redubbed the Isara News Agency's Southern News Desk. At the moment (2015), the desk is supervised by an editor based in Bangkok who occasionally travels to the southern border provinces. The newsgathering unit includes five regular reporters who receive their payment by piece, and some constant contributors.

Table B.2 Summary of news organisations' similarities and differences

Categories	Components	Media Organisations
1. Media platforms	a. Print b. TV c. Online	a. *Matichon* b. *Thai PBS* c. *Manager, Isara*
2. News orientations	a. Political and public policy news b. General news c. Southern conflict issues	a. *Matichon, Thai PBS* b. *Manager* c. *Isara*
3. Media organisational principles	a. Commercial b. Public service broadcasting c. Non-profit/alternative	a. *Matichon, Manager* b. *Thai PBS* c. *Isara*

Appendix D
Research methodology[1]

News Content Analysis

A rolling random sampling was used to select stories from the four selected news organisations that were published/aired/posted from January 2004 to December 2010. The newspaper sample was collected from any section of the print edition, whereas the television sample was collected from two primetime news bulletins (at noon and 7 p.m.) for practicality reasons.[2] The online news sample was collected from stories posted on the dates selected. The sample was collected from the organisations' archive, subscribed news database, and online archive service. The keyword search was applied to extract relevant stories and screen out impertinent ones, using the following key terms collectively: 1) three southern border provinces, and southern border,[3] 2) unrest,[4] 3) insurgency,[5] 4) violence,[6] 5) conflict,[7] and 6) terrorism.[8] This sampling system helped to ensure representativeness and manageability within the selected samples. In the end, 793 stories were selected.

To analyse the reports' news frames, I followed Jörg Matthes and Matthias Kohring (2008)'s *hierarchical cluster analysis* approach to first classify the sample into four broad categories because of the large sample size. I used Robert Entman's definition of frame elements: *problem definition, causal interpretation, moral evaluation,* and *treatment recommendation* (1993, p. 52, original emphasis) as a starting point. This means of analysis not only facilitated the classification of news that contained a wide range of topics, but also corresponded with how the three discourses concerning the southern conflict were distinguished from one another in the Introduction. The four meta-frames were 1) *causes of conflict and violence,* 2) *uses of force,* 3) *repercussions of conflict and violence,* and 4) *solutions,* as explained in Table D.1.

Going through every piece of sample, I categorised which meta-frame group a story belonged to. For stories that contained more than one meta-frame, the analysis would be based on the primary frame – meaning the one that was mentioned first. After the sample was classified into different meta-frame groups, it was further examined and put into the sub-categories with ones that highlighted similar contexts, such as *retaliation against state authority* or *impact on stakeholders,* as shown below. Then, I examined how the stories were reported, whether they were, for example, positive and supportive or negative and critical.

Table D.1 The four meta-frames for the news framing analysis

Meta-frames	Descriptions
1. *Causes of conflict and violence*	Explanations of what caused the conflict and what/who instigated violence in the region
2. *Uses of force*	Aggressive actions, including incidents launched by suspected insurgents and unknown perpetrators such as shooting and bombing attacks, and those caused by state authorities, such as searches, arrests, clashes with suspects, and abuses of power.
3. *Repercussions of conflict and violence*	Situations that ensued as the results of conflict and violence, such as administrative changes and investigations into the responsible parties, contingency security and legal measures, impact on southern communities and victims, and public reactions to the problems.
4. *Solutions*	Policies, instruments, and proposals to solve the conflict, such as political reform, security measures, dialogues, reconciliation, and public involvement.

Table D.2 Components of frames in the *causes of conflict and violence* meta-frame

Frame components

Retaliation against authority

1. Referring to unknown armed groups as being behind the attacks, but not specifically labelling them as "separatist" or "terrorist"
2. Referring to military defector as trainer for militia

Power struggle among interest groups

Referring to disparate interest groups, i.e. drug cartels, local influential figures, etc. as being behind the attacks

State's misdiagnosis and ineffective policies

1. Stating the military-led approach intensifies the southern conflict and violence
2. Stating the competition among political parties enables the conflict's protraction
3. Stating the state officials' incompetency and mistreatment of the locals enable the conflict's protraction
4. Stating the deficiency in intelligence enables the conflict's protraction

Transnational radical Islam

1. Referring to transnational/ Southeast Asia-based armed groups and other influential establishments as supporters of the local insurgent movement
2. Referring to the inappropriate interpretations of Islamic religious teaching as a tool to recruit operative staff

Identity politics

1. Referring to separatist movements as the instigators of violence
2. Referring to the locals' grievance at being mistreated and deprived of identity as the root of the conflict
3. Referring to the long history of power struggle with the Thai state as the root of the conflict

Table D.3 Components of frames in the *repercussions* meta-frame

Frame components

Impact on stakeholders
1. Impact on state officials
2. Impact on the southerners' livelihood
3. Impact on victims
4. Impact on economy
5. Protests by locals
6. Escape (witnesses, suspects)

Governance
1. Reporting authorities' reactions: demotions, transfers, changes of strategies
2. Reporting trials and investigation of suspects and probes on irregularity in the state's mishandling
3. Introducing new/amended political strategies

Public reactions
Reporting about the royal family and general public expressing concerns about the southern situation

Table D.4 Components of frames in the *solutions* meta-frame

Frame components

Governance and political structure
1. Reporting on positive/neutral views of governmental policies in general
2. Reporting on negative views on governmental policies in general
3. Introducing administrative changes i.e. re-establishment of SBPAC, appointment of ministers in charge of southern conflict, etc.
4. Reporting on Thailand's attempts to maintain relationship with Islamic countries and international communities
5. Reporting on political parties' introduction of new strategies for southern constituencies
6. Reporting on budget allocation and spending on southern conflict solutions
7. Reporting on government's reiterating stance that southern conflict is a domestic matter
8. Reporting on positive/ neutral views on special administrative models/ autonomy
9. Reporting on negative views on special administrative models/ autonomy

Quality of life
1. Reporting on improvement in education, community, and healthcare services
2. Reporting on roles of religious institutions in conflict resolution
3. Reporting on improvement in local economy

Appendix D   163

Frame components

Third-party involvement

1. Reporting on the influence of and input from international community i.e. Malaysia's role as mediator/facilitator in dialogues with separatist leaders, the UN's annual human rights situation reports, etc.
2. Reporting on public response and moral support i.e. donations, fund-raisings, opinion poll showing public's concerns about the southern conflict, etc.
3. Reporting on royal family and associate's initiatives
4. Reporting on suggestions on the roles of mass media in southern conflict

Military and policing

1. Reporting about security and public order policy/ operation, i.e. military appointment and management, enactment of martial law and emergency decree, etc.
2. Reporting about crime suppression policy/ operation, i.e. eradication of narcotic drugs in community, police appointment and management etc.

Reconciliation and recognition of local identity

1. Reporting on reconciliation/ peace/ anti-violence campaigns and initiatives
2. Reporting on suggestions to promote recognition of local histories and culture
3. Reporting on suggestions to promote understanding of the region's uniqueness

Justice

1. Reporting on policies/ projects concerning legal actions and investigations into the state's alleged wrongdoing, overhaul of justice system
2. Reporting on healing initiatives for people affected by conflict and violence
3. Reporting on policies/ projects concerning human rights

Counter-insurgency

1. Reporting on positive/ neutral views on dialogues with separatist groups
2. Reporting on negative views of dialogues with separatist groups
3. Reporting on counter-terrorism/ separatism policy (referring to propositions with direct reference to "terrorism" and "separatism")

Others

Reporting on arts and literature about southern conflict and southern culture

---

In-depth interview and news production observation

In-depth interviews with news workers from the selected organisations and those from other media outlets, purposely selected due to their experience and expertise in the subject, were also conducted for further clarification, reflexivity, and retrospective scrutiny of the performances carried out by them and their peers. The interviews were semi-structured, with open-ended questions that enabled interviewees to elaborate on their answers, and allowed for flexible and follow-up questions. The interviews were face-to-face, and all but two interviews were recorded. In all, 31 people were interviewed in-depth, as listed in Table D.5. I also

Table D.5 List of in-depth interviewees

Levels	Matichon	Thai PBS	Manager	Isara	Others
Managerial/ Executives		1. Deputy director of News and Programmes 2. Civil Media Network director		3. Director, Isara Institute	
Editors/ Producers	4. Chief, regional news desk	5. Assistant news director 6. Editor, current affairs programme 7. Producer, southern-issue feature programme	8. Chief, southern news centre 9. Web marketing officer	10. Editor, southern news desk	11. Editor, Aman News Agency 12. Advisor 1, Deep South Watch (DSW) 13. Advisor 2, DSW* 14. Advisor 3 and webmaster, DSW and Deep South Journalism School 15. Co-founder, Patani Forum website**
Field journalists		16. Senior reporter (security affairs) 17–18. Reporters 1–2, southern news centre		19–21. Reporters 1–3	22. Local reporter and photographer, Yala 23. Producer and newscaster, Prince of Songkla University radio 24. Senior reporter, *Bangkok Post* 25. Senior reporter, *The Nation*** 26. Newscaster, National Broadcasting Television, Yala
Stringers/ independent producers	Stringer 3, Pattani*	27. Stringer 1, Pattani 28. Stringer, Yala Province	29. Stringer 2, Pattani		30. Senior freelance journalist 31. Civic community radio practitioner, Pattani

*, ** The interviewees performed more than one role.

Appendix D   165

talked to several other news workers whose input provided me with useful information to understand news production culture.

Notes

1 Part of this section was first published in the author's PhD thesis. For more details on the research methodology, see Chapter 5 of Phansasiri Kularb. 2013. *Mediating Political Dissent: A study of Thai news organisations and southern conflict reporting.* Cardiff University, UK.
2 At the time of this study, *Thai PBS* produces six news bulletins per day: 1) 6 a.m. (Morning News), 2) 9 a.m., 3) noon (Midday News), 4) 5 p.m., 5) 7 p.m. (Evening News), and 6) 11.45 p.m. (Late Night News). The Morning News and Evening News bulletins are 1 hour and 30 minutes. The Midday News lasts 1 hour, and the Late Night News lasts 45 minutes. The 9 a.m. and 7 p.m. bulletins are 30 minutes each. Additionally, there is a top-of-the-hour three-minute news brief five times a day, at 10 a.m., 11 a.m., 2 p.m., 3 p.m., and 4 p.m. The primetime Midday and Evening News programmes generally recap the day's events. Apart from re-using and re-packaging the reports which have already been aired in other bulletins, the programmes also present first-run stories. As a result, the data collected from these two programmes sufficiently represent that day's coverage. Also, to collect every piece of reports on the same day would render repetitive data that did not serve the purpose of this study.
3 The key word search was conducted in Thai language, using the terms three southern border provinces (สามจังหวัดชายแดนใต้ [*sam jang wat chai daen tai*]) and southern border (ชายแดนใต้ [*chai daen tai*]).
4 ความไม่สงบ [*kwam mai sa ngop*].
5 การก่อความไม่สงบ [*kan ko kwam mai sa ngop*].
6 ความรุนแรง [*kwam run raeng*].
7 ความขัดแย้ง [*kwam kad yaeng*].
8 การก่อการร้าย [*kan ko kan rai*].

References

Entman, Robert M. 1993. Framing: Toward clarification of a fractured paradigm. *Journal of Communication* 43(4), pp. 51–58.
Matthes, Jörg and Kohring, Matthias. 2008. The content analysis of media frames: Toward improving reliability and validity. *Journal of Communication* 58(2), pp. 258–279.

Appendix E

List of selected local non-profit media and civil society organisations working on southern conflict issues

No.	Name	Presentation formats/Main platforms	Content emphasis
1	Aman News Agency	News and article/ website and social media	Coverage of local occurrences, produced by local reporters
2	Bunga Raya News	News and article/ website and publication	Coverage of local occurrences, produced by university students in the southernmost provinces
3	The Network of Civic Women for Peace	Article and discussion radio programme/website and radio	Empowering women's participation in conflict resolution and local administration; rehabilitation for victims of violence
4	Deep South Journalism School (DSJ)	News and article/ website (a unit of Deep South Watch)	Coverage of local occurrences and seminars, produced by independent journalists and trained student/youth volunteers
5	Deep South Watch	Analysis and report, article, and blog/website and publication	Decentralisation; Local administrative model; Peace processes and conflict resolution
6	Fine Tune Production and Friends (FTMedia)	Video and audio documentary/social media	Stories about impact of violence and injustice on local people, produced by independent journalists and trained volunteers
7	INsouth Voice (Intellect Southern Thailand)	Article, blog, short documentary/social media	Education for local children, focusing on religious education and participatory democracy
8	Media Selatan .	News and radio programme/website and social media	Coverage of local occurrences, discussions and audience participation, produced by local producers
9	Patani Forum	Article/website	Analytical articles and interviews concerning local identity, produced by reporters, writers, and academics

No.	Name	Presentation formats/Main platforms	Content emphasis
10	Southern Peace Media Volunteer Network	Documentary/social media and public service broadcaster	Stories about the impact of violence on the southerners, the way of life of local people, produced by citizen media producers
11	Wartani	News, articles, blogs, short documentary/website and social media	Coverage of local occurrences, produced by local producers

Appendix F
List of selected publications on the southern conflict by Thai journalists

* Ranked in the order of the year published

Investigative reports/ academic articles/ research

Supalak Ganjanakhundee and Don Pathan. 2004. สันติภาพในเปลวเพลิง *[Peace in the Flame]*. Bangkok: Nation Books.

Supalak Ganjanakhundee. 2009. ชุมโจรในจินตนาการ:ว่าด้วยภูมิรู้ของทหารไทยเกี่ยวกับผู้ก่อความไม่สงบในภาคใต้ [Imagined Bandit's Den: Thai soldier's knowledge about instigators in the South]. ฟ้าเดียวกัน *[Fah Diew Kan]*. January – March 2009, pp. 56–71.

Supara Janchidfah. 2009. บทรำถึงถึงชายแดนใต้: บันทึกได้พรม 5 ปีไฟใต้ [Solioquy to the Southern border: The hidden Memoir of 5 years of Southern Fire]. ฟ้าเดียวกัน *[Fah Diew Kan]*. January– March 2009, pp. 88–104.

Supara Janchidfah. 2009. Peace Intervention as Seen from Below. *Islam in Southeast Asia: Transnational Networks and Local Contexts*. Japan: Research Institute for Languages and Culture of Asia and Africa (ILCAA), Tokyo University of Foreign Studies, pp. 175–204.

Feature

Supara Janchidfah. 2006. *Violence in the Mist: Reporting on the Presence of Pain in Southern Thailand*. Bangkok: Kobfai.

Wimolpan Pita-tawatchai. 2007. เมื่อฟ้าหม่น เจดีย์หัก ที่ปักษ์ใต้ *[Gloomy Sky, Broken Jedi in the South]*. Bangkok: Krung Thep.

Worapot Panpong. 2007. ที่เกิดเหตุ บันทึก 1 ปี ในพื้นที่ 3 จังหวัดชายแดนภาคใต้ *[The Scene: A Memoir of One Year in the Three Southern Border Provinces]*. Bangkok: Openbooks.

Nattarawut Muengsuk. 2009. เป็นเขาและเป็นแขก *[Being the Others and Being Muslim]*. Bangkok: Nakorn Media.

Journalists' experiences in southern conflict reporting

Somkiat Jantaraseema. ed. 2006. ปักหมุด . . . เทใจ: บันทึกประสบการณ์ชีวิตเหยี่ยวข่าวอิศรา *[Memoirs of Isara Reporters]*. Bangkok: Public Communication Foundation Establishment Project.

Passakorn Jamlongrach. ed. 2007. สนามข่าวสีแดง เรียนรู้โต๊ะข่าวภาคใต้ *[The Red News Field: Learning About the Southern News Desk]*. Bangkok: Parb Pim.

Index

Note: Page numbers with *f* indicate figures; those with *t* indicate tables.

adat melayu (Malay customary law) 2
additional threats theory 33
advocate, journalists as 110–11
Al-Jazeera 103–4
alternative perspective 121
arbitrators, journalists as 109–10
Archetti, Christina 80
Askew, Mark 3, 5
ASTV Manager Online *see* Manager
    Online (news website)
Audience Council 105

back gate coverage 81, 94
Bangkok-based staff, factors influencing
    works of 67–71; competition among
    news organisations 68–71; diverse
    views of southern conflict 67–8
Bangkok-centric mindset 71–4, 122
Benson, Rodney 13
Berjihad di Patani (war statement) 9

Chomsky, Noam 14
Civic Network for Women 108, 110
Civil-Police-Military joint command unit
    43 (CPM 43) 3
civil rights, maintaining 41
civil society organisations 166–7
classical approach to journalism 14, 15
competition among news organisations
    68–71
conflict/violence meta-frame, causes of
    31–3, 31*f,* 32*f*; components of 32–3,
    32*f*; frequency of 31–2, 31*f*; identity
    politics 32, 32*f,* 50; power struggle
    among interest groups 32*f,* 33, 42, 50;
    retaliation against authority 32–3, 32*f*;
    state's misdiagnosis and ineffective

policies 32*f,* 33; transnational radical
    Islam 32, 32*f*
contagion effect 14
contextual reporting 109
coordinator, journalists as 109–10
Cottle, Simon 81, 124
crime and conspiracy discourse of
    southern conflict 4–5; features of 10,
    11*t*; journalists' support for 28–9;
    labels used for antagonists and 44*t,*
    45; as most used news frames 42, 51,
    52; news coverage support of 117;
    poverty and 4–5; predominant reporting
    of 50; repercussions meta-frame and
    38; sources and 84–6; Udomchai
    Thammasarorat and 4; uses of force
    news frames and 34
critical approach to journalism 14, 15
cultural chaos paradigm 13
cultural regulation 2

decentralised content 131
decentralised journalistic practice 109
Deep South Watch 65, 88, 107, 110
depth presentation format 45; frequency
    of use 46*t,* 47; writing styles/emphases
    for 45–6
disparate roles of journalism 98–113;
    different conflict portrayals and 98–9;
    as forum for every party 106–9;
    ideology-oriented emphasis 100–2;
    as presenter of truth 102–6; security-
    oriented emphasis 99–100; socio-
    cultural emphasis 100; as supporter in
    conflict resolution 109–11
dominance paradigm 13
Dusun Nyor Rebellion 2

170　*Index*

editorial/production process 59*f*
Elliott, Philip 121
El-Nawawy, Mohammed 104
Emergency Decree on Public
　Administration in State of Emergency 62
enterprise channel, of obtaining
　information 56

Facebook 58
field journalists, reporting difficulties
　of 60–7; information deficit/
　misinformation and 63–4; intimidations/
　threats towards 60–3; personal/
　professional dilemmas and 64–7
field reporting, defined 60
Fink, Katherine 109
fluctuating/oscillating coverage format
　49–52
forum for every party, journalism as
　106–9, 111, 113
front gate coverage 81, 94, 121
functional/professional approach to
　journalism 15–16

going public strategy, of sources 81–2
governance and politics, as thematic group
　28, 28*f,* 31

habitual access 80, 81
Haji Sulong Abdulkader 2, 6
Hallin, Daniel 16, 51
Hasty, Jennifer 82
headline and introduction topics 28–9
Herman, Edward 14
hierarchy-of-influences model 12–13, 122

ideology-oriented emphasis, journalism
　and 100–2
informal channel, of obtaining information
　56
information deficit, field journalists and 63–4
infotainment 13
Internal Security Act 62
Internal Security Operations Command
　(ISOC) 63
intimidations/threats towards field
　journalists 60–3; from above 62; from
　below 62; security laws and 62
Isara see Isara News Agency's Southern
　News Desk (news website)
Isara News Agency's Southern News
　Desk (news website): *Bangkok-centric
　mindset* at 73; comparison of, to other
　news organisations 26–7*t*; coordination

between headquarters and reporters at
　57; cost of southern conflict reporting
　at 70–1; deep South coverage of 104–5;
　depth genre use 47; development of
　158–9*t*; editorial/production process 58,
　59*f*; labels used at 67–8; power struggle
　among interest groups frame and 42;
　problem-solving and 103; profile of
　157–9; royal patronage project headlines
　41; source relationships at 92–3; sources
　of, most cited 85, 107; story length,
　evaluation of 50; thick journalism of
　124; threats against reporters at 61, 62–3
Iskandar, Adel 104
Islamism, Malay nationalism and 7–12

Jemaah Islamiyah member arrest 9–10
jihad, against Thai government 9
jihadist 4
journalism: classical approach to 14, 15;
　critical approach to 14, 15; disparate
　roles of (*see* disparate roles of
　journalism); as forum for every party
　106–9, 111, 113; functional/professional
　approach to 15–16; market demands
　and 13; as presenter of truth 102–6,
　111, 112; role of, in political conflict 12,
　13–16; sociology of 12–13; as supporter
　in conflict resolution 109–11, 113;
　symbiotic relation between political
　violence and 14; Thai, roles of 124
journalists; *see also* disparate roles of
　journalism: as advocate and political
　player 110–11; channels of obtaining
　information 56; as coordinator and
　arbitrator 109–10; field, reporting
　difficulties of 60–7; hierarchy-of-
　influences model and 12–13; news
　source choice of 16; occupational
　requirements of 102; as oxygen
　providers 61; sources of (*see* journalist-
　source relationship; sources)
journalists, southern conflict reporting
　difficulties of 59–71, 75*f; see also* field
　journalists, reporting difficulties of;
　from field 60–7; in newsroom 67–71;
　overview of 59–60
journalist-source relationship 87–95,
　120–1; *see also* sources; being insiders
　and 92–5; contact initiating and 87–90;
　as fluid and dynamic 95; as human
　relation 82; power play between
　82; symbiotic, described 80–2; trust
　building and 90–2

Index 171

King-oua Laohong 5–6
Krungthep Turakij 73

label analysis, news media headlines/
  introductions 43–5, 43*t*, 44*t*, 117–18
Lewis, Justin 15
lines of production, of southern conflict
  news 56*f*

Malay Muslim 2; Deep South Watch and
  65–6; political/cultural identity of 5;
  uprisings, April 28, 2004 5–6, 9; Wan
  Kadir Che Man passage on 6–7
Malay nationalism and Islamism discourse
  of southern conflict 7–12; analyses of 8;
  described 7–8; elements of 29; features
  of 10, 11*t*, 12; news coverage support
  of 117; news framing analysis and 33;
  PULO leader interview concerning
  8–9; radical Islam influence and
  9–10; sources and 84; underground
  organisations involved in 8; uses of
  force news frames and 34
Manager see Manager Online (news
  website)
Manager Online (news website):
  comparison of, to other news
  organisations 26–7*t*; coordination
  between headquarters and reporters at
  57; editorial/production process 58,
  59*f*; profile of 156–7; reported topic
  headlines of 29; royal patronage project
  headlines 41; sources of, most cited
  85; Southern Region page of 105; story
  length, evaluation of 49–50; summary
  and immediacy genre use 47
martial law 62
Matichon (daily newspaper): business
  structure of 153*f*; comparison of,
  to other news organisations 26–7*t*;
  coordination between headquarters and
  reporters at 57; editors' responsibilities
  57; profile of 153–4; reported topic
  headlines of 29; royal patronage project
  headlines 41; sources of, most cited 85,
  107; story length, evaluation of 49–50
McCargo, Duncan 8, 10, 59, 65, 71, 80,
  82, 118, 124, 131
McNair, Brian 13
media *see* news media
media reflexivity 124
millenarian revolt 5
minority's grievance discourse of southern
  conflict 5–7; elements of 29; features of

10, 11*t*; King-oua Laohong thesis 5–6;
  National Reconciliation Commission
  report 6–7; news coverage support of
  117; news framing analysis and 33;
  sources and 84; uses of force news
  frames and 34; Wan Kadir Che Man
  passage 6–7
misinformation, field journalists and 63–4
Murdock, Graham 121

Narathiwat: news coverage and 55; Tak
  Bai District protest clampdown in 6;
  violence in 1; weapons heist in 3, 4
National Front for the Liberation of
  Patani 2
national-level newsrooms, structural
  change in 131
national-level sources, use of 86–7, 86*t*
National Reconciliation Commission
  (NRC) 6–7, 10, 51, 70
National Revolutionary Front 2
nation-building 2
Network Monarchy 8
news framing analysis, in southern conflict
  coverage 31–43; *see also* individual
  meta-frames; conflict/violence meta-
  frame, causes of 31–3, 31*f*, 32*f*; defined
  31; meta-frames frequency 31–2, 31*f*;
  repercussions meta-frame and 31*f*, 34,
  35*f*, 36–8, 36*t*; solutions meta-frame
  and 31, 31*f*, 32, 38–43, 39*f*, 40*t*; uses of
  force meta-frame and 31, 31*f*, 33–4, 34*f*
news media; *see also* journalism: labels
  of, in headlines/introductions 43–5, 43*t*,
  44*t*, 117–18; positions of, in political
  conflict/violence 14–15; relationships
  and 13–14; roles of, in political conflict
  13–16; similarities/differences summary
  159*t*; as state's accomplice 15
news production framework, paradigm
  shift in 131–2
news representation of southern conflict
  26–53; *see also* Isara News Agency's
  Southern News Desk (news website);
  Manager Online (news website);
  Matichon (daily newspaper); Thai
  Public Broadcasting Service (television
  channel); arguments derived from
  findings 52–3; news frames in coverage
  of 31–43; news media's labels for 43–5;
  news themes in 28–31; overview of 26,
  28; presentation formats used in 45–52;
  selected news organisations comparison
  26–7*t*

172 *Index*

newsroom production: conditions/
constraints of 123*f*, 124; defined 60;
factors influencing 112*f*; practices
121–4
Nidhi Aeusrivongse 5
non-profit media/civil society
organisations 166–7
Nossek, Hillel 14

official perspective 121
online social networks 58
oppositional perspective 121

Patani empire 2; Thai-ness and 2
Patani Forum 101, 110
Patani United Liberation Organisation
(PULO) 2, 8–9, 63
Pattani: Kru-Ze Mosque attack in 6; news
coverage and 55; violence in 1
peace dialogues, as solution to southern
conflict 40*t*
personal/professional dilemmas, field
journalists and 64–7
Plaek Phibunsongkram 2
political contest model 13, 16
political player, journalists as 110–11
political violence, newsworthiness of 16
pondok (community-based Islamic
religious school) 2
popular journalism 13
poverty, violence and 4–5
Prem Tinsulanond 3
presentation formats used in southern
conflict reporting 45–52; depth 45–6,
47; fluctuating/oscillating coverage
49–52; platforms used and 47; summary
and immediacy 45, 47; up close and
personal 45, 46; verbatim 45, 46; visual
47–8, 48*t*, 49*t*
presenter of truth, journalism as 102–6,
111, 112
primary definers 81
Prince of Songkla University 107
propaganda model 14
public engagement/participation 131
PULO *see* Patani United Liberation
Organisation (PULO)

Qatari news organisation 104

Reese, Stephen 12, 122
repercussions meta-frame 31*f*, 34–8;
governance frame 34, 35*f*, 42; impact on
stakeholders' frame 34, 35*f*, 36, 36*t*, 37*t*,

38, 38*t*, 42, 50; public reactions frame
34, 35*f*
reporting quality, improvement policies
for 132
reporting southern conflict 55–75; *see also*
news representation of southern conflict;
Bangkok-based staff and, factors
influencing works of 67–71; *Bangkok-
centric mindset* and 71–4; difficulties
of 75*f*; editorial/production process 59*f*;
journalists reporting difficulties (*see*
journalists, southern conflict reporting
difficulties of); overview of 55; southern
conflict coverage, making of 55–9
routine channel, of obtaining
information 56
royal patronage projects, for southern
conflict relief 41–2
Rungrawee Chalermsripinyorat 51, 126

Samatcha Nilaphatama 51, 126
Schlesinger, Philip 121
Schudson, Michael 12, 81, 82, 109, 124
second-class reporters 60
security and public order theme 28, 28*f*,
29, 42, 44
security laws 62
security-oriented emphasis, journalism and
99–100
self-determination and peace processes 51
separatist movements 2–3; peace talks
and 51
shared media 124
socio-cultural emphasis, journalism and
100
socio-economy and culture, as thematic
group 28, 28*f*, 31
solutions meta-frame 31, 31*f*, 32, 38–43;
commercial/not-for-profit organisations
comparison 42–3; components of
38–9, 39*f*; counter-insurgency frame
39–40, 39*f*, 40*t*; governance/political
structure frame 39, 39*f*, 50–1; justice
frame 39*f*, 40; quality of life frame 39*f*,
40; reconciliation/recognition of local
identity frame 39–40, 39*f*, 40*t*, 51; third-
party involvement frame 39*f*, 41–2
Songkla: news coverage and 55; violence
in 1
sources 80–95; *see also* journalist-source
relationship; access to/being approached
by 87–90; blending in and keeping a
distance 92–5; citizen media producers
as 89–90; civil advocates as 89–90;

government as 83–4, 83*t*; journalist, relationship 87–95; locations and bases of, in southern conflict reporting 86*t*; military as 83–4, 83*t*; national-level, use of 86–7, 86*t*; police as 83–4, 83*t*; role of, in news production 80; specialisation of, presented in news content 84–6, 85*t*; symbiotic relationship of, and journalists 80–2; trust building and 90–2; types of, quoted 83*t*

Southern Border Provinces Administrative Centre (SBPAC) 3

southern conflict, Thailand's: cost of reporting 70–1; coverage, making of 55–9; crime and conspiracy discourse of 4–5, 11*t*; discourses of 3–12; diverse views of 67–8; future research in news media and 125–6; history of 1–3; labels of, in headlines/introductions 43–5, 43*t*, 44*t*; Malay nationalism and Islamism discourse of 7–12, 11*t*; minority's grievance discourse of 5–7, 11*t*; Narathiwat weapons heist and 3; national-level source use in reporting of 86–7; news frames in coverage of 31–43; news media role in 13–16; news production culture in 12–13; politics/media, key moments in 134–52; reporting, difficulties of 75*f*; research methodology 160–5; royal patronage projects for 41–2; selected publications on 168; themes in coverage of 28–31, 28*f*; topics in coverage of, frequency of 30*t*

southern conflict coverage, making of 55–9; diversity/complexity of news ecology in 125*f*; editorial/production process 59*f*; factors influencing 112*f*; lines of production 56*f*

southern conflict reporting, diversity/ complexity of 125*f*

southern conflict reporting, recommendations for 131–3; national-level newsrooms, structural change in 131; news production framework, paradigm shift in 131–2; reporting quality, improvement policies for 132; working in tandem 132–3

spheres of consensus, legitimate controversy and deviance model (Hallin) 16, 51, 118–19

spinning strategy 107

state of emergency decree 62

stringers 55–6, 57, 60, 71–2, 85

summary and immediacy presentation format 45; frequency of use 46*t*, 47; writing styles/emphases for 45

supporter in conflict resolution, journalism as 109–11, 113

Tanyong Limo hostage situation 104

terrorism, journalism serving 14

Thai-ification policies 2, 5

Thai news production culture 55–75; *see also* news representation of southern conflict; Bangkok-based staff and, factors influencing works of 67–71; Bangkok-centric mindset and 71–4; journalists reporting difficulties (*see* journalists, southern conflict reporting difficulties of); overview of 55; southern conflict coverage, making of 55–9

Thai PBS *see* Thai Public Broadcasting Service (television channel)

Thai politics/media, key moments in 134–52; 2001-2003 134; 2004 135–6; 2005 136–8; 2006 138–40; 2007 140–1; 2008 141–3; 2009 143–4; 2010 144–5; 2011 146–7; 2012 147–8; 2013 148–50; 2014 150–2

Thai Public Broadcasting Service (television channel): comparison of, to other news organisations 26–7*t*; coordination between headquarters and reporters at 57; depth genre use 47; editors' responsibilities 57; ethics and conduct of 105; far South reporting of 105; news department structure of 156*f*; organisation structure of 155*f*; power struggle among interest groups frame and 42; problem-solving and 102–3; profile of 154–6; reported topic headlines of 29; source relationships at 93; sources of, most cited 85; story length, evaluation of 50; thick journalism of 124

Thaksin Shinawatra 3, 4, 8

thematic focus 131

Thanet Aphornsuvan 7

thick journalism 124, 126

trust building, journalist/source 90–2

Tuchman, Gaye 120

Twitter 58

Udomchai Thammasarorat 4

United Front for Patani Independence 6

up close and personal presentation format 45; frequency of use 46*t*; writing styles/ emphases for 46

uprisings, April 28, 2004 5–6, 9

174 *Index*

uses of force meta-frame 31, 31*f*, 33–4, 34*f*; arrest and suspect surrender 33, 34*f*; by authorities 33, 34, 34*f*, 35*t*; headline comparisons 35*t*; search 33, 34*f*; security reinforcement 33, 34*f*; by unknown actors 33, 34, 34*f*, 35*t*, 50
ustadz (religious teachers) 9

verbatim presentation format 45; frequency of use 46*t*; writing styles/ emphases for 46

visual presentation formats used in southern conflict reporting 47–8; actors featured in 48*t*; contexts of 49*t*

Waisbord, Silvio 81
Wan Kadir Che Man 6–7
Wattana Sugunnasil 9
Wolfsfeld, Gadi 13, 16, 81, 124

Yala: news coverage and 55; stringer 71–2; violence in 1
YouTube 58